⊠ Postal address

☎ Telephone numbe

✎ email address for

🚌 ✈ Directions by road from appropriate airport

SCORECARD

Shows metres/yards from back tee, indicating gold, green, yellow, purple or red rating of holes. (For metres, add 10%, or take appro. more club, compared with yards.) For unrated courses, only selected holes are included: these are generally green, but the selection doesn't necessarily include every green hole on the course.

	m	p		m	p
1	356	4	10	356	4
2	385	4	11	500	5
3	171	3	12	194	3
4	516	5	13	368	4
5	348	4	14	338	4
6	149	3	15	206	3
7	487	5	16	386	4
8	321	4	17	490	5
9	403	4	18	415	4
	3136	36		3253	36
				6389	72

SUMMARY DESCRIPTIONS

Summary description of a rated course in box highlighted in a pale sand colour.

Summary
description box

Particularly enjoyable courses If the box colour is rich sand colour it is one of the 50 rated courses in Ireland that the editorial team regard as the most enjoyable (not just for design, so much as for the whole experience from reservation and arrival to 19th hole).

Particularly
enjoyable course

Measurements: golf in all Ireland is administered by the GUI (Golfing Union of Ireland), but there is no standard as to whether courses are measured in yards or metres. We use the same measuring system as adopted by individual clubs.

ABBREVIATIONS

c'way	=	carriageway
DIY	=	course designed by club, in-house
L	=	left
m	=	metres
NI	=	Northern Ireland
p	=	par (p:3 = par 3, etc.)
R	=	right

rbt(s)	=	roundabout(s)
RoI	=	Republic of Ireland
y	=	yards

? or Unknown – we have been unable to verify the relevant information. If you can help, please email: look@pocket-golf.com.

Previously published

The Pocket Guide to Golf Courses
Spain & Portugal

THE POCKET GUIDE TO
GOLF COURSES

IRELAND

BECKENHAM

All photographs
supplied by
PhotoGolf

First published 2006 by Beckenham Publishing
Limited, Calamint House, PO Box 3339,
Manchester M8 4XX, UK

A catalogue record for this book is available from the
British Library.

ISBN 0-9548040-1-5
10 9 8 7 6 5 4 3 2 1
2010 2009 2008 2007 2006

Design: Robert Updegraff
Print production consultant: Geoff Barlow
Printed in Italy

Photographs © Beckenham Publishing Limited 2006

look@pocket-golf.com   www.pocket-golf.com
www.photogolf.ie   www.photogolf.eu

Half title photograph: *A member of
the world's best greenkeeping team at
p:3 5, Ceann Sibéal.*
Title page photograph: *The most
famous golf photo angle in Ireland –
gold-rated Ballybunion (Old) p:4 11,
seen over the 10th green.*

Acknowledgments

Although the views given in this book
are the personal consensus of the
editors, we could not possibly have
compiled it without the generous
support of so many, including the
numerous golfers whom we have met
during our research. Our thanks go to
all who have helped us, especially
Colin, Jackie, Ali and David Gregan for
so generously and regularly providing us
with shelter and craic in Dublin, and
Allen Lowe, our New Zealand director,
who crossed the world to join us on no
less than 3 of our 5 main research visits
to Ireland. We are indebted to the rest
of our editorial team and our panel of
amateur and professional players, who
have accompanied us on our research
trips. In particular we would like to
thank Arnie & Hilary Cohen, Andrew
Hall, Will Menko, Ivan & Marie Morris
and Sarah Sanderson. On the
production front we have been expertly
and tirelessly guided by Mari Roberts,

A view of the hole with the most intimidating back tee in Ireland, p:4 6 at Wicklow. On the top of the promontory at the right is the tee, immediately below which the cliffs drop into a chasm. The fairway runs across the page to the green on its far left.

our copy editor, Robert Updegraff, our designer (*'si monumentum requiris, circumspice!'* amounts here to understatement) and Geoff Barlow our print production manager – a dream team. Also special and unreserved thanks to annalists of golf club histories, websites and the many other sources: without their work we could never have included as much about the history of golf in Ireland – and indeed to the hundreds of Irish whose welcome has been so generous and entertaining, if not infectiously disarming. Most of all, we have appreciated more than we could ever fully acknowledge the support and, all too often, long-suffering patience of our closer friends and families.

We cannot name everyone who has helped us, but would particularly like to mention the following: Dickon Armstrong, Meriona Armstrong, Tim Browne, Lorenzo Doni, Hugo Donnithorne-Tait, Freddie fforde, Nic fforde, Baden & Eva Foster, Peter Fowler, Hiro & Hiroko Makoto Fujii, Jeff Hall, James Hallett, Oliver Harris, David Head, Scott Macpherson, Paul Maleedy, Ana Mª de la Maza, Sam Millhouse, Stella Millhouse, Lucia Montigiani, Idris Pearce & Anne Meyer, Sara Pearce, Adolfo Rivas, Pat Ruddy, Tom Williams and Juan de Zavala.

Finally, thank you to all the golf clubs for allowing us to play and photograph their courses, without which this book could not have been possible. There was one exception in all Ireland: we would have liked to have included the course at Laytown & Bettystown, but were denied permission to inspect it. From the roadside it looked as if it might be worth at least 🏆🏆🏆 ↗. We hope for a change of heart before the next edition . . .

CONTENTS

This view of gold-rated Ballybunion (Old)'s p:4 6 shows how effective, and on occasions devastating, a greenside combination of natural contours and short grass can be.

USEFUL INFORMATION

Note: Italics denote the 50 courses which the editorial team found to be the most enjoyable.

THE BECKENHAM RATING SYSTEM

Facility ratings

New for the Irish volume is a system to evaluate the quality of the facilities provided at a golf club. The ratings have been assessed by reference to the breadth of facilities provided and their quality: a low rating would be given to a basic course with limited clubhouse facilities, whereas a high rating would be given to one with good (though not necessarily the best) design standards, outstanding facilities including clubhouse, restaurant and hotel, fully-equipped with quality hire clubs, buggies etc and a well-run practice range. We also take into account the quality of the welcome, shop, overall ambience and value for money. These ratings are given on a scale of ♈ to ♈♈♈♈♈, where ♈♈♈ would be the general average for courses over the world. For clubs with more than one course, the rating is applied to the whole facility, not just for an individual course.

Accordingly, in summary, the ratings indicate golf facilities as:

♈♈♈♈♈	exceptional, including hotel standard accommodation
♈♈♈♈	first class, with all facilities necessary for the pursuit of golf
♈♈♈	good, with most facilities the golfer might reasonably expect
♈♈	adequate for golfing requirements
♈	basic for its purpose

Despite the 'basic' tag for ♈, such facilities would not be in this guide if they did not merit inclusion.

Design ratings

We set out to point to excellence rather than weakness. For this reason we have not adopted a '1-10' or 'marks out of 100%' system, where low ratings would inevitably have to be given in some cases, nor (for the same reasons) a star system in which every course is rated. We therefore award between 1 and 3 stars to courses whose design quality is particularly commendable:

★★★ for courses which approach perfection – with the potential to require anything and everything from the golfer, whilst being fair; they must also stand up as a work of art, have presence and no weak holes. There may be fewer than 50 such courses in the world. *Courses worth crossing the world to play.*

★★ for excellence: as for ★★★, but with perhaps the occasional blemish or weak hole causing the distinction – the art and presence factors are still prerequisites. *Courses worth crossing a continent to play.*

★ for courses representing very good design quality – as for ★★, but with perhaps some more blemishes, e.g. some weak holes and/or scoring less in the art/presence department. *Courses worth crossing a country to play.*

↗ rating is given to courses we recommend for a fuller experience of the best in golf course design. *Courses generally (but not always) with the potential for elevation to a star rating.*

In addition to the above 'rated' courses, we have included others on the grounds of interest to the travelling golfer for historical, design, practical, or other reasons as referred to in their individual entries. Their inclusion does not mean that we necessarily endorse their quality of design, even if of interest.

Individual hole ratings

We use a very simple 'traffic light' system: *green – yellow – red*, from strong to weak with yellow representing an 'average' hole. (This average relates to the whole population of golf courses around the world, not just in Ireland.)

Additionally, above green a special *'gold* rating' denotes those few holes that are so well designed and integrated into their surroundings it is difficult to imagine how they could be improved.

A hole worth playing the whole course for – just so you can play that hole.
New for Ireland is the *'purple'* rating: we felt it would be of interest to draw attention to a few selected holes more for their historic or unusual characteristics than for their overall design qualities. Using our normal system, purple holes would otherwise be red, yellow or green (not gold) – they are generally unique (e.g. the blind p:3 5 "Dell" hole at *Lahinch (Old)*).

Criteria used in The Beckenham Course Rating System

We rate the golf courses (from the viewpoint of a right-handed, male scratch amateur, playing the back tee course for the first time – subject to a knowledgeable caddy's advice where appropriate), on two different levels:
i) the golf course as a whole, which we assess for:

Variety – the extent to which the course provides a diversified mixture of golfing tests and design features to provide a breadth of challenge;

Stylistic integrity and consistency – the extent to which the course has a commonality of features and therefore stands together as a whole, rather than comprising a compilation of disparate parts;

Fairness – the extent to which the course and its challenges are openly presented, so that playing errors are due to the player himself making such errors, rather than due to a feature of the course of which the player is not given reasonable notice;

Routing – the extent to which the physical relationship between the layout of the course and the land on which it is set enhances and/or diversifies the golfing challenge (e.g. through changes in the direction of play) and its aesthetic and physical experience; and, to a lesser degree,

History – the extent to which the course has been used for important events, or has otherwise enhanced the game of golf;

ii) each individual hole, for:

Playing challenge – the extent to which the player's physical golfing skills are tested whilst playing the hole; these skills include delicacy of touch as much as sheer physical strength;

Mental challenge – the extent to which the player is required to think his way around playing the hole (e.g. a strategic hole will score more than one where no choices are given to the player);

Use of land – the extent to which the design makes good use of the natural features of the land, or, if artificial, the golfing quality of the land created;

Aesthetics – the quality of the visual, sensual (and occasionally aural) impression provided whilst playing and walking the hole;

Green and greensite – the design quality of the putting surface, and the topography and golfing defences incorporated in the design of the complex immediately surrounding it;

Negatives – give the assessor the ability to downgrade a hole because of particular features which detract from its qualities (e.g. noise pollution, blind shots, reverse cambers, blind bunkers, too steeply uphill, etc.).

Important note: because the hole ratings only make up approximately half of the overall score in rating a course, comparison of courses by their respective numbers of different coloured holes is not a particularly meaningful exercise (e.g. Esker Hills, unrated, has 7 green holes, whereas County Tipperary, *rated ↗, has 6).*

HOW TO USE THIS BOOK

General guide

To quickly choose a 'rated' course you haven't played before, use the star and hole rating system plus the summary description (i.e. the words in the sandy coloured box). For our opinion on the holes of a course you already know, refer also to the hole-by-hole colour ratings (on scorecard). For more detail on featured holes, read the photo captions (gold holes are always included – somewhere in the book). For an explanation of why a hole is red or purple, refer to the smaller print. For more about rated courses, read the main text. For other courses, we include a paragraph of brief notes.

Key

Name of course Facility rating Star rating (if applicable) – see pages 8-9

WATERVILLE ♛♛♛♛ ★

Hackett, Harmon & Mulcahy/T Fazio 1973/2004 €€€ H: M 28, L 36

Name(s) of designer (if two names '&' means co-designers, and '/' means different designers at different years of design shown; years linked by '&' denote same designer(s) in different years).	Price band – for most expensive green fee (i.e. high season weekend, 2005 prices): **€** below €60 or **£** below £40 **€€** €60–€100 or **££** £40–£67 **€€€** €100 – €200 or **£££** £67–£133 **€€€€** more than €200 **££££** more than £133	Maximum **H**andicap requirements (if none, none) for **M**en, **L**adies and **J**uniors (boy/girl – if different); if no junior information given, assume same as for adults. **Best always to take your handicap certificate.**

Important note: there is a huge variety of green fee discounts and packages, which change regularly and would therefore be misleading to include in this book. Our price band system should be used as a general guide as to which courses are more or less expensive relative to the rest.

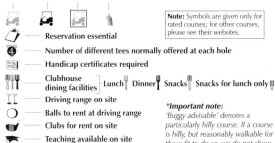

Trolleys: pull trolleys are available to hire at all courses.
Buggy*: available/compulsory/advisable/caddies available

Symbol	Meaning
	Reservation essential
❹	Number of different tees normally offered at each hole
	Handicap certificates required
	Clubhouse dining facilities — Lunch Dinner Snacks Snacks for lunch only
	Driving range on site
◯	Balls to rent at driving range
	Clubs for rent on site
	Teaching available on site
	Easy to lose balls – take plenty

Note: Symbols are given only for rated courses; for other courses, please see their websites.

*Important note:
'Buggy advisable' denotes a particularly hilly course. If a course is hilly, but reasonably walkable for those fit to do so, we do not show the buggy advisable symbol.

✉ **Postal address**

☎ **Telephone number for reservations** – best always to reserve (some courses do not accept visitors every day of the week and a few have annual closures; we do not publish these, as they often change).

✎ email address for reservations; web site url

🚗 ✈ Directions by road from appropriate airport N.B. 'follow road' means follow straight on, straight over all roundabouts, junctions etc. until further instructions; 'sign' means sign for club. We suggest you use our instructions in conjunction with a local map whenever possible. All distances are approximate – RoI uses m and km for distances; NI uses yards and miles.

Scorecard – shows metres/yards from back tee, indicating gold, green, yellow, purple or red rating of holes. (For metres, add 10%, or take approx 1 more club, compared with yards.) For unrated courses, only selected holes are included: these are generally green, but the selection doesn't necessarily include every green hole on the course.

	m	p		m	p
1	356	4	10	356	4
2	385	4	11	500	5
3	171	3	12	194	3
4	516	5	13	368	4
5	348	4	14	338	4
6	149	3	15	206	3
7	487	5	16	386	4
8	321	4	17	490	5
9	403	4	18	415	4
	3136	36		3253	36
				6389	72

Summary description of a rated course in box highlighted in a pale sand colour.

Summary description box

Particularly enjoyable courses If the box colour is rich sand colour it is one of the 50 rated courses in Ireland that the editorial team regard

Particularly enjoyable course

as the most enjoyable (not just for design, so much as for the whole experience from reservation and arrival to 19th hole).

A course name in *italics* denotes a course included in this (or our *Spain & Portugal*) guide (except on the Contents and map pages, where it denotes a *particularly enjoyable course*).

Measurements: golf in all Ireland is administered by the GUI (Golfing Union of Ireland), but there is no standard as to whether courses are measured in yards or metres. We use the same measuring system as adopted by individual clubs.

Abbreviations

c'way	=	carriageway
DIY	=	course designed by club, in-house
L	=	left
m	=	metres
NI	=	Northern Ireland
p	=	par (p:3 = par 3, etc.)
R	=	right

rbt(s)	=	roundabout(s)
RoI	=	Republic of Ireland
y	=	yards

? or Unknown – we have been unable to verify the relevant information. If you can help, please email: look@pocket-golf.com.

PREFACE

Following the success of our guide to the golf courses of Spain & Portugal, we are delighted to publish the next in the series, timed to coincide with Ireland's largest sporting event ever, the 2006 Ryder Cup.

Our purpose continues to be to set new standards for golf course guides. As we go to press, there is no single volume which deals independently, selectively, objectively, critically and in pocket book format to one of northern Europe's most popular, historic and beautiful golf destinations.

We have developed the system used in *Spain & Portugal* (to whose Preface I generally refer). *Ireland* features some important enhancements: a 'facility rating' for the overall standard of the golfing product; a 'purple' rating for holes of unusual design; course presentation in alphabetical order; an introductory photographic tour of some of the best in Ireland (acknowledging, *en passant*, several clubs who have ordered books in advance); an indication of club dining facilities, and a more comprehensive list of places to stay. Encouraged by the positive response to *Spain & Portugal*, we have retained our colour coded hole ratings, and repeat our view that the few clubs with 'red holes' should not take umbrage: readers are encouraged to play courses with 'red holes' as much as those with 'gold holes'.

The change to alphabetical order allows more flow in the design, including larger photographs (as many as space will allow). I refer to my remarks on golf course photography also in the Preface of *Spain & Portugal*, particularly to our desire generally to show holes from the player's viewpoint: too often we see (otherwise excellent) reverse view images which do not show what is required of the player. Whilst we were often very lucky with the weather, we have made a point of showing Ireland as

The vista across the 14th fairway to Tralee's p:4 15th. Words are unnecessary: this has to be one of the most spectacularly beautiful settings for a golf course on the planet . . .

she presented herself to us: be prepared to get wet! The photos in this book, and many others from our substantial library, may be purchased via www.pocket-golf.com or our new dedicated website www.photogolf.ie.

We have structured the book to be used at different levels and for different types of readers – from the travelling golfer, local or holiday house resident, to the armchair tourist, and from players to golf design enthusiasts. To get the best out of it, please carefully read 'How to Use this Book' (pages 10-11). We have made a point of including some of the rich history of golf in Ireland and avoiding interminable hole by hole descriptions.

We are very aware that there is ultimately no right answer to what is or is not good golf course design... We accept that those who disagree with us may have just as valid reasons for disagreeing with, as we have for holding, our opinion (several readers of the manuscript took issue with us over Waterville, in particular). The case may even be put for some red holes to be gold, and vice versa. We welcome your comments to look@pocket-golf.com. Having invested many years in this project, we have rated, photographed, videoed and played on nearly all the courses in the book, with a panel of professional and amateur players from scratch to high handicap, male and female, providing instant feedback. So please savour the consensus opinion of some well-travelled and informed golfers – players of all standards, designers and critics.

A final, personal note: Allen Lowe (our director) and I are both Irish dual nationals, living abroad. It has been a moving experience to have spent so much time in Ireland: we have appreciated alike her outstanding beauty and the consistent generosity of our compatriots.

William fforde, Editor
San Macário in Monte, Italy, May 2006

DESIGN DISTINCTION

Irish Gold

We list here all the 'gold-rated' holes in Ireland:

	No	p		No	p
Ashford Castle	2	4	Lahinch (Old)	2	5
Ballybunion (Cashen)	13	4	Lahinch (Old)	3	4
Ballybunion (Cashen)	15	5	Lahinch (Old)	6	4
Ballybunion (Cashen)	17	5	Lahinch (Old)	13	4
Ballybunion (Old)	6	4	Mount Wolseley	11	3
Ballybunion (Old)	7	4	Mullingar	2	3
Ballybunion (Old)	8	3	Naas	15	4
Ballybunion (Old)	9	4	Narin & Portnoo	8	3
Ballybunion (Old)	11	4	Old Head of Kinsale	2	4
Ballybunion (Old)	16	5	Palmerstown	14	5
Ballybunion (Old)	17	4	Portmarnock	8	4
Birr	7	4	Portmarnock	12	3
Birr	8	3	Portmarnock	14	4
Birr	12	4	Portmarnock Links	16	4
Birr	14	3	Portsalon	2	4
Carlow (Deerpark)	12	4	Rathcore	11	3
Carlow (Deerpark)	16	4	Rathcore	16	3
Carlow (Deerpark)	17	3	Rosapenna (Morris-Ruddy)	14	3
Clandeboye (Dufferin)	4	4	Rosapenna (Sandy Hills)	4	4
Connemara	1	4	Rosslare (Old)	5	4
Connemara Isles	3	3	The Royal Belfast	1	4
Coollattin	12	3	The Royal Belfast	4	3
County Louth	14	4	The Royal Belfast	10	4
County Sligo	4	3	The Royal Belfast	11	3
The Curragh	15	5	The Royal County Down	1	5
Donegal	8	5	The Royal County Down	3	4
Doonbeg	1	5	The Royal County Down	4	3
Doonbeg	3	4	The Royal County Down	9	4
Doonbeg	6	4	The Royal County Down	11	4
Doonbeg	13	5	Royal Portrush (Dunluce)	5	4
Dromoland Castle	8	4	Royal Portrush (Dunluce)	7	4
Druids Glen	13	4	Royal Portrush (Dunluce)	13	4
Enniscrone (Dunes)	13	4	Royal Portrush (Dunluce)	14	3
The European	3	5	Royal Portrush (Valley)	4	5
The European	8	4	Royal Portrush (Valley)	5	4
The European	11	4	Royal Portrush (Valley)	10	5
The European	12	4	Royal Portrush (Valley)	18	3
The European	13	5	Tralee	8	4
Headfort (New)	10	4	Tramore	4	4
The Island	1	4	Tramore	5	4
The Island	4	4	Tramore	13	4
The Island	13	3	Waterville	2	4
The K Club (Smurfit)	2	3	Waterville	11	5
The K Club (Smurfit)	12	3	Waterville	16	4
Killarney (Killeen)	3	3	Westport	15	5
Killarney (Mahony's Point)	18	3	Woodenbridge	14	4

Justifiably one of the most photographed holes in Ireland, Ballybunion Old's p:4 11 is not just a pretty picture, not just a fabulous aesthetic experience running down by the sea (see also photo over 10th green, title page), but a supreme challenge for the player, with strategic use of land, completely natural hazards and a superb greensite. The fairway spreads down in cascades towards the green, leaving many choices for the player to match the infinite conditions. Kerrygold at its best!

Irish purple

We list the purple holes of Ireland and the main reason for their rating:

	No	p	Reason
Ardglass	1	4	Eccentric
Ardglass	7	3	Building as hazard
Athlone	13	4	Doubly blind
Castlerock (Bann)	9	3	Semi blind p:3
Connemara Isles	5	5	Eccentric
The Island	14	4	Narrow
Kirkistown Castle	2	4	Green on top of mound
Kirkistown Castle	10	4	Green on side of mound
Lahinch (Old)	4	5	Historic blind p:5
Lahinch (Old)	5	3	Historic blind p:3
Mount Juliet	16	4	Unusual bunker
Strandhill	13	4	Tiny green

Mackenzie's Design Principles

We summarise the 13 principles essential to good design set down in 1920 by Dr. Alister Mackenzie in his book 'Golf Architecture'. Mackenzie is arguably the greatest golf designer that ever lived. It was surely no accident that his wartime expertise was camouflage: the best golf design leaves you with a feeling that any alterations to the land are so natural that they have been completely disguised.

1) two 9 hole loops;
2) a large proportion of 2 shot holes and at least four 1 shot holes;
3) minimal walking between greens and tees;
4) undulating ground but no hill climbing;
5) every hole different in character;
6) a minimum of blind shots;
7) beautiful surroundings and minimal artificiality;
8) heroic carries and alternative routes;
9) an infinite variety of strokes required;
10) complete absence of having to look for balls;
11) interesting even to a scratch player always seeking ways to improve;
12) enjoyable for high handicappers;
13) equally good in winter and summer.

GOLF RESORT IRELAND

Raising the standards

Although northern European golfers (not least the Irish themselves) generally tend to fly south to play in better weather, Ireland is becoming one of the world's most attractive golf tourist destinations, aided by her recent economic success. This has facilitated a major upgrading of the product over the past 15 years or so – very few clubs seem to sport anything but a new clubhouse (*Shandon Park* and *Rathcore* sharing the prize for design) or a recently refurbished one. Less immediately evident is the huge investment that has been made in bringing golf courses up to modern standards, both in maintenance and infrastructure.

As a result it is pleasing to conclude that, ignoring both highs and lows of course design, the top golf destinations of Ireland can easily compete on the world stage (only to mention some near Dublin, e.g. *Carton House*, *Druids Glen & Heath*, *The Heritage*, *The K Club* and, from 2007, *Powerscourt*), and nearly all the rest are generally well more than adequate for purpose. At the bottom end of the scale, this has not prevented us from including *Castlegregory* and *Portstewart (Old)*, which are of interest as courses in their own right.

How do you do 'Guinness'?

As both my colleagues say, one of the endearing charms of Ireland is the warmth of the welcome and craic. Indeed, for many people the 19th (and, in Ireland, the successive holes – who mentioned Guinness?!) are as much a reason to go there as are the first 18. Here, though, we must air a concern, which may have arisen partly from Ireland's economic success and the expansion of the EU. Especially around Dublin, we have noticed the increasing employment of staff from other European countries, who (quite understandably) have yet to fully absorb the subtleties of either the Irish spirit or the English language. We would encourage the industry to ensure that appropriate training is implemented, or one of Ireland's greatest assets will be lost to a process of homogenisation similar to the one we have seen in course design.

Climate

When to travel? The most obvious period is from May to October, when the average maximum daytime temperature can be expected generally to exceed 60°F (15°C) – more comfortably so in the summer. The most popular courses, especially the famous links of the south west, are particularly busy in September. It can rain often for long periods at any time of the year, yet there is relatively little frost for an island so far north, though 'dank' and 'raw' are words which apply to many winter months. If you wish to play on the normal greens, we advise avoiding the period between Christmas and Easter, as many clubs use winter greens and/or close parts of their course during this period. Whenever you go, take raingear and warm clothes.

The facilities and welcome at Rathsallagh are excellent all year round, winter included. This view is of the lake front right of the 10th green.

Facility ratings

Our new facility ratings are designed to help golfers choose where to play, if their criteria for playing a course is the overall product offered by the club, rather than just the design of the course. The list that immediately follows presents the best facilities in Ireland available in 2006, at all of which there is hotel accommodation. For a list of alternative accommodation, please refer to the *Where to Stay* listings on pages 232.

Finally, new for this volume, the next six spreads comprise a golf-orientated guide to Ireland, supported by photos from our extensive library.

Enjoy the craic and stay slan!

Peter Millhouse, Resort Editor
Guaro, Spain, May 2006

Product Excellence

We list the best golf facilities in Ireland – all rate 🏆🏆🏆🏆🏆:

Adare	Druids Glen Golf Resort	Mount Wolseley
Ashford Castle	The Heritage	Portmarnock Links
Carton House	The K Club	Powerscourt*
Doonbeg	Luttrellstown Castle	Rathsallagh
Dromoland Castle	Mount Juliet	Roganstown

* hotel from 2007

Although close to Dublin's airport, enjoy the peaceful setting of O'Connor's p3:17.

O'Connor's Welcome – Roganstown

This page features modern design by Ireland's prolific Christy O'Connor Jnr: *Roganstown* (see also p 181) is one of his newest courses and also sports a hotel, gym and spa. For visitors to Ireland, it is an ideal place to unwind on arrival (free 15 minute shuttle from airport) and make your base for the north Eastern Dublin courses (notably *The Island,*

p:3 6 – water is never far away here (the hotel's large indoor swimming pool, included!).

Portmarnock and *Portmarnock Links)*. You could also easily play *County Louth* from here, and even make a day trip up to *Royal County Down,* before taking your clubs west . . . (Hotel details, page 236.)

Left *The classic period façade of the hotel entrance belies the quality modern facilities behind it.*

Below *Although routed mainly over former farmland, the placing of several greens near existing trees gives the course a surprising amount of maturity, as seen at p:4 11.*

21

The Dublin Coast – Golf and Craic: Portmarnock Links

Many Irish golf clubs belong to regional marketing groups and good packages are often on offer (see club websites). The East Coast Links (www.eastcoastlinks.com) is one such group, and includes courses on the coast near Dublin such as Bernard Langer's recently upgraded *Portmarnock Links*. If you fly in from the east, as you cross the coast seconds before landing at nearby Dublin airport you will see the course to your right (plus *Malahide* just inland of it and *The Island* across the water to the north). Sitting on the other side of the plane you would see many other courses, including *Howth* and *Sutton* immediately below, with *St Anne's* and *The Royal Dublin* on a long thin island a mile or so to the South. What about *Portmarnock*? It's right underneath you!

The right-hand window seat view: the recent excellent enhancements to Langer's course, which consolidate its ★★ standing, notably comprise new tees (just visible here as darker spots) high in the dunes bounding the sea with excellent vistas.

From the lower tees at his challenging p:3 9th you get a good feel of the superb links atmosphere Langer has created – and the green lies within 50 yds of the sea, over the dunes to the left . . .

The proximity of all these courses, central Dublin, the craic of Malahide to the north and Howth harbour to the south make The Portmarnock Hotel & Golf Links (4 star hotel, conference facilities, corporate golf packages etc; details page 235) an excellent base for a feast of golf, well - and a lot more…

The Portmarnock Hotel overlooks sea and closing holes alike. From the new back tee high in the dunes in a recent scratch competition it took a least a driver and a 2 iron to reach the 18th in two.

The Garden of Ireland – Powerscourt

Mention the subject of golf in Ireland and most visitors think of the courses of the westerly and northerly coastlines, or *Portmarnock*. But you should also consider one the country's most attractive inland areas, the so-called 'Garden of Ireland', below the Wicklow Hills, only half an hour south of central Dublin. The single most beautiful place to play and stay (in a 200 suite 5 star Ritz Carlton, from 2007) is the exclusive Powerscourt Estate, rich in history and home to the Slazenger family since 1961. Here there are two courses, *Powerscourt (East)* and *(West)*, both of championship length, yet playable by all standards, overlooked by the Palladian mansion (see photo page 177) and dominated by the famous Great Sugar Loaf mountain, which rises an almost perfectly conical 1643ft (503m) behind. Stay here also to play *The European*, Pat Ruddy's personal links, and several other courses (garden lovers should play *Druids Glen* in the spring).

This view of West's longish downhill p:3 17th shows the avenue of trees leading away from the mansion and the Wicklow Hills beyond. What you don't see is the bunkers front and right of this excellent undulating greensite.

This view from behind the green of East's p:3 16 hints at the slightly moorland feel to the course's back 9. Playing downhill over a pond to a raised green, don't get too distracted by the aesthetics or your score could suffer…

We include Powerscourt on our list of 'diversions' from the golf – the estate's garden probably dates from the granting of the land in 1609 by James I to Sir Richard Wingfield, the 1st Viscount Powerscourt, and the terraces were formalised in the mid 19th century by Daniel Robertson. The garden has been augmented regularly since, including a magnificent fountain, splendid statuary and, in 1908, the Japanese Garden. The mansion, designed by Richard Castle in 1730, was gutted by fire in 1974 (tragically ironic – on the very night of a party rounding off a long period of restoration). It has since been partially restored and is open to visitors. The extensive garden centre, exhibition and terrace café complete the list. (Accomodation details, page 235.)

With water coming into play around the green, East's long downhill p:5 17 is a challenge for your golfing brain as well as another of the course's scenic gems. McEvoy, its designer, framed the hole with the Sugar Loaf mountain as its backdrop.

Late winter sun casts shadows across the raised green of Faithlegg's p:4 4th and illuminates the woods behind.

The South East – Coast, Hinterland and Crystal

Moving beyond the Garden of Ireland, the beaches of the east give way to the more cliff-faced southern coast. Much of the best golf here is inland (*Carlow*, *Coollattin*, *Gowran Park* and *Mount Juliet*), but don't miss the classic links at *Rosslare* and, if you want to pay for it, the

The exposed medium p:3 11th at Old Head seen from some of the grasses that are strewn around the course.

The approach bunkers and raised green at Fota Island's p:4 6th are defined by the clump of pines standing behind.

experience of *Old Head of Kinsale* (your reaction is likely to depend entirely on the weather you experience). The tour of the Waterford Crystal factory is the most memorable of its type in the whole of Ireland. Nearby are *Faithlegg*, *Tramore* and *Waterford Castle*.

A tour of the Waterford Crystal factory is highly recommended. The factory is on the west edge of Waterford. The highly skilled craftsmen are only paid by the piece: if they make a mistake, there's no money – concentration is guaranteed.

One of the most famous landmarks in Ireland, the Croagh Patrick mountain (763m/2503ft) dominates this view of Westport's p:3 14th. By ringing his bell at the top of the mountain's steep southern screes, legend has it that the saint caused all the snakes in Ireland to plunge to their death.

The Wild West – Ballybunion, Doonbeg, Lahinch and much more

The subject of golf in Ireland leads many to think automatically of the famous west coast links. If you only have a couple of days, this would probably be your best destination, and you should be sure to include *Ballybunion*, *Doonbeg* and *Lahinch*. If you have time for more, consider the spectacular scenery of The Ring of Kerry and/or Connemara and the famous folklore of nearby Croagh Patrick (see *Westport* photo *above*). Other courses to visit would include *Adare*, *Killarney* and *Tralee*. The hotels in Adare (all excellent within their price bracket) would make a good central base for much of this area. Take clothing for the wildest golfing weather you will ever have encountered and hope that you won't need it . . .

A view from behind the ladies' tee at Doonbeg's excellent short p:4 3rd, gold rated for its raised greensite, splendid bunkering, walls as hazards, excellent use of land and aesthetics.

Above *A photo for the archive: Martin Hawtree's recent remodelling of p:3 13 at Dooks has reduced the severe contours on right side of this green, but the original was so memorable we could not omit inclusion of this image.*

Below *The famous courses, such as Waterville (here looking over the 11th tee to the clubhouse), are busy during the summer. Reserve before you travel.*

The North – Golf, spirits and more for giants . . .

The golfing North of Ireland is dominated by three famous links: the underrated *Valley* course at *Portrush*, its *Dunluce* big brother, and the awesome *Royal County Down*. But there is plenty more: relax for a few days in the comfortable hotel at *Rosapenna*, savour the natural features of *County Sligo*, *Enniscrone (Dunes)*, *Ballyliffin (Old)* and the other links at *Castlerock* and *Portstewart*. Inland, Belfast has three particularly memorable courses in *Belvoir Park*, *Malone* and *The Royal Belfast*. If you go to *Portrush*, allow time to see the Giant's Causeway and the Bushmills Distillery – for these, the Bushmills Inn (see page 233) makes a most agreeable base…

Downhill p:5 5 at Castlerock (Bann) provides one of the more spectacular views on the course.

Above The famous panorama looking back over the 3rd green at Royal County Down (Championship), with the p:3 4th (also gold-rated) to its right, and the Mountains of Mourne as the backdrop.

Right Don't miss the 40,000 basalt columns of The Giant's Causeway, one of Ireland most popular tourist destinations. Managed by The National Trust, the visitor centre has an excellent audio-visual exhibition, and a shuttle bus conveys you down to the causeway below.

Below Downhill p:3 11 at Royal Portrush (Dunluce) requires accuracy to avoid sand . . .

ADARE ♟♟♟♟♟ ★★

Trent Jones Snr 1995 €€€ **H:** M 28, L 36, J 36

✉ **Adare Golf Club, Adare Manor, Adare, Co. Limerick, RoI**
☎ + 353 61 395 044
✐ golf@adaremanor.com www.adaremanor.com

🚗 ✈ Shannon: N19/N18 for Limerick, whence N21 for
Killarney; Adare Manor on L after some 11km. Note: this course is
part of the Adare Manor Hotel and Golf Resort, and is separate
from Adare Manor Golf Club, whose entrance precedes.

	y	p		y	p
1	444	4	10	436	4
2	426	4	11	179	3
3	403	4	12	551	5
4	178	3	13	433	4
5	421	4	14	421	4
6	203	3	15	378	4
7	528	5	16	167	3
8	419	4	17	413	4
9	577	5	18	548	5
	3599	36		3526	36
				7125	72

Vintage Trent Jones Snr in grand-scale, majestic arboretum setting (especially back 9 – Jones at his best). Other tee positions compensate for length from back. Lavish, generally open-style bunkering and shaped greensites, often with narrow entrances. Maturity should improve weaker mid-front 9. Water aplenty.

Ireland is best known for its impressive and diverse hand of links courses – they hold all the aces and most of the picture cards. These have mostly been in play for decades, if not a century, but a growing number

The view from back tee to green on dog-leg p:4 15, illustrates the beauty and tranquillity of Jones' design, even directly in front of the manor, which overlooks the river and green from the right.

Accommodation: Adare Manor, Dromoland Castle, Dunraven Arms

Playing lengthily back to the manor, 18 is one of the most demanding p:5s in Ireland: only the bravest will bid to pass on a lay up to near our camera position . . .

of clubs (the odd king, a few queens and jacks) are finessing the inland precedent set by the lakeside splendour of Killarney. Robert Trent Jones Snr's Adare has leapt into the rankings: water here too, but the magnificence lies in the splendour of the arboretum. Some tree gems here: true diamonds (note especially the superb specimen cypress front right of the 13th tee – but no rubber trees: wrong climate!). Jones weaves his course through it all most sympathetically. But it is not just beauty: despite the 3 yellow-rated holes (which may reduce in number with maturity), Adare is one of Jones' best designs in Europe – comparable, say, with Spain's *Sotogrande* ★★ (set in different scenery).

We understand that spades may soon be sharpened to implement Jones' design for a second Adare layout, but the original is no dummy: your game will be severely tested, particularly if you are ambitious in your choice of tee. All the characteristics of a Trent Jones classic are here, not least lavish bunkering, distinctly three-dimensional greens and, of course, water. After the streams and lakes of the front 9 (which includes, it has to be said, a blander section from 5 to 7), the river Maigue features spectacularly on the way home: to succeed in your contract with your opponent, the trick here is to keep your ball above the line (well . . . waterline) right to the end – including the long carry to the green of memorably challenging p:5 18 (see above). Only then, to your heart's relief (and surely with satisfaction), will you cross the final bridge . . .

Accommodation: Fitzgerald's Woodlands House

ARDEE ♟♟♟

Unknown/unknown/Branigan   1911/1982/1990s? €

✉ Ardee Golf Club, Townspark, Ardee, Co. Louth, RoI
☎ +353 41 685 3227
✍ ardeegolfclub@eircom.net   www.ardeegolfclub.com

🚗 ✈ Dublin: M1 north to exit for Ardee; L for Ardee on
edge of town, straight over mini rbt after 300m, R after 50m
(brown sign for Táin Trail); club 200m on L.

Selected holes	y	p
13	202	3
14	546	5
15	405	4
16	368	4
Total	6510	71

Parkland course with pleasant rustic routing and some nice movements in land. Generally good greensites, some raised. With less artificial mounding it might be a candidate for a higher rating . . . p:3 13 is one of the most challenging holes on the course, requiring a carry of some 180yds over water from the tee.

ARDGLASS ♟♟♟

Shaw/D Jones   1896/2003   £   H: M 28, L 36, J 36

✉ Ardglass Golf Club, Castle Place, Ardglass, Co. Down BT30 7TP, NI
☎ +44 284 484 1219
✍ info@ardglassgolfclub.com   www.ardglassgolfclub.com

🚗 ✈ Belfast Int: A26 south to M1 J9; M1 for Belfast, exit J7; A49
to Ballynahinch, whence B2 and R onto A7 for Downpatrick, then B1
to Ardglass (total approx 50 miles); club by sea in town centre.

Purple 1: Stunning seaside vista on leaving oldest clubhouse building in world (with cannons as starting guns), but this short linksy uphill p:4 is rather spoiled by the fact that the raised green is hidden behind a bunker. Could be gold or red, but blended they make . . . purple. Ardglass' remarkable clifftop start only gets better: the 2nd (p:3 over cliffs) and 3rd (p:3 from cliff edge tee over hummocky ground to a raised green) are both close to gold – and the views from the next two tees aren't bad, either . . .

Accommodation: *Ardee*: Boyne Valley; *Ardglass*: Burrendale, Slieve Donard

Purple 7: *quirky p:3 down towards the water – you can't see the putting surface, and in place of bunkers there is a building as a hazard (another one on 16 . . .). Noteworthy.*

	y	p		y	p
1	335	4	10	205	3
2	167	3	11	488	5
3	334	4	12	198	3
4	375	4	13	397	4
5	151	3	14	400	4
6	414	4	15	491	5
7	219	3	16	422	4
8	439	4	17	361	4
9	527	5	18	345	4
	2961	34		3307	36
				6268	70

A dramatic and beautiful hotchpotch of clifftop, open ground and shoreside golf holes, recently extended and woven together into an entertaining course with mountain and island views. Opening and closing clifftop stretch full of character, greens included. Some blind shots, water and wind. Fun to play.

ARKLOW ♟♟♟

FG Hawtree & Taylor/Hackett/Connaughton   1927/1960s/1994–   €

✉   Arklow Golf Club, Abbeylands, Arklow, Co. Wicklow, RoI

☎   +353 40 232 492

✉   arklowgolflinks@eircom.net   www.arklowgolflinks.com

🚗 ✈   Dublin: M1/M50 south becomes M11/N11 to Arklow.
Just after bridge as you approach Arklow, L to sea and follow signs.

Selected holes

	y	p
1	405	4
2	419	4
3	198	3
4	368	4
5	441	4
6	420	4
7	139	3
8	306	4
Total	**6383**	**69**

A harbourside course to watch during a period (as we understand it) of gradual remodelling and 'linksification': on a primarily flat site with small dunes nearer the sea. The first 8 holes have ★★ well within their sights. After this, it turns into relatively disappointing (though not necessarily easier) parkland golf. If these later holes are linksified to the standard of 1–8, the future bodes well.

ASHFORD CASTLE ♈♈♈♈♈ ★

Hackett & Mulcahy   1974   €   H: M 28, L 36

✉ Ashford Castle Golf Club, Cong, Co. Mayo, RoI
☎ +353 94 954 6003
✎ ashford@ashford.ie   www.ashford.ie
🚗 ✈ Galway: R339/N6 to Galway, leaving on N84 for
Castlebar; at Headford R334 to Cross, whence L at church onto
R346 to Cong; club on L just before Cong village.

	y	p
1	320	4
2	340	4
3	381	4
4	128	3
5	354	4
6	494	5
7	370	4
8	279	4
9	161	3
	2829	35

Beautiful 9-hole resort course, set in undulating park with castle (hotel) and lake views. Played for fun, played seriously: a pleasure either way – minimalist 'sandpit' bunkers, surprisingly, work in this context. Unique routing.

As you drive into this castle-hotel estate synonymous with grand-scale luxury, you would be forgiven for thinking that its tree-lined but generally roomy golf course with minimalist 'sandpit-at-best' bunkers is a bit Mickey Mouse. This image belies what is one of the best examples of a hotel course we have seen – admittedly one that should be approached in the right spirit. You come to a place like this for true leisure: sumptuous accommodation, a bit of fishing, perhaps, but nothing too arduous – recreation rather than sport. You find a course without any rough (except for the very wild shot), not of any serious

p:3 9 - note the rectangular shape of the bunker left of the green (and, yes, the castle is pay and play, too!).

length, whose few bunkers may be exited by putter – a glorified municipal pitch and putt? We beg to differ.

Ashford Castle was designed by Eddie Hackett under the watchful eye of none less than Mr JA Mulcahy, shortly before he masterminded the links at *Waterville*. Ashford earns a ★ because it is a perfect design for its purpose – a place to relax and have a bit of fun: no titanium-drive-required-just-to-get-to-the-fairway golf here. Even so, it can be played at two levels: for fun and don't worry about the score, or set up as a serious challenge, especially with several raised greensites (e.g. 1–5 and 8). But the highest marks are earned for the almost unique routing: you go round in two circles, with the final 4 holes intertwined around the first 5, all wonderfully fitted to the graceful folds of the land (especially at 2, which earns gold primarily for this). The aesthetics are superb – a park with occasional views of the castle and lake, and some majestic trees, especially the huge cypress beside the 3rd green/4th and 7th tees, which also forms a backdrop for the 6th hole. Strategic qualities as well – most notably

The green at golden p:4 2, seen across and over the fold of land that swallows up mis-hit approaches . . .

at right-to-left sweeping dogleg p:4 3, where you can choose either to cut the corner through/over the trees (as Tom Watson once did), or to play the hole's full length by driving into a valley and then up to the green.

Christy O'Connor Snr was professional here in the opening years.

ATHENRY ♟♟

Hackett/Connaughton   1991/2005   €

✉ Athenry Golf Club, Palmerstown, Oranmore, Co. Galway, RoI
☎ +353 91 794 466
✎ athenrygc@eircom.net   www.athenrygolfclub.net
🚗 ✈ Galway: R339 away from Galway; R onto N18; L onto N6 for Dublin; L on R348 to Athenry; under railway bridge and L, then L again, club on R.

Selected holes		
	m	p
12	175	3
16	367	4
17	143	3
Total	5718	70

Mainly tree-lined, compact parkland course: two loops of 9 holes with four greensites recently enhanced. Note: two p:3s through woods (downhill 12, and 17), and medium long p:4 16 (straight away through trees over gently but interestingly moving land to a mounded and bunkered new greensite).

ATHLONE ♟♟

McAllister/F Hawtree/Hackett/Connaughton   1892/1972/1985/2005   €

✉ Athlone Golf Club, Hodson Bay, Athlone, Co. Roscommon, RoI
☎ +353 90 649 2073
✎ athlonegolfclub@eircom.net   www.athlonegolfclub.ie
🚗 ✈ Dublin: M1/M50 south; exit 7 onto N4/M4/N6 for Galway; from Athlone bypass R onto N61 for Roscommon; R to Hodson Bay after 2km; club on L before Hodson Bay Hotel.

Selected holes		
	m	p
2	140	3
6	177	3
11	390	4
13	396	4
15	300	4
Total	6175	71

A parkland esker course, recently partially remodelled, with some quite steep undulations, water and some testing greensites. As well as 13 (*below*) you may also have fun with p:3 2 (the roadside fence excepted), p:3 7 challenging over water and p:4 11 (greenside water).

Purple – 13: *a memorable and spectacular esker (see Birr, p 55) roller-coaster hole, which would have worked well as an old fashioned 'bogey' 5, but doesn't really work as a p:4, because both drive and 2nd shot are at best semi-blind.*

Ballinrobe's p:3 16, our favourite hole – see comments in the text below.

ATHY

Larkin & Barret/Suttle/Howes   1906/1993/2004   €

✉   Athy Golf Club, Geraldine, Athy, Co. Kildare, RoI

☎   +353 59 863 1729

✏   info@athygolfclub.com   www.athygolfclub.com

🚗 ✈ Dublin: M1/M50 south; exit 9 N7/M7/M9 for Carlow; at Kilcullen (5km along M9) R onto N78 to Athy; on approach to Athy R at lights for Kildare; club 2km on R.

Selected holes		
	y	p
5	517	5
11	176	3
Total	**6475**	**72**

Set over rolling ground with a pleasantly natural feel, a partially tree-lined course, some of which has recently been enhanced by Howes. 5 and 11 are particularly memorable. Some water. Don't make the graveyard at 16/17 your own!

BALLINROBE 🏆🏆🏆

Hackett   1995   €

✉   Ballinrobe Golf Club, Clooncastle, Ballinrobe, Co. Kerry, RoI

☎   +353 94 954 1118

✏   info@ballinrobegolfclub.com   www.ballinrobegolfclub.com

🚗 ✈ Knock: N17 south for Galway; 10km after Knock, N60 for Claremorris, where L for Galway/N17; then R onto R331 for Ballinrobe; approaching which after some 20km, club on L during a series of bends.

Selected holes		
	m	p
2	410	4
4	478	5
10	365	4
16	160	3
Total	**6354**	**73**

A generally fairly flat parkland course, locally well regarded, with some mounding and a few heathland features (such as gorse narrowing the entrance to medium p:3 7) and some grander sets of trees near and in front of the clubhouse – a period building, making a pleasant distinction from the many, albeit most often excellent, modern clubhouse buildings in Ireland. Some good greensites and nice bunkering – especially at our favourite hole, p:3 16, whose challengingly front-bunkered green is impressively set beneath of a clump of trees (above).

BALLYBUNION 🏆🏆🏆🏆

✉ Ballybunion Golf Club, Sandhill Road, Ballybunion, Co. Kerry, RoI

☎ +353 68 271 46

✎ bbgolfc@iol.ie   www.ballybuniongolfclub.ie

🚗 ✈ Kerry: N23/N22 to Tralee; N69 to Listowel; R553 for
Ballybunion (9km), where follow road to seafront and round to L;
club entrance 1km on R.

CASHEN ★

Trent Jones Snr   1984   €€   H: M 24, L 36

	y	p		y	p
1	522	5	10	324	4
2	377	4	11	146	3
3	154	3	12	210	3
4	350	4	13	395	4
5	314	4	14	400	4
6	155	3	15	487	5
7	378	4	16	164	3
8	605	5	17	479	5
9	478	5	18	368	4
	3333	37		2973	35
				6306	72

American/links hybrid with rather narrow undulating fairways leading to generally raised, small, often tiered greens in stunning seaside setting. Long – but at some holes well-placed drives will roll down hills, significantly shortening second shots. Some out-of-place artificiality, but nice echoes of less hilly, less scenic Old course (e.g. consecutive p:5s and p:3s). Wind!

With the possible exception of a Colt or Mackenzie, anyone accepting a commission to design a second course in the dunes alongside *Ballybunion (Old)* was risking trouble. It was somehow fitting that the opportunity was given to Trent Jones Snr, himself a hybrid (British born, yet the 20th century's most famous American golf-course designer), with

Gold rated p:5 15 can play every which way, depending on the wind. Be careful: the approach shot is deceptive, as you'll often play it sheltered from the wind; anything short is marked 'return to sender' . . .

Short p:5 17 - one of the most exposed holes here. With a good score in the making, your heartbeat reflects the wind speed. On in two - for glory, or sheer lunacy?! Up to you . . .

no track record with traditional links. He clearly relished the opportunity and the result, rather neutered by subsequent revisions, is fascinating. Some may argue that it is also an example – by exception – of how it sometimes pays to keep to one's core business. Jones thought it was one of his finest, a view apparently supported by many members of the club (a club which then changed it!). Others felt the mixture just didn't work.

We stand in the middle of the love-it-or-hate-it debate. True, the greensites are all but too small (yielding few chip-and-run links opportunities), but how can one criticise a course for being 'un-links-like' when it is so undeniably on links ground? For some, the holes are too long and the fairways too narrow for such a windswept site. For others there are some very cleverly designed holes and the stunning views from dunes (on an even bigger scale than *Ballybunion (Old)*) mitigate for the demanding length. Our mid-position is no cop-out: we see this course as

---

For readers interested in Jones' original design, we summarise the changes made to it:

1	Tee moved from near entrance gate up to near clubhouse, turning hole into dogleg.	12	Was a short sharp left-to-right dogleg p:4 on top of dunes between current 11th green and 13th tee. The green, on top of the dune to left of current 12th, was driveable – over a perditious abyss. The climb from 11th green to 12th tee became known as 'heart attack hill' – perhaps explaining its demise. (Note that Jones' design thus did not include consecutive p:3s.)
2	Tee moved away from above 8th green (i.e. near 9th tee,) to the left and lower.		
3/4	Unchanged.		
5	Unchanged, except grass on direct line to green from tee is now cut rather than left completely wild.		
		13	Unchanged.
6	Unchanged.	14	Basically unchanged: fairway widened and smoothed out, removing some blindness.
7	Erosion problems: fairway was too close to sea. It has had to be severely fortified to stop erosion, including banks added to left, closing off view of sea.	15	Unchanged, though green is now perhaps marginally bigger on left.
		16	Unchanged (an experiment with tee on other side of the dune to give protection from wind was discontinued).
8	Unchanged.		
9	Unchanged, except rough is gentler (as generally over whole course).	17	Original tee was a little further back, and landing area for second shot has been flattened and widened.
10	New green: original was lower, long and narrow green with friendly mounding, more exposed to sea.		
		18	Landing area for drive has been widened and flattened.
11	Unchanged.		

---

a demonstration of the difference between old-style British Isles links and new-style American target golf. Give the man credit: Jones had been around long enough to understand what a links course was. He also knew that if you look west from Ballybunion, the next course is somewhere in America. His Irish links course does exactly that – it looks to the New World of golf, while acknowledging its historic location. So, for example, the mass of rough dunes grass (which is now cut shorter than Jones intended) in front of the shelf green at short

For many, medium long p:4 13 at Ballybunion (Cashen) is the best hole on the course. But its design is also an illustration of the modern trend towards tee to green golf being played in the air.

p:4 5 plays as fatally as the water in front of Jones' many American lakeside greens, while the shelves down which the fairway of p:5 15 cascades pay homage to the similar feature at *Ballybunion (Old)*'s famous p:4 11. Sure, you only have to walk out of the clubhouse the other way for evidence that Cashen is far from the greatest course in Ireland, yet, in the history of golf design, its statement is somehow unique.

You don't need perfect weather to enjoy the aesthetics of Ballybunion (Old), but you do need a steady nerve for your short game here: shortish p:3 8 rewards a well-aimed teeshot, but everything else will give you trouble, as is very evident from the tee. Most of us have our green-criss-crossing days: make sure it isn't one of yours when you come here! This hole wins gold on all counts. (The green on the right is the winter green.)

OLD ★★★

Various/Simpson & Gourlay/Watson 1893/1941/1995 €€€ H: M 24, L 36

	y	p			y	p
1	392	4		10	359	4
2	445	4		11	453	4
3	220	3		12	192	3
4	520	5		13	484	5
5	524	5		14	131	3
6	364	4		15	212	3
7	432	4		16	499	5
8	153	3		17	385	4
9	454	4		18	379	4
	3504	36			3094	35
					6598	71

Fashioned by nature, world-class seaside links. Massive dunes, eccentricities and irregularities. Every hole different, yet harmonious and fair. Slightly blander townwards section comes early in a round which builds, through sometimes penal, short-game-testing shore-liners and undulations, to a roller-coaster climax. Wonderful greensites. Views. Wind!!

Superlatives are commonplace in the consistent praise for Ballybunion (Old) ever since its late 19th-century inauguration. This is a links course that is different, yet one that, for those well acquainted with the genre, should come as no surprise. Different, because everything here is on a larger scale than anywhere else: not just in the height of the sandhills (which run rather more across the course from land to sea than on many links), but in the finesse it requires of your short game (e.g. the demands of the severe run-offs around the 8th and 9th greens). No surprise? Well, ultimately, there are no rules to links design, so you should expect anything and everything. And that is what you get.

A view of the seaside green of Ballybunion (Old)'s gold-rated p:4 7 (there is a winter alternative, inland). This green is more raised than it looks, and long. Take your par and move on quickly – if you can . . .?!

And yet, despite its incredible dimension, the fairways (played to scratch, as it were) are devoid of blind shots and of a kindly length. While comparisons are often made with *Lahinch (Old)* (its near neighbour – there is no right answer as to which is better), Ballybunion (Old) is the benchmark against which all natural golf courses should be tested. (In saying this, we respect Viscount Castlerosse's 1934 wisdom, expressed in his *Sunday Express*, that 'The Old Course at St. Andrews . . . is not a golf course. It is a miracle.', and, in passing, mention the near perfection of Royal Melbourne.) So, measure the appealing eccentricities of a Cruden Bay, the fairness and honesty of a Muirfield, the remote challenge of a Royal Dornoch, the windswept exposure of a Royal St George's, the surprises and naturally irregular character of a St Enodoc, the dimension and bunkers of a *Royal County Down*, the seaside holes and views of a Turnberry, the dunes of a Royal Birkdale, the length and

Gold is earned at p:4 9 primarily because of the raised green and short grass run-offs.

p:3 15, seen from the tee, where you may need anything up to driver to reach the raised slopes of the green.

Above *A sample of the roller-coaster finish (15–18: down-and-long; across-and-up; down-and-round; up-and-round). Viewed here with one's back to the sea, 16 is a sweeping right-to-left dogleg shortish p:5 up to a green perched between the dunes on a brow opposite the graveyard in front of the 1st tee. Cut off as much of the corner as you dare, but risk too much and your match will receive a premature burial . . .*

threats of a Carnoustie, even the Kiwi understatement of a Paraparaumu: measure them all by reference to this remarkable links. And, when you have played all these (and no doubt many others), to which would you most want to return? If your answer is 'Ballybunion', you will be in the company of thousands of golfers, exemplified by no lesser linksman than Tom Watson.

Right *The dimension of the dunes of downhill right-to-left medium p:4 17 has to be experienced to be believed. The line of your teeshot (down towards the shore) will dictate how short your approach could be to a green (seen here from the dunes above left of the approach) that often seems as small as the bunker does large. Be careful: the slightest hint of a following wind can put you on the beach. (Conditions can change quickly here: this photo was taken within minutes of our shot of 16 - above.)*

Research is inconclusive as to who was responsible for the design of Ballybunion (Old). It is generally accepted that the current layout was significantly influenced by the mid-1930s report of Tom Simpson (who considered it so perfect that he changed very little) and Molly Gourlay (look for the touch of a female designer, respected alike for her passion for p:3s and brilliant play), while (more likely) James McKenna, the first pro at Lahinch, and (less likely) Old Tom Morris and James Braid may have played some part. Surely the difficulty here is a compliment to Mother Nature, whose ingredients on site are so naturally suited for all that is golf that the course could almost be said to have, at the very least, routed itself – most notably at the roller-coaster finish? It goes beyond imagination, yet works.

BALLYLIFFIN

✉ Ballyliffin Golf Club, Ballyfiffin, Inishowen, Co. Donegal, RoI

☎ +353 74 937 6119

✎ info@ballyliffingolfclub.com   www.ballyliffingolfclub.com

🚗 ✈ Derry: A2 Londonderry, across Foyle bridge, then A2 north/R238 for Moville; L onto R240 at Quigley's Point for Carndonagh, whence R238 to Ballyliffin; club on R before village.

GLASHEDY ↗

Ruddy & Craddock   1995   €€   H: M 28, L 36

	y	p		y	p
1	426	4	10	397	4
2	432	4	11	419	4
3	428	4	12	448	4
4	479	5	13	572	5
5	177	3	14	183	3
6	404	4	15	440	4
7	183	3	16	426	4
8	422	4	17	549	5
9	382	4	18	450	4
	3333	35		3884	37
				7217	72

Large-scale modern dunes course in sublimely remote windswept setting with wonderful views over hills and sea. Generally long holes will challenge the best players (whatever the elements), but there's plenty of room to accommodate the rest of us, especially from the more forward tees. Generally large, relatively flat greens. Watch out for hidden bunkers.

A shot from Glashedy's 7th tee, giving a full view of right to left dogleg p:4 8 (right) and (top left) sight of the 9th fairway and green, running towards the clubhouse, a barge amidst a heaving sea of dunes . . .

OLD ★

Hackett/Faldo 1973/2005 €€ **H:** M 28, L 36

	y	p		y	p
1	400	4	10	330	4
2	420	4	11	396	4
3	350	4	12	206	3
4	492	5	13	431	4
5	176	3	14	538	5
6	374	4	15	407	4
7	181	3	16	413	4
8	384	4	17	160	3
9	389	4	18	553	5
	3166	35		3434	36
				6600	71

Wonderfully natural links course on relatively level ground overall, but whose fairways are often like rough seas, with wave after wave of eccentric little undulations giving a truly old-fashioned links feel. Relatively flat, natural-feel greensites. Pleasant to find a links not always requiring long irons or woods for the 2nd shot. Setting: as for Glashedy.

Note: the course was being lengthened by some 300 yards as we went to press.

A visit to Ballyliffin will be hard to forget – here are some extracts from our notes:
- the most northerly golf in all Ireland (Old and Glashedy – well, Glashedy just wins);
- the most natural course you'll ever play (Old, especially pre-construction of Glashedy);
- the most unnatural natural course you will ever play (Glashedy): reflect on this at the 37th;
- the most dramatic views of wild sea, rocks and mountains – 360 degrees' worth (Old and Glashedy);

- every kind of weather, and worse… and better (Old and Glashedy);
- the only course where it is almost possible to get seasick driving a buggy (Old) – the fairways are sometimes calm, sometimes rippled and often covered in wave after wave of subtle, and not so subtle, undulations, all wonderfully natural;
- one of Ireland's new genre of 'dunes' courses (Glashedy), so named because the course sits more on top of the dunes than more naturally within them like a true links course (Old);

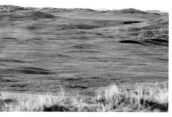

A view up Old's p:4 2, showing both the subtle undulations of the fairway and Faldo's generally simple, often incisive and always effective bunkering, which has significantly added quality to the course.

- p:3s the stronger element of the course (Glashedy); p:3s the weaker element of the course (Old);
- greensites of diverse interest, because they are so natural (Old) (we love 4); greensites you cannot miss, visually (Glashedy);
- one of Ireland's most fun-to-play courses (Old);
- one of Ireland's courses that most consistently tests you with 3 irons and/or woods for your second shots (Glashedy);
- one of the courses most likely to rise from * to ** (Old) – primarily due to the added definition of Faldo's classy re-bunkering;
- one of the courses where you are likely to curse the designers for including blind bunkers (Glashedy; Old p:3 17);
- a club with an entrepreneurial history, if ever there was one: from nearly swamped by the sea (Old, 1974), nearly bankrupt (Club, 1978 – saved by the Bazaar and Raffle Committee; 1984 – saved by the

You cannot avoid Ballyliffin's remote natural duneland serenity, seen here from left of the fairway of Old p:4 10. (N.B. The green has been moved back since this shot was taken.)

£100 draw; £100,000+ in credit by 1986!), to new clubhouse, a huge barge, serenely anchored amidst the heaving seas of fairways (1987), new course (Glashedy, 1995) and growing worldwide repute.

They might just be worth a visit . . .

BALLYMASCANLON ♔♔♔♔

Ruddy & Craddock   1989   €

✉ **Ballymascanlon Hotel and Country Club, Dundalk, Co. Louth, RoI**
☎ **+353 42 935 8200**
✎ **info@ballymascanlon.com   www.ballymascanlon.com**
🚗 ✈ **Dublin: M1 north for Belfast to end of m'way R at rbt, L at next rbt onto R173 for Carlingford; club is at Ballymascanlon House Hotel 400m on L. (M'way works may change m'way exit.)**

Selected holes

	y	p
3	169	3
4	454	5
5	150	3
7	395	4
18	415	4
Total	5763	68

Relatively short but reasonably well-designed hotel course (ideal for its purpose), in pleasant parkland/woodland setting on gently rolling ground with several water hazards and some interesting raised greens. The good 3–5 p:3 p:4 p:3 run, ending in front of the dolmen, makes the best of the views to distant hills, while there are some good water-carrying challenges at p:4 7, and the relatively new p:4 18, which crowns a strongish finish.

Braid would be pleased to see that the effect of the front bunkers has endured at p:3 7 – well short, they make the green look closer than it is: a favourite device of his (British examples being at Walton Heath, Gleneagles, Hankley Common, etc.).

BANGOR 🏆🏆🏆 ↗

Braid & Stutt   1935   £   H: M 28, L 36

✉ Bangor Golf Club, Broadway, Bangor, Co. Down BT20 4RH, NI
☎ +44 28 912 709 22
✉ bangorgolfclubni@btconnect.com   www.bangorgolfclubni.co.uk
🚗 ✈ Belfast Int: M2 to Belfast whence A2 to Bangor, on whose ring road L at Gransha rbt (signposted Town Centre); after 1/2 mile R onto Fairfield Rd, then 50yds later L onto Broadway; club on R.

y	p			y	p	
1	351	4		10	438	4
2	493	5		11	319	4
3	359	4		12	194	3
4	471	5		13	384	4
5	463	4		14	175	3
6	354	4		15	408	4
7	192	3		16	510	5
8	409	4		17	159	3
9	392	4		18	339	4
	3484	37			2790	34
					6410	71

Mature parkland course, rising to higher ground in middle of each 9 hole loop. Several doglegs and some good bunkering, occasionally fronting greensites. Large, often tiered greens may generally be monoplane, but flat they are not. Extensive (including distant sea) views. Uphill holes more than balanced by those downhill. Some revisions (e.g. p:3 12 greensite) to Braid's original.

Opposite *From left of the approach to Beaufort's p:3 17, you see the ruins of Castle Core (centre, on horizon). But from the tee, this testing hole aims straight at the mountains of Macgillycuddy's Reeks (background, left).*

Accommodation: Shelleven House; *Beaufort:* Aghadoe Heights Hotel, Castlerosse Hotel

BEARNA 🏆🏆

Browne   1996   €

✉ Bearna Golf Club, Corboley, Bearna, Co. Galway, RoI

☎ +353 91 592 677

✎ info@bearnagolfclub.com   www.bearnagolfclub.com

🚗 ✈ Galway: R339 into Galway, leaving on R336 along the seafront west for Spiddle; after about 7km R in Bearna away from sea; follow signs to club, on L.

Selected holes

	m	p
11	350	4
13	120	3
Total	6174	72

Distant and closer views of the sea abound on this excellent site, whose design thus has potential for enhancement over time. The often boulder- and bog-strewn surrounds are reminiscent of *Connemara* and *Connemara Isles*. A few holes stand out, notably shortish p:4 11 with a second shot over a creek to a green that is a little further away than it looks, and downhill short p:3 14 over a pond, with the wilderness stretching beyond.

BEAUFORT 🏆🏆🏆

Spring   1994   €

✉ Beaufort Golf Club, Churchtown, Beaufort, Killarney, Co. Kerry, RoI

☎ +353 64 444 40

✎ beaufortgc@eircom.net   www.beaufortgolfclub.com

🚗 ✈ Kerry: N23/N22 to Killarney, then N72 west for Killorglin; after 7km L across Beaufort bridge and R into village; continue for 2km; signs to club on L.

Selected holes

	y	p
12	482	5
17	192	3
Total	6598	71

Parkland course in full view of Macgillycuddy's Reeks: well-conceived holes which, perhaps with enhancement over the years, have potential for higher rating. The ruins of Castle Core (*below*) stand impressively beside the raised 13th green. Stone was taken from the castle to build the Georgian house that is the centrepiece of the Churchtown Estate, within which the course is laid out. The entrance to the course is lined with 200-year-old trees, and the pineapples that crown the gate pillars are a traditional symbol of the hospitality that endures.

BELMULLET (CARNE GOLF LINKS)

Hackett 1993 € **H:** M 28, L 36

✉ Belmullet Golf Club, Carne, Belmullet, Co. Mayo, RoI
☎ +353 97 822 92
✎ carngolf@iol.ie   www.carnegolflinks.com
🚗 ✈ Knock: N17/N25/N26 to Ballina, whence N59 to Bangor; there R onto R313 to Belmullet; follow signs to Carne from Belmullet airport; club 3km on R.

	m	p		m	p
1	366	4	10	465	5
2	183	3	11	332	4
3	376	4	12	300	4
4	473	5	13	482	5
5	378	4	14	133	3
6	363	4	15	366	4
7	162	3	16	154	3
8	365	4	17	399	4
9	327	4	18	495	5
	2993	35		3126	37
				6119	72

Undulating links, whose mainly rather disappointingly to-and-fro front 9 routing belies the spectacular vistas of the back 9, which run out to sea and back through massive dunes. Minimal bunkering, but little needed. Some putting surfaces move more than others. Study your yardage chart carefully, as the course's eccentricities could otherwise mislead your eye. Wind!

The dunes surround Carne's p:3 16 like the broken walls of a Roman amphitheatre, more ruined on the sides than behind. On the tee, imagine standing on the of the outer walls of the Colosseum, aim at the gladiators centre stage and wait for the wind to roar, in place of lions or spectators.

Even with modern equipment, Colt's legacy does not need stretching – at 192 yds, p:3 4 is long enough: the bunkers speak for themselves, whilst the green cascades unevenly down from back to front.

BELVOIR PARK ♟♟♟♟ ★

Colt & Alison   1927   ££   H: M 28, L 36

✉ Belvoir Park Golf Club, 73, Church Road, Newtownbreda, Belfast BT8 4AN, NI

☎ +44 289 049 1693

✎ info@belvoirparkgolfclub.com   www.belvoirparkgolfclub.com

🚗 ✈ Belfast Int: A57/M2/M1 south; exit 2 L onto A55 ring road for Newcastle, Bangor etc; follow A55 (Stockman's Lane, Balmoral Ave, R onto Malone Rd, Milltown Rd, Belvoir Rd) for some 4¼ miles from M1; L onto Ormeau Rd (A24); after 300yds (with shopping centre on R) L and immediately L again onto Church Rd; club on R before top of hill.

	y	p			y	p
1	277	4		10	479	5
2	411	4		11	183	3
3	428	4		12	483	4
4	203	3		13	399	4
5	513	5		14	187	3
6	390	4		15	509	5
7	434	4		16	220	3
8	141	3		17	439	4
9	493	5		18	408	4
	3290	36			3307	35
					6597	71

Classic Colt layout, which only improves as the round progresses. Undulating mature parkland setting with front 9 to left and back 9 to right, below traditional clubhouse. Dramatic bunkering with an excellent old-fashioned feel (notably at front of p:3s), around some seemingly tame putting surfaces (be careful!). Private club in residential oasis.

It was on the instigation of Sir Anthony Babington, the Attorney General, that Harry Colt was invited in 1926 to lay out the course at Belvoir (pronounced 'Beaver') Park, a design which has remained

This view from tee to green at p:3 8 shows the freshness of the excellent bunkering – a credit to Colt, club and greenkeepers alike: overall, the splendid raised greensite renders a sense of achievement from just a par.

largely unchanged since its inception. Yet at first sight Colt might hardly recognise it today, thanks to the impressive programme of tree planting, implemented over the years. (Colt was not a particular fan of trees, but he would surely have remembered the splendid oaks and beeches which he integrated into his design and still adorn the course.) But he would also be impressed by the memorable freshness the bunkering seems to retain, almost as if he (and his partner Alison) had only left the course a few weeks earlier. While it is unlikely that all Colt's original bunkering remains intact, this seems to be a club that has not been frightened into removing the tougher bunkers to placate its more difficult (or should we say less talented?) members. The way the bunkers surround the greens almost in waves, particularly at the excellent batch of p:3s (most notably 4 and 8), is a delight to the eye (if not to the mind, club in hand, on the tee!).

It is also particularly refreshing to find a 'haven' golf course so close to a city centre. The road to the course is unassuming, and the car park yields no view. Only on the other side of the clubhouse do you first discover the well-tended oasis (bedecked with majestic trees) that lies below. Indeed, the relative peace is a feature of several courses that lie close the centre of Belfast. Two honourable exceptions to Belvoir's peace: the Irish Open Championship was held there in 1949 and 1953 (won by Harry Bradshaw and Eric Brown, respectively), with more than 10,000 attending.

The course only gets better as you go round: the front 9 comes as a preparation for the more undulating and dramatic back 9. The climax is at right-to-left longish p:4 17: the drive must be well placed, as the dogleg comes fairly late, and the second is over a valley with a stream, up to a raised bunkered green. Par here does indeed feel like birdie.

BIRR ★★

Bancroft 1893/1911 € **H:** M 28, L 36

✉ Birr Golf Club, The Glenns, Birr, Co. Offaly, RoI
☎ +353 509 20082
✎ info@birrgolfclub.com   www.birrgolfclub.com
🚗 ✈ Dublin: M1/M50 south; exit N7/M7 for Limerick; at Roscrea (some 110km from M50) R onto N62 to Birr; club 3km north from Birr on R439 for Banagher.

	m	p			m	p
1	311	4		10	325	4
2	324	4		11	390	4
3	130	3		12	356	4
4	325	4		13	364	4
5	461	5		14	174	3
6	438	5		15	226	3
7	369	4		16	302	4
8	169	3		17	350	4
9	413	4		18	397	4
	2940	36			2884	34
					5824	70

Well worth the detour from your journey east or west, a course you really have to see and will want to play. Fabulous routing up, over and round eskers squeezes 18 holes into space for 12. Some blind shots, but plenty of space over the hills. Good, well-bunkered, occasionally raised greensites.

A true hidden gem, with a long history, rewards a drive into the centre of Ireland, but not too inconvenient for those travelling from Dublin to the famous links on the west coast. Birr is the classic Irish esker course.

Birr first strikes gold at roller coaster strategic p:4 7: a ridge runs away from right to left, the more it nears the direct line to the hole, the longer the carry. Cut off as much as you dare: failure leaves a blind second.

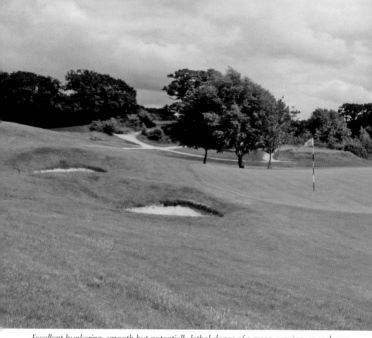

Excellent bunkering, smooth but potentially lethal slopes of a green running up and over a brow, and (lined by gentle esker slopes) aesthetics all combine to make gold at p:3 14.

More than 10,000 years ago, this area was shaped by the powerful natural forces of the melting Ice Age: streams that flowed in tunnels beneath the retreating glaciers deposited rounded ridges of gravel and sand, known as 'eskers'. Match a few folds of eskered land with an inspired golfer and a course could almost lay itself out.

Birr is an incredibly compact layout (on only 120 acres, when an average course requires at least 150), with the feel of an inland links on this

p:3 8, marks the start of Birr's spaghetti junction of crossover holes: the 15th plays from right to left over the back of the green – but from a higher level, so you don't notice it.

uniquely rolling ground (none of the other esker courses lies wholly within the eskered ground). Lots of old-fashioned fun: blind/semi-blind shots at 1, 2, 4, 7, 9, 11, 12, 13, 17, 18; excellent, often raised small undulating greens that seem to belong naturally to the land. Its fine collection of no less than four gold holes all have excellent balance between risk and reward, skill and fun, up and down. All worked within a theme, stated simply at the first, and developed as the round progresses. The compactness yields its own

spaghetti junction: 8, 9, 13 and 14 all seem to cross over each other – yet it works, helped by the fact that the holes are on different levels (a technique also used by Norman at *Doonbeg*). However, as we go to press, we hear that plans to include some more land are being considered. The consequent changes may relieve the congestion at spaghetti junction. Time will tell whether this amounts to just another bolognese, or a genuine improvement in the design. We hope the latter: the course deserves it.

This view from the tee of p:4 12 shows (near the bottom) the ridge, sweeping from left down to right, which must be carried to see the green for your second. The many other qualities of this hole are more subtle.

BUNDORAN ♛♛♛

Butchart/Vardon/Swan   1903/1936/2006   €

✉ Bundoran Golf Club, Bundoran, Co. Donegal, RoI
☎ + 353 71 984 1302
✎ bundorangolfclub@eircom.net   www.bundorangolfclub.com
🚗 ✈ Knock: N17/N4 to Sligo; N15 for Donegal, after 35km
reaching Bundoran; on north side of which L to Great Northern Hotel;
club on R of hotel.

Selected holes

	m	p
7	324	4
8	359	4
9	363	4
11	382	4

Total **5688** 70

Ideal for holiday golf, an open clifftop course adjoining hotel on generally gently sloping land, with extensive views of town and sea. Recent rebunkering by Howard Swan has added quality. Wind!

Red – 9: greensite too close to the hotel.

CARLOW (DEERPARK) ♛♛♛♛ ★

Barcroft/FG Hawtree & Taylor/Simpson & Gourlay/Steel
1922/1926/1937/1984 & 1994   €€   **H:** M 28, L 36

✉ Carlow Golf Club, Deerpark, Carlow, Co. Carlow, RoI
☎ +353 599 131 695
✎ carlowgolfclub@eircom.net   www.carlowgolfclub.com
🚗 ✈ Dublin: M1/M50 south; exit 9 onto N7/M7/M9/N9 for
Limerick/Naas/Carlow; club on R 1km before Carlow.

	m	p		m	p
1	401	4	10	279	4
2	292	4	11	393	4
3	131	3	12	344	4
4	354	4	13	152	3
5	503	5	14	416	4
6	165	3	15	354	4
7	398	4	16	401	4
8	397	4	17	139	3
9	373	4	18	482	5
	3014	35		2960	35
				5974	70

A traditional 'inland links' feel predominates at this wonderful heathland course, which well uses its ideal naturally undulating over-and-around-hillside site, with little need for bunkers and where even the occasional blind shot seems to work. Several superb greensites. A little water. Extensive views.

Opposite: Seven counties are visible from bunkerless, medium-short p:4 12 on a clear day, but the immortal challenge of the second shot is invisible from the tee: the fairway is narrowed on the left by a huge depression (mostly out of shot all below the green). God only can help you there, so perhaps wise to avoid it.

Accommodation: Clanard Court, Mount Wolseley

This view, from the right of Carlow's excellent p:4 7, shows its sweep over folds from right to left up to a sloping green. The slightly adverse camber is acceptable here, as it helps open up the hole. Wonderfully natural.

Dating from just one year back into the 19th century, and originally known as the Leinster Golf Club with a 9-hole course at Gotham ('a sporting course with all kinds of queer and unpleasant hazards' – *Irish Independent*, 8 May 1936 – within 3 miles of Carlow station), Carlow Golf Club has a distinguished history and equally distinguished list of course designers.

The club moved to a new course at Deerpark in 1922, designed by Cecil Barcroft, the multi-talented barrister and longtime secretary of *The Royal Dublin*. A contemporary reflection on one of the effects of the move is recorded in the club history: 'There appears to have been an increase in "usage" of caddies and golf balls as the more difficult terrain of the new course was having a dual effect – increased "wear and tear" on the caddies and a dramatic increase in the loss of golf balls.' Although there are significant rises (notably at 4, 11 and 16), it cannot be said that today's layout is unduly demanding. Barcroft's course survived for only 4 years before major changes by JH Taylor and FG Hawtree – changes that introduced the routing that remains largely recognisable today. This is a credit to all three designers, and to the club (which carried out the works

We suspect that medium p:3 17 may have seen the mid-1930s touch of Molly Gourlay, Tom Simpson's colleague and a p:3 specialist. With 5 bunkers around the multi-level green, the only place to miss it is . . . well, somewhere else on the green!

itself), with further enhancements in 1931 when they discussed the subject with no less than Alister Mackenzie – though it is not clear if he influenced any aspect of the layout. In 1937 the course was graced by a halved exhibition match between Gene Sarazen (Open Champion, 1932) and Australian Joe Kirkwood (one of the first big-money tour players with only a few wins to his name), which included an incident at p:3 3 in

Long p:4 16 is another natural gem, which has remained substantially in its original form. You drive across the 15th fairway over mounds into a valley with your second slightly right over more mounds rising to a natural, sloping greensite.

which Sarazen queried the printed yardage, after playing short – the hole was re-measured before dinner, where it was announced that it was indeed 5yds longer!

The club has kept up the pedigree of its design advisers over the years. In 1936 Tom Simpson was accompanied by his fellow designer Molly Gourlay (see *Ballybunion (Old)*, page 45) and it is worth musing how much her input may have been, as three short holes (6, 13 and 17) are given particular praise in the *Irish Golf Review* of 1938. Minor changes were made by the club in the early 1940s and John Morrison made recommendations, perhaps the most notable of which was not taken up: to move the 16th tee to the left of the 15th green.

The changes since 1984 have been on the advice of Donald Steel, including a significant woodland management programme and alterations to 10 and 18. If ever you need to prove the fallacy of the proverb 'too many cooks spoil the broth', you only have to play at Carlow.

PS A certain C. O'Connor Jnr was pro here from 1969–75; his salary was increased from £8 to £12 in 1973!

Note: Howes' promising 9-hole Oakpark loop, on less undulating ground than its neighbour and less minimalist in style, is not covered by our research.

CARTON HOUSE

MONTGOMERIE ★

Montgomerie & Eby   2003   €€€   **H:** M 28, L 36

✉ Carton House Golf Club, Maynooth, Co. Kildare, RoI

☎ +353 16 286 271

✎ golfshop@carton.ie   www.carton.ie

🚗 ✈ Dublin: M1/M50 south; exit 7 onto N4 for Galway; exit
Leixlip west; R148 for Maynooth; club on R before Maynooth.

	y	p		y	p
1	456	4	10	465	4
2	414	4	11	477	4
3	220	3	12	210	3
4	605	5	13	338	4
5	474	4	14	408	4
6	394	4	15	554	5
7	192	3	16	462	4
8	552	5	17	176	3
9	391	4	18	513	5
	3698	36		3603	36
				7301	72

Assuming not tricked up for
professional play, a moderately
undulating grassland course
playing distinctly better than first
appears. Description 'inland links'
may be a touch inappropriate, but
the cavernous bunkers are more
avoidable than they seem, giving
sense of achievement. On a good
day, the large undulating raised
greens can be fun. On a bad day
. . . well, that's golf!

The Carton House estate boasts
two distinctly different 'designer
label' modern courses, for which no small amount of credit is due to Stan
Eby (Montgomerie) and Tim Lobb (O'Meara) of European Golf Design, a
company that specialises in supporting the design of courses by tournament
professionals. This is not to take credit away from Messrs Montgomerie and
O'Meara, but it is important to realise that the profession of designing golf
courses is completely removed from that of playing them. The rich history
of the art well demonstrates that it has generally been better practised by

*Shorter p:4s are often the best: Montgomerie's 13th is no exception – the putting
surface is hidden from the tee by the brow in which the left hand bunker is set.
Carry it if you dare, to open up the back right pin position.*

61

Montgomerie's p:5 15, turning from left to right through these bunkers up to a green backed by the woods, may play shorter if you go for it in two, cutting corners. But this brings the challenging right-hand greenside bunker more into play . . .

non-professional golfers: Harry Colt was a lawyer and Alister Mackenzie a doctor, after all. And some of the world's most famous courses are the canvases of people who designed relatively little. (George Crump, an hotelier, designed the course that has consistently been ranked No 1 in the USA; yes, he was assisted by Colt, and others posthumously, but Pine Valley's unique penal island fairways and greens were Crump's original concept. This was the only course he designed.)

What we have at Carton House are two grand-scale layouts. Open land, with a few magnificent trees, has been completely resculpted for the 'Monty' into rolling artificial grassland, strewn with often cavernous bunkers and swales that provide excellent definition, all of which earn it the misleading marketing title of an inland links. If so, it is a links at which the traditional links art of 'bump and run' play cannot often be practised, due to the combination of generally raised greens and bunkers. (To see a true inland links, go to Ganton in Yorkshire, England, a course over the uneven and eccentric folds of linksland from which the sea has receded over millennia.) Better to praise the course for what it is, rather than what it is not: this is a long and often demanding modern layout, which came of age as the venue of the 2005 and 2006 Irish Opens, yet one which can be enjoyed by the rest of us, provided we play from the tee appropriate to our handicap. The greens are large, fast and have some tricky undulations, but most of us will be playing here primarily for leisure, so enjoy them in the same spirit of fun that Monty and Eby must have had in their design. (After the 2005 Open, it was rumoured that Colin had promised to redesign, at his own expense, the 18th, which slopes rather too much towards the river, but nothing has happened to date.)

The O'Meara runs over the hills and dells of a park, whose variety gives the course a less distinct identity than its consistently grassland brother. Slightly more of a resort course, it is also best played from the appropriate tee – from the back it stretches to over 7000yds. Its thrilling climax comes at 14–16, which require four spectacular carries over the river Rye: two p:3s, both downhill over water, but otherwise different in character, yet both as pretty as they are challenging, and a twisting p:5 in between that offers a heroic opportunity to reach the attractive green in two – take it if you dare.

Pretty downhill p:3 14 marks the start of O'Meara's testing run of three holes with four river crossings.

O'MEARA ↗

O'Meara & Lobb   2002   €€€   **H:** M 28, L 36

Caddies on request

	y	p		y	p
1	438	4	10	427	4
2	380	4	11	431	4
3	534	5	12	396	4
4	210	3	13	390	4
5	373	4	14	185	3
6	560	5	15	557	5
7	154	3	16	180	3
8	462	4	17	561	5
9	378	4	18	390	4
	3489	36		3517	36
				7006	72

This reverse view of O'Meara's p:3 16 shows the beauty of the setting. The 15th green is also visible through trees on the left.

Large-scale modern course (resort-ish from the front, tough from the back), routed up, around and down a hill within a fairly open park, the downhill teeshots part compensating for the uphill holes. Challenging finish (notably at penal yet picturesque 14–16 where the river Rye has been spectacularly brought into play). Interestingly sloped, generally raised greensites.

CASTLE ♟♟♟♟ ★★

Barcroft/Colt/Howes   1913/1919/2005   €€   H: M 28, L 36

✉ Castle Golf Club, Woodside Drive, Rathfarnham, Dublin 14, RoI
☎ +353 1 490 4207
✎ info@castlegc.ie   www.castlegc.ie

🚗 ✈ Dublin: M1/M50 south; at exit 11 (Tallaght), L to Templeogue
on N81; 200m after PO, go R onto R112 (Springfield Av), which
becomes Lower Dodder Park Rd/Braemor Rd; R into Woodside Drive
after lights, club on R as road turns L.

	y	p		y	p
1	492	5	10	190	3
2	433	4	11	401	4
3	149	3	12	348	4
4	317	4	13	132	3
5	372	4	14	391	4
6	418	4	15	187	3
7	177	3	16	529	5
8	347	4	17	500	5
9	452	4	18	411	4
	3157	35		3089	35
				6246	70

Classic lush, mature parkland course (generally turning from a coniferous to deciduous feel as the round progresses) over generally gently sloping ground in a compact, intra-residential setting, whose recent excellent upgrading Colt would surely have endorsed. Superb, excellently bunkered, often sloping greensites require precision right from the tee to score well.

Set in the middle of one of the smarter residential areas of Dublin on very gently sloping land, with exception of one valley with a stream (well used: brought into play in no less than three of the p:3s), Castle is a distinguished club with a distinguished membership and course. For a different perspective of the club and some of its members, we refer you to

Short p:5 1 establishes quality from the start: the morning shadows conceal a cross bunker, waiting to swallow up erroneous second shots. The excellent, raised bunkered green requires a precise shot, even if you go for it in three.

Excellent bunkering before and around the rising green make 4 a challenging short p:4 – risk and reward both at a premium.

some of the early pages of *The Life of O'Reilly* (ISBN 1932202153, by tour caddy John O'Reilly, with Ivan Morris). For a perspective of the course, we refer you to your own future experience, because this is one you must play. We offer what follows solely to encourage you to do so.

Castle has a history of association with pedigree golf designers: Barcroft (1913, with Hood and Pickeman); major revisions, which fashioned the base for today's layout, by Colt (1919); later touches by Hackett and most recently by Howes. Although this is rightly considered to be a Colt course, all credit must go to Jeff Howes and the club for the recent major enhancement (it is normally committees who commission designers, and then, it must be said, often interfere too much – but not here, it would seem!). What you will see is primarily the original routing with a full set of new greensites, which, while clearly of Howes' design, also respect Colt's principles. We feel that the old master would have happily congratulated Howes on bringing the course up to date, while leaving the golfing challenges he had intended. We refer

Another splendid green at medium p:4 5, expertly bunkered, with a good variety of pin positions across its slopes.

to our photos, but notice how everything seems to work: strategically bunkered short p:5 (1st); heavily bunkered short p:4 (4th) ; bunkers on the inside rather than outside of doglegs (5th); interestingly sloping putting surfaces (several); for a relatively tight tree-lined course, trees generally kept out of play (Colt disliked them as hazards), etc. All in a well-managed, pretty parkland setting – perhaps best when the blossom is out. Have we said enough?

One of the surprises of our research, maybe, but we award ★★ with confidence.

CASTLECOMER 🏆🏆

Ruddy 1975, 2000 & 2004   €

✉ Castlecomer Golf Club, Drumgoole, Castlecomer, Co. Kilkenny, RoI

☎ + 353 56 444 1139

✎ info@castlecomergolf.com   www.castlecomergolf.com

🚗 ✈ Dublin: M1/M50 south; exit N7/M7/M9/N9 for Carlow. At
Kilcullen fork R onto N78 for Athy; follow signs to Castlecomer, whence
N78 for Kilkenny; club 1km on L.

Selected holes		
	m	p
5	425	4
10	495	5
Total	6180	72

Hybrid and interesting (particularly for the diversity of
design evident from what would appear to have been
rather different budgets), a mixture of the original 9 holes
(1970s) on lower, lusher ground, part of which was
improved by Ruddy in 2000, and 9 new holes built over
a difficult site on and around the top of a hill in 2004.

CASTLEGREGORY 🏆

Spring 1989   €

✉ Castlegregory Golf Club, Stradbally, Castlegregory, Co. Kerry, RoI

☎ + 353 66 713 9444

✎ castlegregorygolf@oceanfree.net castlegregory_golfclub.com

🚗 ✈ Kerry: N23/N22/N21 to Tralee, whence N86 for Dingle; at
Camp R for Stradbally/Castlegregory; first R in Stradbally village and
follow road to beach – club after approx 1km (sign).

Selected hole		
	m	p
8	365	4
Total	2632	34

An 18-hole course opened here in 1896, but it declined
due to the long train journey from Tralee. Today the site
hosts a 9-hole links course, set between Lough Gill and
the sea, overlooked by Stradbally mountain and
Beenoskee, a truly spectacular location which, with the exception of 1, 2
and most notably 8, is not wholly matched by the design. Still, it is worth a
look on the way back from Dingle, should you have some spare time.

CASTLEISLAND 🏆🏆

Spring 2002   €

✉ Castleisland Golf Club, Doneen, Castleisland, Co. Kerry, RoI

☎ +353 66 714 1709

✎ managercastleislandgolfclub@eircom.net www.castleislandgolfclub

🚗 ✈ Kerry: R onto N23 to Castleisland, then L onto N21for Limerick;
club on L near top of hill.

An upland course with (in the right weather) dramatic views over
Castleisland to Macgillycuddy's Reeks, set, as it were, on terraces up

	m	p
4	187	3
7	404	4
9	176	3
Total	6041	71

which the course initially runs, before coming straight down and crossing a valley to another swathe of sloping land over which it runs more up and down. The design won't faze you, but if you don't have a better game further down the road to Killarney from Limerick, stop here: it's hardly off the main road.

CASTLEKNOCK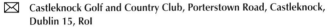

Gaunt   2005   €€

✉ Castleknock Golf and Country Club, Porterstown Road, Castleknock, Dublin 15, RoI

☎ +353 1 820 5600

✎ teetimes@castleknockgolfclub.ie   www. castleknockgolfclub.ie

🚗 ✈ Dublin: M1/M50 south; at exit 6 (Castleknock) R over M50 onto N3; at 1st rbt L and round to R, turning L onto Castleknock Rd after 200m; 1km after crossing over M50, R onto College Rd; after 1km R at lights; after 800m, bear L at lights, round bends and under M50, approx 1km after which club/hotel on L.

Selected holes

	y	p
3	219	3
6	479	5
8	596	5
11	158	3
15	350	4
Total	6703	72

Red – 6 and 8: Two p:5s that can be shortened to p:4s by cutting the corner, potentially interfering with play on other holes, including 7th greensite.

Appearing to use the best of modern golf infrastructure (dark tarmac cart paths excepted), a new parkland course (with five p:5s and five p:3s) set over former farmland with some stronger undulations mid-front 9. Some penal water, including the impressive parallel p:3s with which each loop ends, stadium-style, in front of the clubhouse – both being tee-water-green holes, with a large bunkered double green. (NB Our inspection was cursory as the course had only just opened when we saw it. We use the proposed long-term hole numbers.)

Testing 521yd p:5 10 requires a carry over a stream, which is semi-blind from the fairway. Stray left and it only gets worse . . .

CASTLEROCK

BANN ★

Kane   1985   £   **H:** M 28, L 36

✉ Castlerock Golf Club, 65 Circular Road, Castlerock, Co. Londonderry BT51 4TJ, NI

☎ +44 287 084 8314

✎ info@castlerockgc.co.uk   www.castlerockgc.co.uk

🚗 ✈ Belfast Int: A57/M2/A26 north past Ballymena for Coleraine; follow signs for Limavady on A37, R onto B201 less than 1 mile after crossing river; over rbt and L onto A2; after 4 miles R into Castlerock; when road turns sharp L, turn R: club 50m on L.

Natural links running up, over, round, down and between large sandhills on a remarkable piece of land, with spectacular views over the Bann Estuary. Often narrow and quirky (e.g. semi-concealed p:3 9), with generally small greens, the course's design feels a century older than its years. Much more than the excellent training ground that it also is. Wind!

Bann			Mussenden Links					
	y	p		y	p		y	p
1	301	4	1	367	4	10	391	4
2	367	4	2	375	4	11	509	5
3	92	3	3	523	5	12	430	4
4	153	3	4	200	3	13	382	4
5	491	5	5	477	5	14	192	3
6	337	4	6	347	4	15	518	5
7	288	4	7	418	4	16	157	3
8	276	4	8	411	4	17	493	5
9	141	3	9	200	3	18	357	4
	2446	34		3318	36		3429	37
							6747	73

Purple – 9: *Mound in front of the green, homage à the famous 5th at Lahinch (Old), but you can see a bit more of the target here.*

The flamboyant Sayers was an accomplished acrobat and would surely have done his party trick of cartwheeling around the green had he birdied the infamously testing 4th, known as Leg of Mutton for the (almost isosceles) triangle formed by the green (base), stream and railway (sides), which almost close at the gun-platform tee (apex).

MUSSENDEN LINKS ★

Caddies on request

Sayers/Colt/D Jones   1908/1925/2002   £££   **H:** M 28, L 36

A fine complement to its better-known neighbours, a links through dunes to more open lower ground between the Bann estuary and railway mid-round. Capitalise on the milder start before the stronger tests begin at the 4th tee, respecting the often uneven ground and occasional water hazards. Heed the movement on well-bunkered greens. Sea views.

One of the very few courses designed by Ben Sayers, the longstanding professional at North Berwick GC, Scotland, best known for his club-making. Although since revised, the Scottish feel to this course endures through the dunes of the opening and closing sections to the more open ground between the river Bann and the railway beyond. The links contain several opportunities for more or less physical exertion (according to the quality of your play), including the water running around the front of p:4 6th green, and climbs into dunes to recover errant shots. Equally remarkable are the grass armchair in which the 7th green sits, and the mound in the middle of the 12th fairway, which for a first-time player can give an optical illusion that you are playing a hole that rises over a hill, whereas it is just, yes, a mound in the middle of the 12th fairway (concealing the green). The sporting downhill p:5 17th tumbles listlessly down the hill, giving excellent sea views and, near the green, a glimpse of one of the Causeway Coast's hidden gems, the Bann course.

Whether or not there is any truth in the story we heard – that building-contractor members of the club, hearing that development of the duneland between the Mussenden Links and the sea as a golf course was soon to be banned, quickly brought out their bulldozers ahead of the ban – the books ascribe the name of Frank Pennink (the renowned designer of

Vilamoura (Old) ★★, Portugal and many other courses) to the 9-hole Bann course. But the same books say that this course was built in 1985, whereas Pennink died in 1983! Rather than our normal quest for the truth, because it is such a colourful (and indeed plausible) tale, we prefer here to imagine that all of the above may be true: Pennink designed the course before he died, but it had not been implemented when the ban was mooted, so the members got out their bulldozers before it was too late. Whatever the case, the result is one of the most natural golf courses we have ever seen on a remarkable set of dunes immediately above the Bann estuary. Yes, it is quirky (e.g. p:3 9), has consecutive p:3s (why not? – the best use of the land) and is often narrow, with occasional blind shots and small greens. But relish the sheer fun and challenge of land so well used for its purpose (a fun 9 holes after lunch, practice or perhaps even golf with just a 5 iron?).

CEANN SIBÉAL

Caddies on request

Hackett/O'Connor Jnr   1972/1988   €€   **H:** M 28, L 36

✉   **Ceann Sibéal Golf Club, Ballyoughtra, Ballyferriter, Co. Kerry, RoI**

☎   **+353 66 915 6255**

✎   dinglegc@iol.ie   www.dinglelinks.com

🚗 ✈ **Kerry: N23/N22/N21 to Tralee, whence N86 to Dingle; R559 NW for Ballyana, where L for Baile an Fheirtéaraigh (Ballyferriter); 1km after which R for Smerwick (sign); club on R after approx 1km.**

The 9th is an example of a good uphill p:4. Crossing a stream off the tee, the incline in the hole's key playing positions is gradual, leaving the raised green in clear view.

	y	p		y	p
1	401	4	10	197	3
2	227	3	11	523	5
3	370	4	12	161	3
4	367	4	13	465	5
5	202	3	14	342	4
6	550	5	15	410	4
7	415	4	16	366	4
8	360	4	17	428	4
9	449	4	18	504	5
	3341	35		3396	37
				6737	72

The most westerly course in the British Isles – a hardy native, design uninfluenced by trends from across the ocean, over which its relatively gentle slopes sometimes offer dramatic views. Good start and finish. The stream can occasionally be lethal. Some good greensites, occasionally raised (some recently enhanced). Better than its up-and-down routing suggests.

CITYWEST ♛♛♛♛
CHAMPIONSHIP

O'Connor Jnr   1994   €

✉ Citywest Golf Resort, Saggart, Co. Dublin, RoI

☎ +353 1 401 0500

✎ info@citywest.com   www.citywesthotel.com

🚗 ✈ Dublin: M1/ M50 south; exit 9 onto N7 for Naas; exit for N82/Citywest Business Park; club at Citywest Hotel.

Selected hole

	y	p
9	430	4

Total 6266 69

Note: the course was being lengthened as we went to press but it will remain p:69.

Well located on the edge of Dublin, a relatively flat parkland hotel course with several water hazards and some testing holes, whose relatively weak routing has been complicated by the erection of additional hotel space. However, as a hotel course for leisure break/relaxation golf, it well suits its purpose.

LAKES

O'Connor Jnr   1994   €

Selected holes

	y	p
7	393	4
8	161	3
10	374	4
11	137	3

Total 5154 65

Shorter, more punchy design, which we prefer to the Championship Course, with generally well-conceived greensites and plenty of water. The holes are tightly laid out on land that gently slopes up and away from pro shop at the start. Several entertaining holes with penal (or semi-penal) water carries to reach green.

Note: *Palmerstown (PGA National)* course p. 162 is part of the same group.

CLANDEBOYE 🏆🏆🏆

✉ Clandeboye Golf Club, 51 Tower Road, Conlig, Newtownards, Co. Down BT23 7PN, NI

☎ +44 28 91 271 767

✎ contact@cgc-ni.com   www.cgc-ni.com

🚗 ✈ Belfast Int: M2 to Belfast; A20 to Newtownards; follow signs and A21 for Bangor; after 2 miles, L for Conlig; after ⅓ mile R (sign) into Tower Rd; club at top of hill.

AVA

Robinson/von Limburger, Alliss, Thomas & McAuley   1933/1971   £

Selected holes

	y	p
2	524	5
6	183	3
7	312	4
8	542	5
9	309	4
11	432	4
Total	**5755**	**70**

Ava's 2nd green with p:3 3 (over the gorse) beyond.

A particularly charming front 9: some short p:4s, blind shots and one seriously challenging hole (renowned uphill p:5 2 – pro's tip: 'miss the fairway and you're dead'!). This loop is set over a series of disused lead mines, resulting in some eccentricities, e.g. the 7th fairway 'Hell's Bells' has apparently 'sunk' considerably since it was originally laid out, explaining the rather unusual into-a-pit-and-up-to-the-green character of the hole.

DUFFERIN   ★

Robinson/von Limburger, Alliss, Thomas & McAuley   1929/1971   £

H: M 28, L 36   **N.B. After wet winter weather check if open.**

	y	p		y	p
1	388	4	10	443	4
2	179	3	11	153	3
3	420	4	12	517	5
4	403	4	13	384	4
5	190	3	14	176	3
6	520	5	15	503	5
7	370	4	16	424	4
8	455	4	17	375	4
9	409	4	18	433	4
	3334	35		3408	36
				6742	71

Well-designed out and back layout running gently down from higher gorsy heathland to lower more ex-farming country section with trees and water. Spacious, with everything to scale, and widespread sea and distant peak views, good bunkering and subtle, often raised greens – and there's the fun Ava course.

Clandeboye is a 36-hole golf complex whose clubhouse is on a hillside, a few miles south of Bangor, with outstanding views of the mountains of Mourne, the Isle of Man, Arran, Ailsa Craig, the Mull of Kintyre and the Ayrshire coast. The first course here was designed in 1928 by William Renwick Robinson, a local linen merchant with a passion for golf and a talent for landscaping, and the club was formed in 1933. History abounds: the courses lie on the edge of Lady Dufferin's estates and the legendary Conn's stone still stands between Dufferin's 16th green and 17th tee. Major

Irish championships were held here until, as the club's website plainly puts it, in the early 1970s there was a 'very fierce argument among club members', culminating in an Extra Special General Meeting at which the future design of the courses was approved.

Dufferin's p:5 6 contains some demanding bunkering, particularly around the green.

In 1969, Baron Bernhard von Limburger, the leading German designer (whose *Atalaya (Old)* ↗ on the Costa del Sol, Spain is well worth playing), aided by Peter Alliss, Dave Thomas and local engineer TJM McAuley made a proposal that would result in 36 holes. One original loop of 9 over what is now the upper part of the Dufferin course was substantially remodelled, with 9 new holes introduced below. These two loops have become (with some minor changes since) the Dufferin course. A new back 9 was then added in the land adjoining the entertaining holes, which are now the front 9 of the Ava, to complete a second 18.

Fierce argument or not, the result has been successful in that the members can now enjoy a demanding test over the Dufferin, while still having a lot of fun with the Ava. Indeed, we understand that many members prefer to play the Ava, but the Dufferin is a serious test of golf: a well-designed, well-bunkered and spacious layout with everything to scale, albeit with a few semi-blind/blind drives.

Medium-short downhill p:4 4 looks tight all the way along, but there's more room than you think – room indeed for a nugget. The hole swings a little left down over some excellent rougher ground (foreground) to a raised greensite.

Right to left dogleg medium p:4 1 earns gold for its natural qualities, including the perfectly positioned stream, which preys on you up the left hand side, and its excellent raised greensite.

CONNEMARA 🏆🏆🏆 ★

Hackett 1973 € **H:** M 28, L 36

✉ Connemara Golf Club, Ballyconneely, Clifden, Co. Galway, RoI

☎ +353 95 235 02

✉ links@iol.ie   www.connemaragolflinks.com

🚗 ✈ Galway: R339 to Galway, whence N59 to Clifden, then L onto R341 for 9km to Ballyconneely; R and follow signs to club (6km).

Caddies on request

	y	p		y	p
1	381	4	10	427	4
2	413	4	11	193	3
3	164	3	12	445	4
4	382	4	13	212	3
5	381	4	14	513	5
6	203	3	15	412	4
7	572	5	16	431	4
8	465	4	17	499	5
9	436	4	18	526	5
	3397	35		3658	37
				7055	72

Note: the rating applies to holes 1–18; the 3rd 9 is unrated.

Excellent use of land and well-placed bunkering at this remote, windswept yet serene links with distant views of the Twelve Pins across the bogs with which the course harmonises, wildly strewn with boulders and understated water features. Well worth the trip. The use of raised tees makes it psychologically easier to play to raised, generally small, mildly sloping greens. Wind!

It required the faith of a local curate, Father Peter Waldron, to drive on a group of local golfing enthusiasts to build what is one of the remoter courses in Ireland – it is indeed a long way to a long course, but it is worth every bit of it. Hackett well knew how to use land best to route a golf course, and somehow his understated design here emphasises the remoteness of its location. The land is open to the sea to the south and over the bogs to the distant mountains northwards, and much of the centre of both 9s is relatively flat, yet edged (particularly on the back 9) by slightly higher ground. By often placing tees and greens on the more interesting edges of this bleak playground (most notably towards the close – 14 and 15 are the best examples), he gave the course a wonderful character, which is becoming increasingly respected with the passage of time. The almost constantly turning routing also ensures that you will face the wind, whichever direction it blows. Hackett's legacy has been followed by the construction of more tees slightly raised above the fairways. If there is a weakness it lies in the parallel routing over flat ground of some of the earlier holes (especially 4–5). But, sure of an ace with his splendid opening hole, Hackett knew that it was

'C' COURSE ③

	y	p
19	365	4
20	222	3
21	322	4
22	389	4
23	176	3
24	380	4
25	441	4
26	372	4
27	478	5
	3145	35

best to get the weakest part of the site out of the way early in the round – and distract the player with sea views in the process. The course finishes with two p:5s that are as challenging as any other pair up or down the coast.

Sadly, Hackett (and his successor) both died during the design/implementation of the 3rd 9, opened in 2000 without further input from a professional designer, which perhaps explains why they

There is not one ounce of protection from the wind at excellent long p:3 13, from a raised tee across a valley to a raised green.

are weaker. But don't miss the spectacular long p:3 2nd (i.e. 20) right beside the ocean. Any club could be required here: with a strong wind against, it must be at least a driver . . .

On 3rd July 2005, it was on the 8th fairway that the intrepid Steve Fossett landed his replica Vickers Vimy Atlantic biplane, re-enacting Alcock and Brown's first non-stop transatlantic flight of 1919.

p:4 14 is perhaps the best example of the success of Hackett's raised-tee-raised-green design concept; challenging long p:3 20 is in the upper left background.

CONNEMARA ISLES ♟♟ ★

Ruddy & Craddock   1991   €   H: M 28, L 36

✉ Connemara Isles Golf Club, Annaghvane, Lettermore, Co.
Galway, RoI

☎ +353 91 572 498

✐ connemaraisles@eircom.net   www.connemaraislesgolfclub.com

🚗 ✈ Galway: R339 into Galway, leaving on R336 coast road through
to Costelloe/Casla, where L and L onto R343 (over bridge); after 3km R at
Radio na Gaeltachta for Lettermore; follow signs R (500m past pub on
corner); club at end of road.

	y	p
1	323	4
2	354	4
3	159	3
4	270	4
5	412	5
6	165	3
7	284	4
8	481	5
9	186	3
	2634	35

A wild and simply tended 9 holes on a wild and
simply awesome site, with fabulous vistas of
Connemara across the sea, which all too
regularly comes into play. Some holes are
rather unorthodox, but the * is earned because
the design just 'goes for it'. Wind, water, sea,
rocks, boulders, raised greens, an island green,
a cop-out green, bracken, wilderness – golf!

It is fitting that one of the more extraordinarily individual golf courses we
have seen lies in one of the more extraordinary settings – in a way one
makes the other, in that an adventurous design was perhaps required to
balance the surroundings. The course is laid out over a saddle of land
between two sides of a promontory, and, via a causeway, on an island.

After a relatively unassuming opening p:4 with a raised green, the view
across the sea to the mountains unfolds. From the 2nd tee the initial
impression is of a long downhill p:4 with a very long 2nd over the Atlantic
to a green on the island – it comes as a relief to discover that this is in fact
the 3rd green. The 2nd is another raised, small green round to the right,
concealed by a mound. On the 3rd tee you take your ball's destiny into
your hands: is it for the crustaceans now, or will it survive a couple of holes

This is what you see (with the tide out) on the 3rd tee – the sloping green is clearly visible (on the right), and so is everything else! Now imagine the wind . . .

more? The 3rd plays straight across the ocean to a severely tiered green set on a bouldered promontory. Crossing the causeway to the island, you'd be forgiven for thinking that the next tee is on the rocks beyond the green, only reached by a rowing boat. Almost . . . The 4th tee is on some other rocks, but boat not required – a respite hole, after a teeshot over water, it's a shortish p:4 down the length of the island. The p:5 5th is unique (*see photo below*). Now, for downhill p:3 6, you turn to perhaps the best view of the bay and mountains beyond (*again, photo below*). A lull follows with a relatively gentle p:4 and p:5 (though with a testing wall and approach shot at the latter), before one reaches the cop-out. The design for the 9th is clearly visible: an island green linked to the clubhouse by a small causeway, which would make it one of the most awesome finishing holes in the game – were it not disused. Instead, a replacement raised green lies inland, between some small trees. For most of us, at over 180yds from the back, it will still be good to finish with a 4…

Purple – p:5 5. *An uphill hole from the island back to the main part of the course, measuring less than a normal p:5, and with very unusual topography. With the wind in the right place, tigers could drive 230yds+ across the sea (to near the 6th green – right, below sea), which would leave a short iron up to the green, but short hitters may require four shots to get there. This is because it may take at least two shots to position the ball to play the sea carry required to get off the island! So you may have to play driver (tee at far end of island, centre right), short iron lay-up, over the water 3rd and then pitch up to the green (4th). Unusual, but who said that golf wasn't fun?*

COOLATTIN

Unknown/McEvoy   1918/1997   €   H: M 28, L 36

✉ Coollattin Golf Club, Shillelagh, Co. Wicklow, RoI
☎ +353 55 291 25
✒ coollattingolfclub@eircom.net   www.coollattingolfclub.com
🚗 ✈ Dublin: M1/M50 south becomes M11/N11 to Gorey
(some 70km from M11 start), whence R on R725 to Carnew (16km),
then R to Coollattin; arriving there, at T-junction L and R into club.

	y	p		y	p
1	307	4	10	165	3
2	185	3	11	490	5
3	383	4	12	122	3
4	407	4	13	516	5
5	202	3	14	384	4
6	581	5	15	390	4
7	391	4	16	261	4
8	340	4	17	460	4
9	367	4	18	163	3
	3163	35		2951	35
				6114	70

Set mainly within the former gardens of an historic park, a course doubled to 18 holes by McEvoy, who said it was his best. We agree, primarily because of the fine arboretal routing and walled garden features, which more than make up for the weaker holes on more open ground. Some challenging greensites. Specimen trees. Rhododendrons reward a late spring visit.

McEvoy's unique 12th, set within the estate's walled garden. Rabbits should still find this a difficult place to get at: the raised green rejects anything not true. The bunkers are only just visible from the tee, minimising disturbance to the original atmosphere.

Accommodation: *Coollattin:* Marlfield House, Mount Wolseley

A view of p:3 9 from the approximate line of Mackenzie's tee. The hole is now played from the right, over the bunker, and is only marginally less fearsome than before – notice the steps in the green.

CORK (LITTLE ISLAND) 🏆🏆🏆 ↗

A Mackenzie/Cotton, Pennink & Lawrie/Thomas   1927/1975/1986
€€ **H:** M 28, L 36

✉ Cork Golf Club, Little Island, Cork, Co. Cork, RoI
☎ +353 21 4353 451
✎ corkgolfclub@eircom.net   www.corkgolfclub.ie
🚗 ✈ **Cork:** N27 for Cork; R onto N25 for Waterford, through tunnel; after 2km R onto Little Island, over rbt, ignore sign for Little Harbour GC; about 300m onto island R at xrds (sign); L into club after 100m.

	m	p		m	p
1	341	4	10	386	4
2	463	5	11	455	5
3	285	4	12	300	4
4	410	4	13	156	3
5	528	5	14	397	4
6	302	4	15	377	4
7	169	3	16	309	4
8	396	4	17	354	4
9	180	3	18	384	4
	3072	36		3118	36
				6192	72

With a parkland start and finish, this moderately undulating out-and-back course opens up, after two excellent shore-liners, into Mackenzie's fun-to-play central quarry holes (several worthy of ★★). Some excellent raised greens with tricky contours. Estuary views.

COUNTY LOUTH ★★

Caddies on request

Simpson & Gourlay/Steel/Steel & T Mackenzie   1938/1993/2005

€€€ **H:** M 28, L 36

✉ County Louth Golf Club, Baltray, Drogheda, Co. Louth, RoI

☎ +353 41 988 1530

✎ reservations@countylouthgolfclub.com
   www.countylouthgolfclub.com

🚗 ✈ Dublin: N1/M1 north for Belfast; exit for Drogheda North
after toll bridge, following signs to Drogheda; over 3 rbts, then first
L for Termonfeckin; follow road behind hospital to major junction (filling
station opposite), L here and immediately R (before Maxol station); at
next major junction L onto Termonfeckin Rd; over first xrds, then R at the
next onto R167 for Baltray (6km); club close to sea at end of road.

	y	p		y	p
1	454	4	10	429	4
2	523	5	11	470	4
3	544	5	12	410	4
4	379	4	13	421	4
5	173	3	14	332	4
6	531	5	15	167	3
7	163	3	16	429	4
8	421	4	17	207	3
9	419	4	18	559	5
3607	37		3424	35	
			7031	72	

Understated, gently undulating,
natural links course, with fewer
eccentricities than many,
excellent minimalist bunkering
and generally smallish greens
(playing even smaller in wind).
Effective use of relatively small
differences in elevation, in front
of higher dunes closing off sea
views, except on 14th tee. Fun
to play. Wind!

Affectionately and commonly known after the local village as 'Baltray',
County Louth was founded in 1892. The original links are reputed to
have been designed by a Scot with the curious name of 'Snowball'.
However, Cecil Barcroft, the respected Dublin designer, is also recorded

*This view of p:5 2 well illustrates the merit of placing hazards inside rather than
outside the turns of doglegs: such positioning challenges players to carry them and
shorten the hole; hazards on the outside yield no motivation for such 'heroic' play.*

*With a kindly wind, modern equipment has made medium short p:4 14 drivable by
tigers, but look at the landing area (foreground) and greensite: endless subtleties.
There are so many ways of playing this marvellous hole that it cannot escape gold.*

as having had a hand here, no doubt building on the Scottish original. In
any event, the current layout is the product of a partnership between the
flamboyant Tom Simpson and Molly Gourlay, the leading lady golfer with
whom he regularly worked in Ireland in the 1930s. Some updating,
including new tees to lengthen the course and revision to the order of
playing the holes, was carried out in 1993 by Donald Steel's firm. A
more ambitious renovation was undertaken recently by Tom Mackenzie
(of the same company) with 11 new tees and new bunkers on 9 holes,
plus a new 2nd green and extensions to the 6th and 7th greens.

But Baltray is much more about links golf than the details of those
whose names go against the design: this is such an outstanding piece of
land that golf could be played in infinite ways across it. Indeed, it is
perhaps only because of its slightly offbeat, pleasantly rural locality that its
reputation is not as high as the big Dublin courses, such as *Portmarnock*.

Although edged on the sea-side with higher dunes, rather like at St
Andrews the central area used for play does not contain particularly
huge differences in elevation – yet Baltray is by no means flat. It does
not take much imagination to invent new holes across its wonderful
folds. The key to the successful design in such circumstances lies as
much in what the designers choose not to do as in what they do do. In
the marketing of many modern courses, it is alarming how often you see
the word 'natural'. This word can only be genuinely used where the
shape of the land is good enough for it to be left alone. If you know a
golf marketing copywriter, perhaps you should bring him/her to Baltray
for a game, if not an education in understatement . . .

COUNTY SLIGO ★★

Colt, Alison & A Mackenzie   1927–31   €€   **H:** M 28, L 36

✉ County Sligo Golf Club, Rosses Point, Co. Sligo, RoI

☎ +353 71 917 7186

✎ Reserve via website   www.countysligogolfclub.ie

🚗 ✈ Knock: N17/N4 north to Sligo, whence (near start of N15) R281 for Rosses Point (8km); club is at end of road.

	m	p		m	p
1	347	4	10	351	4
2	278	4	11	397	4
3	457	5	12	486	5
4	150	3	13	162	3
5	438	5	14	394	4
6	405	4	15	367	4
7	393	4	16	196	3
8	412	4	17	414	4
9	153	3	18	336	4
	3033	36		3013	35
				6136	71

Note: we understand that the course is to be enhanced by Merrigan in 2007.

Sublime, strategic links. Clever routing over three separate sections: initially up and down a hill, then over a linksy plain to a farther piece of duneland (and back), all in front of the spectacular Benbulben mountain. Inviting drives, precision-requiring raised/sloping greensites, well-placed streams, challenging bunkering, run-offs – and one blemish (17). A classic. Wind!

County Sligo (aka 'Rosses Point' after the village at which it is located) is famous for many reasons: celebrated amateur golf events (notably the West of Ireland Championship); the brothers Yeats (WB and JB, writer and painter); the

Longish p:4 14 twists from right to left and then left to right around sand and a stream to an excellent greensite. Everything is in the right place (or not, if you're having an 'off' day . . .). A par here is very satisfying.

adjoining hotel named after them; Bernhard Langer's remark: 'I went for one round, and stayed two weeks', and much more. But the enduring reason is the quality of the golf course, the brainchild of Harry Colt.

The original links had been laid out in 1894 by George Combe (inventor of the world's first handicap system and a founder and first secretary of the GUI) and extended to 18 holes by William Campbell in 1906. By the mid-1920s the 'West of Ireland' was becoming sufficiently successful to warrant a more challenging test of golf. The tender was won by Hawtree and Taylor, but they could not offer a sufficiently early start date, so Colt's higher offer was accepted.

Well demonstrating the qualities of short grass as a hazard, the slopes of the raised greensite at medium short p:3 4 rewards finesse more than muscle. Exposed to the winds above Sligo's central plain, a birdie here is a rare pleasure.

The view from the gun-platform tee of County Sligo's short p:5 5; p:4 6 runs right to left above it and the higher ground for 9-12 appears immediately below the distant water.

In 1927 Colt marked out the routing, the most important contribution to the success of the course, employing his preference for maximising the natural potential of the site with minimal movement of earth, continuous, if sometimes subtle, changes in direction and challenging greens (not wholly welcomed by the members!). The only exception was the construction of the 17th green, in a position requiring a long period of excavation, which was necessary to bring the course efficiently back to the clubhouse. Thus the course was only fully completed in 1931, when Colt sent Hugh Alison, his assistant, to bunker it. (Mackenzie is also credited, but his contribution may only have been made 'back at the office', as Colt's partner.)

Alison was known for his often deeper, more incisive bunkering style than Colt's, evidence of which remains visible. However, with three distinct sections of land to cover, Colt's routing was the key to success here. The rising land around the clubhouse encompasses 1–4 and 18 (the climb to the top is efficiently dealt with by the short p:4 2nd). A lower plain (once the site of the local racecourse) is used for 5–8 and 13–17. Here Colt provides variety: a gun-platform tee introduces the area, allowing big drives down short p:5 5 and a clear view of the dead ground in front of the green (*above*); changes in direction (7 and 8 most obvious, others more subtle); raised greens (most of them); water (most notably the stream that strategically twists along and across 14), varying bunker challenges and more. Finally, beyond the plain, the course climbs to a swathe of duneland, which houses 9–12. Here the holes are no less testing and maximise the aesthetics, aiming directly at the impressively screed, flat-topped Benbulben mountain, before turning back straight down to the ocean, above which the 12th green sits serenely – or menacingly, according to the elements.

Note: The further 9 holes, more recently built in the 'plain' area, are not covered by our research.

COUNTY TIPPERARY

Walton 1993 € H: M 28, L 36

✉ County Tipperary Golf and Country Club, Dundrum House Hotel, Dundrum, Co. Tipperary, RoI

☎ +353 62 717 17

✎ dundrumh@iol.ie   www.dundrumhousehotel.com

🚗 ✈ Dublin: M1/M50 south; exit N7/M7 to Portlaoise, whence N8 to Cashel, then R onto R505 to Dundrum; follow signs to hotel.

	y	p			y	p
1	388	4		10	464	4
2	367	4		11	510	5
3	198	3		12	170	3
4	366	4		13	582	5
5	343	4		14	424	4
6	178	3		15	368	4
7	561	5		16	424	4
8	419	4		17	387	4
9	470	4		18	464	4
	3290	35			3793	37
					7083	72

Parkland, occasionally tree-lined hotel course in two loops of 9 over rolling land with streams and ponds. Rating due mainly to a strong section mid-round. Reasonably well-bunkered medium-size greens, some raised. Doglegs, and some strategically placed trees and bunkers, challenge. (Also known as 'Dundrum'.)

Notice that the central bunker here at Dundrum's p:3 3rd is well short of the putting surface. This is not so evident from the tee – nor is the potentially swirling effect of the trees on the wind.

This view of downhill medium p:4 5 shows both the natural, common land features of the more open part of the terrain and the constant presence of the best greenkeeper known to man.

THE CURRAGH ★

Caddies on request

Hammersley & Close   1901   €   **H:** M 28, L 36

✉ **The Curragh Golf Club, Curragh, Co. Kildare, RoI**

☎ +353 45 441 714

✎ curraghgolf@eircom.net   www.curraghgolfclub.com

🚗 ✈ Dublin: M1/M50 south; exit 9 N7/M7; leave M7 at exit 10 for Newbridge/The Curragh; 1st exit from rbt onto R413 for Kilcullen; R after 2km, club after 200m at top of hill.

	m	p		y	p
1	477	5	10	170	3
2	335	4	11	400	4
3	272	4	12	391	4
4	187	3	13	285	4
5	322	4	14	460	5
6	341	4	15	459	5
7	483	5	16	124	3
8	166	3	17	412	4
9	407	4	18	344	4
	2990	36		3045	36
				6035	72

The oldest course in Ireland: wonderfully natural, freely grazed by the world's best greenkeepers. Set on undulating ground, with a partially tree-lined 'common land' feel and a weaker section nicely out of the way by the 5th tee. Some glorious holes show how, on a good site, there is need for neither bulldozers nor excessive bunkering. Understated greensites.

The Curragh is a plain of nearly 5000 acres some 45km west of Dublin. Owned by the Department of Defence, it has long been home to the military and, because of its unique natural grass sward, to the horse racing business and the world-famous racecourse. It also houses the oldest golf layout in Ireland. The game has been played here since

1852, when the Earl of Eglington, Lord Lieutenant of Ireland, played golf on the Curragh with a Col. Campbell of the Queen's Bays.

The club itself was formed some 30 years later. In 1883 the *Irish Times* announced: 'Maj Gen Fraser, VC, CB, Commanding the Curragh Brigade, has sanctioned the formation of a garrison golf club. The Rules of the Club will be the same as those of The Royal and Ancient Club of St Andrews.' Membership of the club was, however, restricted to Officers of the British Curragh Garrison. By 1889 there was a course of 18 holes and, by 1897, 9 holes for the ladies.

There are few details of the origins of the present course, because all records were removed when the British army evacuated in 1922. However, it is known that, in the early days, the layout was often changed to meet military requirements. Barracks, parade

Gilded p:5 15 is another wonderfully natural hole, with a fairway full of movement leading to a superb greensite.

grounds, ranges and even a water tower now stand on the site of many fairways and greens. What is also known is that, in 1901, a Col Hammersley and Major Close laid out a course to the east of the military camp. Play continues in this area today. While this is unquestionably the oldest extant course in Ireland, we do not know which holes date back to 1901, nor indeed for sure if any are even older.

One final piece of interest: in 1910 the title 'Royal' was conferred – correspondence between the club and the British Home Office has confirmed that the title remains valid.

Some holes at The Curragh are more tree-lined, as at downhill p:5 1, simply but very effectively bunkered.

The most uneven ground at Donegal is that closest to the shore, most notably at p:5 8, where it rolls marvellously – all over the shop. Your task is to choose the best strategy for the elements of the day. (Oh, and then successfully to implement it . . .)

DONEGAL (MURVAGH) 🏆🏆🏆 ↗

Caddies on request 🏌️🛺

Hackett/Ruddy   1976/2000   € **H:** M 28, L 36

✉ **Donegal Golf Club, Laghy, Co. Donegal, RoI**

☎ +353 7497 34054

✎ info@donegalgolfclub.ie   www.donegalgolfclub.ie

🚗 ✈ Derry: A2 to Derry; A5 to Strabane; R over frontier onto N15 for Donegal; before which L on N15 for Ballyshannon; at Laghy R to Mullinasole, 2km after which club (sign) on R.

	m	p		m	p
1	485	5	10	361	4
2	425	4	11	371	4
3	195	3	12	543	5
4	469	4	13	166	3
5	179	3	14	521	5
6	469	5	15	367	4
7	391	4	16	228	3
8	502	5	17	325	4
9	368	4	18	399	4
	3483	37		3281	36
				6764	73

Large-scale, fairly modern, windswept links, which can play every meter of its prodigious length. Set over generally fairly flat ground, the best holes are in the more undulating dunes that divide the course from the shore and run close to the middle of the links. Large, occasionally sloping greens. Excellent finish. Some sea views.

Accommodation: *Donegal:* Lake House;
Dooks: Aghadoe Heights, Castlerosse, Killeen House

DOOKS ♟♟♟ ★★

British Army/Hackett/M Hawtree 1889/1973/2003–6 €
H: M 28, L 36

✉ Dooks Golf Club, Glenbeigh, Co. Kerry, RoI
☎ +353 66 976 8205
✎ office@dooks.com   www.dooks.com
🚗 ✈ Kerry: N23 into Farranfore (adjoining airport, south),
whence R on R561 to Castlemaine; here L onto N70 through
Killorglin for Glenbeigh/Ring of Kerry; R just before Caragh Bridge
(sign) to club, 2km on L.

Caddies on request

	y	p		y	p
1	389	4	10	559	5
2	318	4	11	172	3
3	375	4	12	368	4
4	180	3	13	170	3
5	445	4	14	406	4
6	479	5	15	349	4
7	470	4	16	378	4
8	185	3	17	397	5
9	506	5	18	425	5
	3347	36		3224	35
				6571	71

Natural windswept links with stunning views. Few bunkers, as few are necessary over the irregularly but gently undulating holes crossing land that slopes gently towards the sea; more heathery and gorsy towards the close. Splendid greensites – some raised, others contoured with the land. Excellent phased remodelling just completed.

Dooks is the oldest golf club in Kerry, founded in 1889, when the establishment of an artillery range nearby brought in army officers (from the Black Watch regiment) who introduced the locals to golf.

The authentic traditional-feel bunkering and classic greensite at Dooks' medium p:4 1 whets your appetite for the golf, even before you cross the brow revealing the course's widespread sea views.

Newly fashioned p:3 4 at Dooks shows that (despite exceptions elsewhere in Ireland), modern links greensites (yet with all the traditional challenges) can be crafted with today's equipment – and of course the wind never stops . . .

If you are new to links golf, take a look at the land beyond the course, especially to the left of the 15th tee. You will see how the terrain must have looked before it became a golf course – it doesn't take much imagination to see that it was almost one already. Identify suitable positions for greensites first (e.g. prominent spots – not necessarily always raised); then work back across the land to determine your teesites; as for hazards, there are natural bunker sites all over the place, etc. Introduce some sheep as greenkeepers.

It may seem a long way from modern desert courses in Arizona, but this is how golf began – we may prefer to play on sanitised modern courses, but we forget the history of course design at our peril. You can see it all here.

Martin Hawtree's excellent remodelling has now been completed. We reserve final judgement until his work has matured, but enough has already been done to raise our rating from ★ to ★★. On our last visit there were still four holes to go, the plans for which impressed. Dooks is very much *not* just a course on the way to Waterville: it ranks higher and deserves more attention, from local and longer-distance golfers alike.

The scenery often takes centre stage at Dooks. Behind the green of challenging p:4 14 you can see the 11th green, and, beyond it, examples of the form of this terrain before, with relatively minor adjustment, it became a golf course.

DOONBEG ♛♛♛♛♛ ★★★

Norman 2003 €€€ **H:** M 28, L 36

✉ Doonbeg Golf Club, Doonbeg, Co. Clare, RoI

☎ +353 65 905 5246

✎ reservations@doonbeggolfclub.com www.doonbeggolfclub.com

🚗 ✈ Shannon: N19/N18 to Ennis, whence N67 for Kilrush; R at
Knockalough onto R484 for Creegh, whence L for Mountrivers
Bridge, where join N67 for Doonbeg, before which club on R.

	y	p			y	p
1	567	5		10	580	5
2	426	4		11	148	3
3	361	4		12	401	4
4	592	5		13	500	5
5	373	4		14	111	3
6	370	4		15	405	4
7	227	3		16	205	3
8	582	5		17	424	4
9	175	3		18	464	4
	3673	37			3238	35
					6911	72

Raw links golf on a modern course that feels centuries old. Out and back with a fabulously natural feel among sea dunes and inner linksland, each hole presents a different variation within a consistent theme, full of eccentricities and undulations (natural-feel greens included). Good mix of harder and easier holes. Generally generous fairways, awesome bunkering. Wind!

Having won the Open twice, Doonbeg's designer is more than familiar with links courses, but for the course to leap into our *** rating, even on a site as good as this, he must have produced something rather special.

The key is the way he has laid out his theme at the start and then developed it over the 18 holes, with sufficient variety to test every golfing skill, yet with stylistic consistency and integrity. Integrity from the firm links introduction: splendid p:5, with pot bunker awaiting second shot, green dwarfed by sandhills – everything belongs. Integrity through the holes on the gentler, but often no less eccentrically undulating inner land featured with walls, streams and awesome (often grass-wisped) bunkers – some so natural they seem to have grown out of the ground. Integrity during the course's three visits to the cauldron of dunes lining the shore (at 5–7, 9 and 13–16).

It is also a course that will bring out all the emotions of golf. It may be an elements-battling day of sheer survival, or a benign one wafted with smells of sea and grass. It may be the shame of being caught out by the left-hand 'sucker' pin position of superbly subtle, walled shortish p:4 3 (best to play for the centre of the raised bunkered green, as the left side is very shallow). It may be the terror of the bunkering around the 6th green. It may be the feelings inspired by the p:3s: strength in an understated arena (7), nerve at a shoreline apex (9), drama (11), rawness over the sea (14 – see photo caption), or vulnerability to risk

p:5 1 looks relatively benign from in front of the tee, with the green below the highest point of the dunes. This player's-eye view shows the relatively generous width of the fairway, but by the time you reach your drive, your mind may well have come to dwell on the mid-fairway pot bunker that awaits a misjudged second . . .

(16). It may be the fizz of shots to sizzling duneland greens (e.g. 13 and 15). Or it may even be the tease of the semi-blind final drive to the shoreside exposure of longish p:4 18. Whatever the cause, your heartbeat will accelerate . . .

Of course, we have a few quibbles: the bunker in the middle of the 12th green – why not make it more clearly visible from the fairway? Also, the lower land on the 10th and 17th could perhaps be made a little more interesting (though on the credit side, it is good to have the occasional respite). But none of these make any hole weak enough to miss out on ***; rather, they suggest potential for a higher rating within this ranking.

Limiting factors have often contributed to great art (e.g. Beethoven's deafness): Doonbeg seems to be no exception. Norman was restricted from routing the course through much of the duneland – to protect a rare tiny snail. Instead of having to deal with the common problem of how best to route a course out and back along shoreline and amid dunes ('Do I give the most dramatic land to the front 9, the back 9 or a mixture?'), Norman was only allowed to visit the multi-dimensional shoreline area at what on a plan look like pinch points (notably at the convergence of the 5th, 13th and 14th greens and 6th, 14th and 15th tees). Yet these have resulted in some of the highlights of the course: would the unfolding delight of seeing the sea over the brow of medium p:4 5 have come so early in the round? Would the course have included both the raw undulations (and menacing bunkering)

Medium p:4 6 is the first of Doonbeg's holes up in the dunes to run parallel to the shore. The depth of the bunkers is greater than a photo could ever convey. The green falls away frighteningly to a lower section beyond the bunkers on the right. (The 13th green is in the foreground.)

of the 6th and 13th holes (both excellent greensites) had not the routing been so tight (the back 6th tee requires a shot over the line of the 14th and over the 13th green)? This problem has necessitated a creative solution – the 6th tee was placed sufficiently high in the dunes to reduce the feeling that you are playing over two holes – just as the back tee for majestic p:4 15 takes play over the 5th fairway, but from so much higher ground that you hardly notice it.

At Doonbeg Norman has both achieved his philosophy of 'least disturbance' and respected the maxim: 'To do nothing, yet leave nothing undone'.

With tees out of shot left, short p:3 14 is as obvious as it is dramatic. While it has been well lauded for its spectacle and drama, relative to the rest of the course it feels rather crude. But Norman's thesis is one of variations within a general theme. On most holes the course speaks for itself, often set against a seemingly simple backdrop. Here Norman lets the backdrop speak for itself and keeps the course simple.

Gently uphill medium-long p:4 8 plays all its length and wins gold for its combination of aesthetic excellence and golfing challenge, all linked to the way in which it moves around the edge of the woods. The bunkering at the multi-tiered green is excellent.

DROMOLAND CASTLE

Wiggington/Kirby & Carr   1961/2004   €€   **H:** M 28, L 36

✉ Dromoland Castle Golf Club, Newmarket on Fergus, Co. Clare, RoI

☎ +353 61 368 444

✎ golf@dromoland.ie   www.dromoland.ie

🚗 ✈ Shannon: N19/N18 for Ennis; past 1st exit for Newmarket on Fergus, take 2nd main junction on N18 (Clare Inn and course visible on R); follow signs for Newmarket on Fergus; entrance to Dromoland Castle 1km on L.

	y	p		y	p
1	381	4	10	351	4
2	462	4	11	543	5
3	197	3	12	413	4
4	472	5	13	159	3
5	429	4	14	443	4
6	590	5	15	267	4
7	179	3	16	455	4
8	407	4	17	227	3
9	298	4	18	572	5
	3415	36		3430	36
				6845	72

Recently significantly improved with Kirby's remodelling, an undulating parkland hotel course, which generally gets better as the round progresses, with back 9 circling lake in front of castle. Playing all its length with testing, often raised greens, this will challenge your finesse as well as your strength. Some excellent shortish p:4s.

Red – p:3 7: A token red for a very simple mistake. From the back tee we could not see the green (nor the lake beside it). This was primarily because the shrubs in front had been allowed to grow too much. We accept that they may since have been cut back, but the cutting would have to be very severe to make the green visible. We use this example to make the point that all too often growth goes unnoticed at golf courses.

DRUIDS GLEN GOLF RESORT

✉ **Druids Glen Golf Resort, Newtownmountkennedy, Co. Wicklow, RoI**

☎ **+353 1 287 3600**

✎ Druids Glen: **info@druidsglen.ie**
Druids Heath: **druidsheath@druidsglen.ie**
Both: **www.druidsglen.ie**

🚗 ✈ **Dublin: M1/M50 south becomes M11/N11; exit to Newtownmountkennedy; L to Kilcoole, leading to major T-junction, whence L for Druids Glen,
which is on R after 200m, or R for Druids Heath, which is on L after 200m.**

DRUIDS GLEN ↗

Caddies on request

Ruddy & Craddock   1995   €€€   H: M 28, L 36

	y	p			y	p
1	445	4		10	440	4
2	190	3		11	522	5
3	339	4		12	174	3
4	446	4		13	491	4
5	517	5		14	399	4
6	476	4		15	456	4
7	405	4		16	538	5
8	166	3		17	203	3
9	389	4		18	450	4
	3373	35			3673	36
					7046	71

Unique, in that it is a garden as much as a golf course, wending its way around the occasionally undulating estate (walls and all) into which it has been set. Full of mature specimen trees and a variety of water hazards, it is long with large greens and reasonably flat putting surfaces. The two horticultural prize-winning gardens are p:3s 8 and 12. Indulge: see them in May.

We have to admit that this is not our favourite golf course. It is our favourite garden with a golf course in it.

The problem is that the garden is better than the course: its rating is founded on a high score in the aesthetics department. Have no doubt, set

The late sun bathes a May view of the relatively arboreal horticultural introduction: Druids Glen's p:4 1st runs gently down from the clubhouse to a raised green.

95

Downhill p:3 12 brings you the nearest to Eden in golf, especially in May.

in the middle of the 'Garden of Ireland', it is a beautiful place to play golf and we encourage you to do so, if only to see what can be done by a dedicated team of green-keeping horticulturalists. The club also has a very enlightened wildlife policy, especially for the abundant kingfisher population.

Druids Glen is especially good in spring when the rhododendrons and azaleas are in bloom, as our photos illustrate. But don't get too carried away: there are several hidden bunkers – you are at highest risk if you allow yourself to be too distracted by the horticultural show. You should also savour the excellent 19th,

Played down from a tee from high right above the foreground in this view, with two water carries and lots more, gold-rated p:4 13 is the best golfing challenge at Druids Glen.

Accommodation: Marriott Druids Glenn, Porterhouse Inn, Powerscourt

Woodstock House. It is one of Ireland's finest period clubhouses, with each room dedicated to Irish historical figures. Built in 1770, it was the centre of the Woodstock Estate, originally part of Sir Thomas Wentworth's estates in southeast Ireland, then sold to Lord Tottenham (Bishop of Ferns and Clogher) in 1826 and taken over in 1990 by the consortium who developed the course.

Druids Glen has hosted the Irish Open no less than four times in its short history, the winners being Colin Montgomerie (1996 and 7), David Carter (1998) and Sergio García (1999 – his first professional win). In 2002 it hosted the Seve Trophy.

DRUIDS HEATH ↗

Caddies on request

Ruddy 2003 €€

H: M 28, L 36

	y	p			y	p
1	464	4		10	426	4
2	561	5		11	250	3
3	233	3		12	492	4
4	519	5		13	420	4
5	202	3		14	171	3
6	467	4		15	500	5
7	466	4		16	513	4
8	449	4		17	447	4
9	439	4		18	415	4
	3800	36			3634	35
					7434	71

With widespread views over sea and the Wicklow mountains, a challenging layout on fairly hilly heathland, whose rolling fairways, natural quarries, water, occasional trees, deep bunkers and large undulating greens will test all your golfing skills. Study your yardage chart carefully for hidden hazards (including the first of two lakes at spectacular downhill p:5 2). Wind!

Red – 13: *too much is left to chance for the drive – semi-blind to a severe left down to right sloping fairway, which, in the circumstances, also leaves too much to chance for the watery second shot. The presence of a sign on the tee to tell you where to play is symptomatic.*

DUNDALK ♟♟♟

Braid/Alliss & Thomas   1905/1975   €

✉ Dundalk Golf Club, Blackrock, Dundalk, Co. Louth, RoI
☎ +353 42 932 1731
✎ manager@dundalkgolfclub.ie   www.dundalkgolfclub.ie
🚗 ✈ Dublin: M1 north to Dundalk, whence south on R132 for
Castlebellingham; after 2km, L onto R172 to Blackrock; club on L 1km
after Blackrock Inn.

Selected holes		
	m	p
2	370	4
5	158	3
10	461	5
17	173	3
Total	6206	72

Mature parkland course, generally becoming more
tree-lined as the round progresses, on gently rolling
ground with some occasionally more dramatic
elevations, which can render a few shots semi-blind.
However, in the case of shortish p:4 14, the mound
contributes to the quality, though this hole would
possibly be even better if the prospect of driving it
from the tee were made a little more tempting.

EDMONDSTOWN ♟♟♟

McAllister/McEvoy & Cooke   1944/2002   €€

✉ Edmondstown Golf Club, Edmondstown Road, Rathfarnham,
   Dublin 16, RoI
☎ +353 1 493 1082
✎ info@edmondstowngolfclub.ie   www.edmondstowngolfclub.ie
🚗 ✈ Dublin: M1/M50 south to exit 12 for Firhouse/Ballyboden; L at
exit, straight over 1st two rbts; R at 3rd onto Edmondstown Rd (R116);
club on L after about 1km, opposite Chemserve.

Selected holes		
	m	p
6	382	4
10	310	4
17	196	3
Total	6011	71

Recently enhanced tree-lined course on mildly
sloping ground with some views over fashionable
south Dublin. Some good greensites, but take care in
your approach to others whose putting surfaces are
less visible from the fairways. Two newer holes (10
and 11) lie below the clubhouse.

A view of Edmondstown's downhill p:4 18 from left of the fairway.

The huge dune to the left dominates Enniscrone (Dunes)'s medium short p:4 12, seen here from the brow at the beginning of a fairway that swoops down before rising to a green nestling in the sandhill.

ENNISCRONE (DUNES) ♔♔♔ ★★

Hackett/Steel & Ebert   1974/2003   €€   H: M 28, L 36

✉ **Enniscrone Golf Club, Enniscrone, Co. Sligo, RoI**

☎ **+353 96 362 97**

✎ **enniscronegolf@eircom.net   www.enniscronegolf.com**

🚌 ✈ **Knock: N17 for Sligo then L to Ballina, whence N59 north, then L onto R297 to Inishcrone; club on L as you approach village.**

	y	p		y	p
1	373	4	10	359	4
2	556	5	11	170	3
3	208	3	12	345	4
4	523	5	13	350	4
5	450	4	14	542	5
6	424	4	15	421	4
7	534	5	16	514	5
8	170	3	17	149	3
9	395	4	18	465	4
	3633	37		3315	36
				6948	73

Challenging links primarily up, down and through awesome dunes in sublime beachside setting. Flatter-looking middle section is . . . not flat, but one of strongest parts of the course. Inviting downhill teeshots, eccentric undulations and greensites with some very entertaining putting surfaces, often raised, all conspire to make you wish to return. Wind!

This engaging course is a hybrid, incorporating both of the two main types of land used for links courses. It is possible to allocate most types of 'links' holes into two categories:

Type A: A hole set over land with, overall, relatively little difference in elevation (often the maximum variation within the overall plane of a hole is little more than 10ft), yet with almost infinite irregular variations and subtleties combining to render the best of natural golfing challenges – every hole on the Old Course at St Andrews falls into this category.

Type B: A hole that may well use all the subtleties of Type A, but also features the often significant differences in elevation offered by sand dunes (sometimes as much as 100ft) – exemplified by most of the holes at *Ballybunion (Old)*.

Downhill gold-rated medium-short p:4 13, seen from the right of the brow which, if driven, can leave a short, yet testing approach to set up that birdie . . . If the wind is against, it can play quite differently. An example of a hole on 'Type B' land.

The majority of links courses have a combination of the two types, because what we know as 'linksland' tends to be a mixture of sand dunes that have been blown up by the sea winds, and, behind them (i.e. away from the prevailing wind), land that is lower and flatter, for the very reason that the dunes have protected it from the wilder ravages

A view of one of many excellent holes on the flatter ('Type A') land: par at long p:4 5 becomes a tall order if you drive into a fairway bunker . . .

of nature. So the two types of land are so often found together because the one (Type B) helps create the other (Type A).

As anyone who has played the Church Course at St Enodoc, Cornwall (one of the best examples of a primarily Type B course) will confirm, Type Bs tend to be more instantly spectacular than those that are 100% Type A. But As can be just as good, if not better, than Bs: As are often more understated and subtle, resulting in more enduring appeal to players. Although Bs lie primarily in dunes, they naturally fit within them; indeed, in the pre-bulldozer days when most links were laid out, the often huge dimensions of such land made it almost impossible for much earth (i.e. sand) to be moved, a good thing because it guaranteed natural golf.

At Enniscrone we have an area of massive sand dunes bordering the sea (i.e. B), inland of which is a large area of A. Hackett laid out the original course here mostly over the A land. The A holes that remain

(5–10) are some of the best on the course, but Steel and Ebert's remodelling introduced much more B land (notably 2–4 and 14–16).

Why do we go to such length with all this A and B stuff? Ireland is about the only country in the world where genuine (as opposed to artificial, hotter-latitudinal, make-believe) linksland has been used for golf courses in the bulldozer age. Enniscrone is one of the few courses (along with *Doonbeg* and perhaps *Ballybunion (Cashen)*) where the designer has given enough respect to the B land to enable the natural charm and eccentricities of such land to prevail. Although the land for the newer holes has undoubtedly been smoothed out a bit (compare 14–16 with Hackett's 11–13), it still feels that the holes fit within the dunes rather than having been imposed on top of them. This is not to say that some of the newer seaside courses of Ireland don't represent good design. It is just that we would prefer not to call them links courses. We prefer to call them 'dunes' courses, one of the best examples of which is *Rosapenna (Sandy Hills)*.

For a modern links course, Enniscrone (Dunes) is a delight.

Note: The 3367yd p:36 9-hole Scurmore course lies on the flatter ground inland of the Dunes course and is not covered by our research.

ESKER HILLS

O'Connor Jnr   1996   €

✉   **Esker Hills Golf Club, Tullamore, Co. Offaly, RoI**

☎   **+353 50 65 5999**

✎   **info@eskerhillsgolf.com   www.eskerhillsgolf.com**

🚗 ✈   **Dublin: M1/M50 south; exit 7 N4/M4/N6 to Killbeggan (approx 77km from M50), just after which L onto R436 for Clara; L at junction with N80, for Tullamore; club soon up on R.**

Selected holes

	y	p
4	391	4
5	167	3
8	354	4
10	306	4
13	196	3
14	356	4
15	187	3
Total	**6626**	**71**

p:4 7 seen from the tee: even with a view restricted by trees, the smooth roll of the esker land is evident.

Some two-thirds of this generally engaging course runs attractively up, over, down, round and through eskers (definition: see *Birr* p. 55), yielding several fun holes (notably 4–8, 10, 13–15). The rest have less charm, but the wide-ranging rustic views compensate. Reasonably large, occasionally sloping greens add to the challenge. Hilly.

THE EUROPEAN ★★

Ruddy   1992–   €€€   **H:** M 28, L 36

✉ The European Club, Brittas Bay, Co. Wicklow, RoI
☎ +353 40 447 415
✎ info@theeuropeanclub.com   www.theeuropeanclub.com
🚗 ✈ Dublin: M1/M50 south, becomes M11/N11; about 40km from start of M11, L at Jack White's Inn for Brittas Bay; R onto R750 for Arklow; club on L after 3km.

	y	p		y	p
1	424	4	10	466	4
2	160	3	11	416	4
3	499	5	12	459	4
4	470	4	13	596	5
5	409	4	14	195	3
6	210	3	15	415	4
7	470	4	16	415	4
8	415	4	17	432	4
9	427	4	18	477	4
	3484	35		3871	36
				7355	71

Optional extra holes:

7a	166	3	12a	205	3
Out	3650	38	Back	4076	39
Total (20)				7726	77

A golf-design enthusiast's personal, if slightly eccentric, statement amounting to 20 beautiful, testing modern links holes, lovingly enhanced perennially, routed mainly along plateaux between some high dunes, with a great run along the shore. The sleeper-faced bunkers and moderately undulating greens will test your game and give many a thrill. Wind! Private.

A view from the 15th fairway back over gold-rated p:5 13, running back initially along the shore from the flag (lower middle right) then up right into the dunes, to shore-liner golden p:4 12; p:3 12a is below the highest dune.

Having been entertained generously by Pat Ruddy and his family on more than one occasion, we confine ourselves to some extracts from our notes:

- Democracy and the design/running of a successful golf club generally do not go hand in hand.
- Many of the most successful courses have been designed/are run by an oligarchy, if not an autocrat – often almost delighting in the fact of being answerable to nobody – from Pine Valley, Augusta National and Valderrama downwards.
- Such places also thrive because they can get on and do things, with a fine disregard for the interminable process of committees.
- But they also thrive on a touch of . . . well, if not eccentricity, then character. (Pine Valley has often been described as more bunker than golf course – but that is what George Crump, its original owner and designer, wanted.)

Gold-rated p:4 8 runs between the dunes to a bunkerless raised green.

- Here, Pat Ruddy is the president, the president is the founder, the founder is the owner, the owner is the unceasing designer, the designer is the manager, and the manager (and his family) almost exclusively do almost everything there is to be done – which includes making the unforgettably delicious apple pie.
- On arrival you are given a welcome card, explaining the European's philosophy, including: 'It is important to understand that we are in the process of establishing perhaps the last great golf links to be created.' A fine ideal, which has a realistic chance of being achieved (including, sadly, the word 'last': there are very few links sites left anywhere for

new golf use) – even if it takes the 100+ years the same card mentions. Another extract: 'the belief that manners, space and time, rather than money, should be the governors of access to our links'.

- We first played it in the summer. On an early evening, ideal for golf, William waited with his camera for two hours on top of the dunes for the sun to re-emerge from the clouds. Not one player came by.
- Greg and William returned for another inspection. It was a cold, dank, drizzly, grey September day. Pat offered to drive us all over the course – in his car, of course!
- The course has 20 holes: 7a and 12a, both p:3s, may be played optionally, or, as Ruddy puts it: 'If there are 20 fine golf holes out there, why stop at 18? We are here to play golf!'

Ruddy's three putt green at golden 12 can be more than a passing challenge, but, at 459yds, there's much to do even before you reach its football pitch putting surface . . .

- Ruddy is also founder of the Great Three Putt Society: the 12th green is 127yds long (longer than the widest double green at St Andrews) – he wishes to restore the art of three putting, as opposed to 'the disappointing version' of the same.
- The bunkers are walled with railway sleepers (US – ties), a traditional feature of some Scottish links, more recently revived in the US by the famous designer Pete Dye. The contrast of the dark wood against the otherwise soft green landscape gives the course its unique character, and (unlike the bunkers on some other Ruddy courses) you cannot fail to spot them. Unusually, the sleepers here lie at an angle, so there is an element of luck, in that your ball can hit a bunker face and bounce back onto the fairway, or into the bunker, or worse . . .
- The 13th green is U-shaped, with the bottom of the U nearest the fairway and a bunker inside the bottom of the U. If you're on the wrong half of the green, you can try putting the ball (roulette-style) round the sleeper slopes of the bunker and back onto the other part of the green (who said golf wasn't fun?).
- With 3 holes (7, 13 and 14) ranked in *The 500 World's Greatest Golf Holes* (ISBN 1579652379, Peper and editors of *Golf Magazine*), a book whose views we sometimes accept (as here), the golf is good.
- It is a long course, so heed Pat's words: 'In its essence, golf is a game of skill. We make no apology for the fact that the thoughtless and inept player may suffer on our links. It was not created for such players. Yet even a beginner will enjoy a game here, subject to having some sense and choosing the correct teeing-ground and then playing within one's skills.'

The European is that kind of a place.

FAITHLEGG

Caddies on request

Merrigan 1993 € **H:** M 28, L 36

✉ Faithlegg Golf Club, Faithlegg, Co.Waterford, RoI
☎ +353 51 382 241
✎ golf@fhh.ie   www.faithlegg.com
🚗 ✈ Dublin: M1/M50 south; exit 9 N7/M7 for Naas; M9/N9 past Carlow to Waterford, where cross bridge and L; follow N25 along quayside and R; then L onto R683 for Clohernagh/Dunmore; 2km beyond ferry signs, L to Faithlegg; club on L after 4km.

	y	p		y	p
1	290	4	10	487	5
2	494	5	11	420	4
3	154	3	12	438	4
4	350	4	13	493	5
5	418	4	14	510	5
6	205	3	15	367	4
7	420	4	16	166	3
8	388	4	17	432	4
9	153	3	18	444	4
	2872	34		3757	38
				6629	72

A parkland course with some splendid specimen trees on ground that slopes gradually from the top of the park (with hotel in centre) to the reaches of Waterford Harbour, in view of Waterford Castle on the opposite shore. With some well-defended greensites, the design is more appealing from fairway than tee. The p:3s (and one industrial view) are all engaging.

The surprisingly non-unattractive industrial view (and residential accompaniments) are more than complemented by the splendid tree around which dogleg downhill p:4 8 turns.

The raised and tiered bunkered greensite of longish p:4 is dominated by the intriguing shape of the grandstand without seats beyond the 1st fairway which appears behind it. Play out to the left to reduce the threat of the greenside bunker.

FOTA ISLAND

O'Connor Jnr & McEvoy/Howes 1993/2001 €€ **H:** M 28, L 36

Caddies on request

✉ Fota Island Golf Club, Carrigtwohill, Co. Cork, RoI

☎ +353 21 488 3700

✎ reservations@fotaisland.ie www.fotaisland.ie

🚗 ✈ Cork: N27 for Cork; R onto, and follow, N25 for Waterford, through tunnel; after some 8km R onto R624 for Cobh; club on R after 1km.

	y	p			y	p
1	409	4		10	500	5
2	461	4		11	168	3
3	165	3		12	428	4
4	548	5		13	208	3
5	544	5		14	417	4
6	376	4		15	476	4
7	179	3		16	417	4
8	478	4		17	222	3
9	424	4		18	507	5
	3584	36			3343	35
					6927	71

Mostly spacious, gently undulating parkland course (with several specimen trees) in two 9-hole loops, with pretty inland tidal views. In the comparatively cramped, watery start to the back 9, the golf can be more fun but the design weaker. Strong finish. Large, gently undulating greens not too tightly bunkered. Venue of Irish Open 2001 and 2002.

Note: a further 9 holes by Howes is under development as we go to press.

GALWAY

A Mackenzie/Hackett/DIY & Connaughton   1925/1994/2005

€€ **H:** M 28, L 36

✉ Galway Golf Club, Blackrock, Salthill, Co. Galway, RoI

☎ +353 91 522 033

✎ galwaygolf@eircom.net   www.galwaygolf.com

🚗 ✈ Galway: R339 into Galway, leaving west on R336 along seafront; club is on R 5km from centre, past end of promenade at Blackrock, Salthill.

	m	p		m	p
1	287	4	10	398	4
2	142	3	11	188	3
3	394	4	12	474	5
4	354	4	13	125	3
5	403	4	14	382	4
6	396	4	15	362	4
7	475	5	16	389	4
8	343	4	17	314	4
9	185	3	18	363	4
	2979	35		2995	35
				5974	70

Pleasant, parkland-with-gorse layout recently upgraded, including remodelled 1–4 by sea, 4–18 running inland over a reasonably gentle hillside. Fairway undulations, some fairly attractive bunkering and raised greensites (notably on the upgraded holes) add to the challenge. Nice sloping greens. Home to the O'Connor clan (Jnr born nearby and caddied here).

This view of downhill medium p:4 14 shows off Galway's wonderful setting, most visible from its higher reaches.

GALWAY BAY 🏆🏆🏆🏆

O'Connor Jnr   1993   €€

✉ Galway Bay Golf and Country Club, Renville, Oranmore, Co. Galway, RoI

☎ +353 91 790 711

✎ info@galwaybaygolfresort.com   www.galwaybaygolfresort.com

🚗 ✈ Galway: N6 east to Oranmore, then R for Renville and follow signs.

Selected holes

Note: closed in 2006 for enhancement; scheduled to re-open 2007.

	y	p
12	400	4
17	349	4
Total	6586	74

A grand-scale hotel course, laid out over fairly open ground, mainly sloping gently down to water hazards in a small valley between the clubhouse and the sea, which adjoins several holes. Widespread views over, and adjoining, Galway Bay. Wind!

GLASSON 🏆🏆🏆🏆

O'Connor Jnr   1993   €€

✉ Glasson Golf Club, Glasson, Athlone, Co. West Meath, RoI

☎ +353 90 648 5120

✎ info@glassongolf.ie   www.glassongolf.ie

🚗 ✈ Dublin: M1/M50 south; exit N6 to Galway on Athlone bypass; take 1st exit, for Cavan N55; in Glasson village L by Village Restaurant club; 2km on L.

Selected holes

	y	p
5	199	3
8	432	4
12	406	4
15	185	3
Total	7205	73

Red – p:4 12: Almost geometrically right-to-left dogleg downhill to a green in front of the hotel with severe adverse camber. A real shocker.

Overlooking Lough Ree, a hotel course on generally sloping former farmland. Some holes have spectacular views, but these are generally not matched by the design. We would like to have been more positive, because it is a popular course and has an excellent practice facility, also with good views.

GLEN OF THE DOWNS 🏆🏆🏆

McEvoy   1997   €€

✉ Glen of the Downs Golf Club, Coolnaskeagh, Delgany, Co. Wicklow, RoI

☎ +353 1 287 6240

✎ info@glenofthedowns.com
www.glenofthedowns.com

🚗 ✈ Dublin: M1/M50 south; exit N11 past Bray; L for Delgany/ Greystones, then L up steep hill before Delgany Inn; club on L after 2km.

Selected holes

	y	p
1	181	3
8	404	4
10	382	4
Total	6443	71

Exposed hillside layout with good sea and hill views (including nearby Sugar Loaf mountain). Some challenging holes, especially p:3s (including well-bunkered p:3 1 with tricky green divided in the middle by a spine running directly away from the tee) and the 5-tier double green for 8 and 10. Pleasant modern clubhouse.

The view from the tee at Gold Coast's medium p:4 15 with the tide out. Now imagine it with the tide in . . .

GOLD COAST 🏆🏆🏆

Hewson/Fives   1939/2000   €

	m	p
Selected hole		
15	361	4
Total 6171		72

✉ Gold Coast Golf Club, Ballinacourty, Dungarven, Co. Waterford, RoI

☎ +353 58 440 55

✎ info@clonea.com   www.clonea.com

🚗 ✈ Cork: East on N25 for Waterford; approx 1km after Dungarvan R onto R575 and follow signs to Gold Coast Hotel; club just past hotel near shore.

A gently sloping part-parkland part-clifftop course, which, despite the often rather cramped and parallel routing, contains some holes with spectacular views, including one 'drive over the beach' challenge (15). Wind!

GORT 🏆🏆🏆

O'Connor Jnr   1996   €

	m	p
Selected hole		
5	155	3
12	303	4
Total 5974		71

✉ Gort Golf Club, Castlequarter, Gort, Co. Galway, RoI

☎ + 353 91 632 244

✎ info@gortgolf.com   www.gortgolf.com

🚗 ✈ Galway: N18 for Limerick; in village of Gort follow signs to Kilmacduagh; then follow signs to Castlequarter; club on R.

A fairly open course with occasional trees, hedges, walls, ponds and good views over the nearby lakes and wetlands, routed from the clubhouse down, through and across the hills and valleys of its rolling terrain. Some good greensites (notably 12 and 15, both raised), and memorable p:3 5 in the valley. The club was founded in 1924 and for 50 years used a different site, but it was prone to winter flooding. After an interim move, it is now settled at the present location. The whole area is well known to Christy O'Connor Jnr: he came to live in Gort in the early 1980s, and was made an honorary life member of the club after breaking Henry Cotton's 50-year-old record in the 1985 Open at Royal St George's, Sandwich (won by Sandy Lyle).

GOWRAN PARK ★

Caddies on request

Howes   2001   €   **H:** M 28, L 36

✉ Gowran Park Golf Club, Gowran Park, Co. Kilkenny, RoI

☎ +353 56 772 6699

✎ gowranparkltd@eircom.net   www.gowranpark.ie

🚗 ✈ Dublin: M1/M50 south; exit N7, then M9/N9 for Waterford, past Carlow and through Gowran; shortly after, club is at racecourse on L.

	m	p			m	p
1	482	5		10	174	3
2	350	4		11	368	4
3	383	4		12	540	5
4	403	4		13	150	3
5	160	3		14	482	5
6	334	4		15	360	4
7	356	4		16	193	3
8	447	5		17	377	4
9	147	3		18	404	4
	3082	36			3048	35
					6110	71

Consistently good holes on an imaginative, entertaining, yet understated and rarely arduous routing inside, over and around a racecourse – more wooded in the country, more heathland on course. Five testing p:3s. Excellent greensites and bunkering. Some water.

Gowran Park is one of the best inland golf bargains in Ireland. Indeed, if you need to balance out the higher cost of a day's golf at nearby *Mount Juliet*, you need go no further. Jeff Howes (who was Nicklaus' man on site at Juliet) has laid out a completely different and sporting course with 7 greens inside the railings of what has become, since its first meeting in 1914, one of the

A grandstand view of longish left to right p:4 3, which attractively moves around bunkers on the inside of the turn. Even money on a par?!

We love the humour of medium p:4 7 – if ever there was a hole crying out to be named, this is it. We leap out of our fairly high stalls onto the flat, wonderfully parallel to the real thing on the left (the striped mowing emphasises the joke to all but the blinkered). If you've paced it well off the tee, take care: your next shot could still unseat you… Got it? 'The Water Jump'!

top trial racecourses in the British Isles. (Levmoss first won here and went on uniquely to win the Ascot Gold Cup and the Prix de l'Arc de Triomphe. Other famous horses trialled here include Arkle, Nicholas Silver and Foinavon.) We would bet that the golf course was itself trialled on a fairly low budget, but in our evaluations we can make no allowances for how much (or not) a course has been backed. What we assess is what we see, and, inspecting as many courses as we do, the 'spend' on the design and construction of a course normally becomes apparent fairly quickly.

You can see the quality of design even before you are under starter's orders. As you walk across the course to the course, preview the excellent opening p:5: you will soon discover its well-bunkered approach and subtly mounded greensite.

Equally, there is no excuse for a designer for accepting too low a budget for a course. He must design as his budget allows – or make a refusal to his prospective client.

Here, Howes has accepted his budget and made the best of the running with it. The result: the holes on good land for golf have seen relatively little investment (e.g. 1, where the shape of the land was ideal for an excellent hole, with only minor alterations), whereas more has had to be spent in the woods to achieve success (e.g. 4 and 5, which have both been shaped through the trees) – even here, we suspect the land to have been very much on Howes' side, so all credit to him for the routing.

No photo-finishes here: this is a clear winner.

GRANGE ♔♔♔♔

Hood/Braid   1910/1929   €€

✉   Grange Golf Club, Whitechurch Road, Rathfarnham, Dublin 16, RoI
☎   +353 1 493 2889
✎   grangegc@eircom.net   www.grangegc.com
🚗 ✈ Dublin: M1/M50 south; at exit 12, L to Ballyboden on R113;
club after 2km at junction with Whitechurch Rd (entrance is R fork
between R113 and Whitechurch Rd).

Selected holes

	m	p
1	173	3
4	375	4
7	377	4
8	186	3
9	340	4
11	179	3
12	299	4
13	295	4
14	436	5
Total	**5396**	**68**

Golfing home of two Irish greats: David Sheahan
(amateur, unbeaten in the Walker Cup) and Paul
McGinley (famous for his 2002 Ryder Cup winning
putt); a historic club. Unique in starting with 2 p:3s,
and having 24 holes, it yields pleasant parkland golf
over gently sloping ground in a peaceful setting, with
some raised greens.

*The cross bunker at p:3 11 foreshortens its appearance: played over a small valley
in front of the tee, this hole uses the land well.*

Corsican pines mark the edge of Greenore's 17th, a relatively short p:5 which thus provides a late chance to improve your score.

GREENORE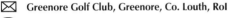

Caddies
on request

Baillie/Hackett/Ruddy & Craddock 1896/1973/1991 € H: M 28, L 36

✉ Greenore Golf Club, Greenore, Co. Louth, RoI

☎ +353 429 373 212

✎ greenoregolfclub@eircom.net www.greenoregolfclub.com

🚗 ✈ Dublin: N1/M1 north to Dundalk; ignore signs to Dundalk south and centre, at end of M1 follow signs from 2nd rbt to Carlingford R173; after about 15km R fork onto R175 for Greenore; club on L as you approach Greenore.

	y	p			y	p
1	218	3		10	154	3
2	562	5		11	523	5
3	409	4		12	424	4
4	409	4		13	436	4
5	420	4		14	149	3
6	130	3		15	360	4
7	419	4		16	438	4
8	412	4		17	492	5
9	323	4		18	369	4
	3302	35			3345	36
					6647	71

A good mix, despite stylistic inconsistencies, of traditional-feel links and newer holes, occasionally made dramatic by trees (note rare Corsican pines). Minor but distinct elevations and some good small greensites. Surprisingly romantic lough-side setting with some excellent vistas. Three p:3s stand out: 6, 10 and 14, plus p:4 16. Some water. Wind – beware from northwest!

HEADFORT

✉ Headfort Golf Club, Kells, Co. Meath, RoI

☎ +353 46 924 0639

✎ info@headfortgolfclub.ie   www.headfortgolfclub.ie

🚗 ✈ Dublin: M1/M50 south; exit 6 for N3/Navan; after 15km club on R, 500m before Kells.

NEW ★

O'Connor Jnr   2000   €€   **H:** M 28, L 36

	m	p			m	p
1	400	4		10	378	4
2	480	5		11	163	3
3	345	4		12	366	4
4	157	3		13	392	4
5	400	4		14	510	5
6	516	5		15	398	4
7	170	3		16	508	5
8	384	4		17	180	3
9	377	4		18	391	4
	3229	36			3286	36
					6515	72

One of the most beautiful inland Irish courses, well and spaciously routed through woods and pinetum, opening out onto moderate parkland slopes in front of Headfort House, with water frequently in play – best to go there at blossomtime. The better holes are generally those in the woods, but few disappoint. **Large greens with mostly gentle undulations. Enjoy!**

The members of this club are blessed with one of the most beautiful inland settings for golf in Ireland: on the eastern edge of Kells lies Headfort House, which dates from 1780, and its estate, which runs down to and over the river

Headfort New's medium p:3 7, seen from the edge of the woods on the right: with water left, only a straight shot will do.

After a teeshot over water, gold-rated p:4 10 curves attractively to the right round trees to a slightly raised bunkered greensite. It makes excellent use of natural features.

Blackwater. Golf began here in 1930 with 9 holes, extended to 18 in 1956. Having purchased the land for this course (the Old) in 1987, the club was fortunate to be offered the stunning piece of land between the house and the river in 1998, which includes a pinetum (including some splendid Asiatic specimens collected by the former Lord Headfort), abundant rhododendrons and shrubs, some set on islands midstream.

Uphill p:4 5 plays the longest of all holes at Headfort (New) against its par; the attraction of contour mowing here is self evident.

   Christy O'Connor's layout for the New unfolds a tour round this magnificent estate, currying our interest with regular transitions between the woods, riverside and more open

The glade which contains Headfort (New)'s p:3 11 frames a distant view of Headfort House.

parkland in front of the house. With careful development over time, this course could easily earn a higher rating, especially if the bunkering were given a flair equal to the excellence of the site and routing.

OLD

DIY/DIY   1930/1956   €

Selected holes

	m	p
3	369	4
4	444	5
8	144	3
9	318	4
12	356	4
13	351	4
17	326	4
Total	**5973**	**72**

Parkland course with undulating fairways (admirably defined with contour mowing at our visit) over gently rolling ground, the maturity of whose trees render a beautiful setting. Some testing holes, occasionally with fairly narrow raised greensites. A good second course for visitors to *Headfort (New)*.

A view from behind Headfort (Old)'s well-bunkered p:3 8 shows some of the majesty of the course's mature parkland features.

With the pin on the right, long p:3 4 at The Heritage rewards only the best of shots; the sensible play is not to take on too much water.

THE HERITAGE ♔♔♔♔♔ ↗

Caddies
on request

Howes & Ballesteros 2003 €€€ H: M 28, L 36

✉ **The Heritage Golf and Country Club, Killenard, Co. Laois, RoI**
☎ **+353 502 45 500**
✎ reservations@theheritage.com   www.theheritage.com
🚗 ✈ Dublin: M1/M50 south; exit 9 onto N7/M7 for Limerick; after some 35km exit onto N7 to Monasterevin; after 3km R at Roadhouse Café (sign); club in Killenard village after 3km.

	y	p		y	p
1	406	4	10	526	5
2	572	5	11	332	4
3	431	4	12	491	4
4	214	3	13	473	4
5	460	4	14	572	5
6	455	4	15	175	3
7	189	3	16	397	4
8	533	5	17	225	3
9	421	4	18	447	4
	3681	36		3638	36
				7319	72

Grand-scale deep-budget course, set over gently sloping land with several water hazards, extensive bunkering and many good holes, but the wide fairways make many of the hazards feel out of play. Yet this makes it easier to score, especially as the good drainage provides a lot of run. (Was it designed for the power golf of the future?) Lavishly equipped hotel and spa.

Accommodation: *Headfort:* Boyne Valley; *The Heritage:* Clanard Court **117**

HERMITAGE 🏆🏆🏆

McKenna/unknown/Hackett   1902/1938/1940s & 1950s   €€

✉ Hermitage Golf Club, Ballydowd, Lucan, Co. Dublin, RoI

☎ +353 1 626 8491

✎ hermitagegolf@eircom.net   www.hermitagegolf.ie

🚗 ✈ Dublin: M1/M50 south; exit N4 for Galway; use Lucan exit to U-turn for Dublin, club almost immediately on L.

Selected holes

	m	p
3	348	4
6	299	4
7	201	3
8	395	4
10	151	3
11	520	5
15	455	5
16	368	4
Total	6060	71

Very narrowly missing ✈, a beautiful mature tree-lined parkland course, whose centenary was in 2005. The front 9 is set on gently rising land above the clubhouse (NB long challenging downhill p:3 7), before the course takes you, via spectacular medium downhill p:3 10, down to the banks of the Liffey and gradually back up again via some good holes, and others with some blind shots. Some well-bunkered greens. (A course with 19 holes, in that in the winter a different downhill p:3 10th is played.)

Red – 16: Too much uphill and blind all in one go.

HOWTH 🏆🏆🏆🏆

Braid & Stutt   1929   €

✉ Howth Golf Club, Carrickbrack Road, Sutton, Dublin 13, RoI

☎ +353 1 832 3055

✎ manager@howthgolfclub.ie   www.howthgolfclub.ie

🚗 ✈ Dublin: M1 for Dublin; L at exit 3 onto N32 for Malahide; straight across all jncts/rbts until (after about 6km) T-junction with coast road at Baldoyle; here R and immediately fork L onto Strand Rd (R106); after level crossing, straight over fork junction (becomes R105); club on L after about 1.5km up hill.

Selected holes

	m	p
3	375	4
15	137	3
Total	5634	71

Open hillside/heathland course with spectacular views every which way over Dublin, the sea and most of the links courses in the area. With several tees and greens shelved into hillside, Howth has a nice old-fashioned feel. Both loops of 9 emanate uphill from the clubhouse, so you can also play this course to keep fit, with the added bonus that the routing gives you two series of downhill drives on the way back. Uphill p:4 3 requires accuracy off the tee to avoid the stream which meanders across the fairway at driving distance. The view at short p:3 15 with Dublin Bay as the backdrop is a particular favourite: anything from a wedge to a wood may be required here.

A view from left of the fairway of the opening longish p:4. There is more room than you think but the rising green will test you, especially if you have not fully warmed up.

THE ISLAND ♛♛♛ ★★

Unknown/F Hawtree & Hackett/Howes/M Hawtree
1890/Unknown/Unknown/1990   €€€   H: M 28, L 36

✉ The Island Golf Club, Corballis, Donabate, Co. Dublin, RoI
☎ +353 1 843 6205
✎ info@islandgolfclub.com   www.theislandgolfclub.com
🚗 ✈ Dublin: M1 north; Lissenhall exit (R132), following signs for Donabate; at 1st rbt take 3rd exit, 2nd exit from 2nd rbt (R126); pass Newbridge House then 2nd R; follow signs to club on R.

Caddies on request

	m	p			m	p
1	397	4		10	489	5
2	362	4		11	393	4
3	396	4		12	401	4
4	318	4		13	192	3
5	339	4		14	316	4
6	299	4		15	507	5
7	412	4		16	139	3
8	278	4		17	391	4
9	153	3		18	421	4
	2954	35			3249	36
					6203	71

Winding unpretentiously through a peninsula of dunes with extensive sea views, a sublime natural links, whose holes often seem heroic but are pleasantly tolerant of minor errors (e.g. slightly wayward drives), giving you confidence in playing its undulating fairways, revetted bunkers, often raised natural greens and challenging back 9 (some p:4s feel like p:5s). Wind!

Purple – 14: *Wonderfully old-fashioned natural bunkerless links shortish p:4, with incredibly narrow fairway and green, playing even narrower in the wind.*

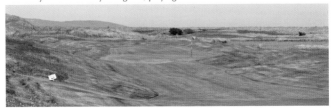

The view across p:3 16, and its superb 'raised-with-run-offs' green, well illustrates The Island's wonderful links setting across the estuary from Malahide.

In September 1887 four enterprising men rowed across the water from Malahide to the spur of duneland immediately north, with the mission of creating a golf course they could use on Sundays, when play was prohibited at their *Royal Dublin* club.

In those pioneering days this wonderful site for natural links golf was, for communications purposes, almost as good as an island, and the clubhouse remained near the jetty opposite Malahide until the boat service was discontinued in 1973. The early members routed the course through the valleys within the dunes, as it was impracticable to do anything else. This resulted in some rather narrow fairways. With the coming of road access and development of machinery, the course has

The excellent combination of natural features, and its tempting shortness, is what yields gold at p:4 4.

been remodelled and extended on several occasions (and we understand that more upgrading is planned for the front 9). However, the spirit of the original is still clearly visible, notably at remarkable 14, which was the original first hole: this bunkerless shortish p:4 must have one of the narrowest fairways in the world.

PS WG Grace brought a group of friends here to play golf and cricket (the 11th hole has been known as the Cricket Field ever since). He was out first ball!

A view from the tee over the valley to the green of challenging long p:3 13 – the rising ground in the foreground is deceptive, as the green is much further away than it looks.

THE K CLUB

- The K Club, Straffan, Co. Kildare, RoI
- +353 1 601 7300
- hotel@kclub.ie   www.kclub.ie
- Dublin: M1/M50 south; exit 9 onto N7; after approx 15km R for Straffan (sign); club on L before village; entrance to Smurfit clubhouse precedes Palmer clubhouse (but access possible from both to both; follow signs).

PALMER ↗

Palmer, Seay & Minchew   1991   €€€€   **H:** M 28, L 36

	y	p		y	p
1	584	5	10	418	4
2	450	4	11	413	4
3	182	3	12	170	3
4	428	4	13	568	5
5	213	3	14	440	4
6	446	4	15	478	4
7	555	5	16	430	4
8	424	4	17	173	3
9	401	4	18	537	5
	3743	36		3627	36
				7370	72

Peaceful, gently rolling parkland course with lakes and the Liffey much in play. The variety of tees mitigate for length off the back. Occasionally testing fairway bunkering rewards accurate driving. Well-contoured putting surfaces on greensites sometimes difficult to find. Respect this 2006 Ryder Cup challenge, or it will have you for breakfast!

NB Ryder Cup/tournament course: loops reversed, except 9 and 18 stay the same.
'RC' numbering on captions indicates Ryder Cup order of play.

The award of the 2006 Ryder Cup has made the K Club's Palmer Course a very special 'K': as the first Irish venue for the biennial transatlantic duel, it has become the toast of all Ireland – a reputation only to be enhanced over the years by the memories of this historic

1: (RC10, below) A long p:5, which curves gradually from left to right around trees to a well-bunkered green, seen here through the trees right of the approach.

2: *(RC11, above) Majestic parkland trees on the left and right dwarf the fairway and water's edge green of this longish p:4.*

3: *(RC12, right) A side-on view of this tee-water green p:3 shows the magnificence of the combination of water and trees on this part of the course.*

4: *(RC13, left) Water again comes into play – down the right of this longish right to left dogleg p:4.*

5: *(RC14) A challenging p:3 over water and sand, but we take issue with the unnecessary artificial waterfall behind (left) – it does nothing for the golf.*

event. This is a full-size modern golf course, with an American feel, which will test your ability to hit the ball long and straight, yet it is set in an unmistakably rich and green Irish setting.

But for all its demanding and

6: *(RC15) A relatively bland long p:4 which gently turns from right to left; to a greensite that could have been better defined.*

7: *(RC16) Coming at a critical point for Ryder Cup play, 7 is a theatrical hole: this just-reachable-in-2 p:5 witnesses as many match-losing as match-winning shots.*

8: *(RC17) A new back tee brings the Liffey onto this watery line at this longish p:4. If played sensibly, the water is more of an aesthetic feature than a golfing hazard.*

competently designed challenges and the fun of some of the water holes (especially 7 and 16), for golf-course-design buffs the Palmer Course is only the cereal. Their hunger here for the 'full Irish' will be better met by the newer Smurfit course.

To celebrate the Ryder Cup, we publish here a photograph of every hole on this historic course.

9: *(RC 9) Guide your drive over the bunkers and between the trees at this long p:4 – otherwise there is no chance of a par.*

10: *(RC1, above) The greensite at this longish p:4 lies beyond a stream and is partially concealed behind the mound on the left (11 is visible through the trees behind).*

11: *(RC2, right) An uphill p:4 which plays longer than its yardage due to the rising ground and raised, bunkered greensite.*

12: *(RC3, below) A medium p:3, protected by a pond and bunkers, with room out to the right for those with aqua- or arena-phobia on the tee.*

13: *(RC4, above) The long carry over bunkers from the tee of this downhill double dogleg long-ish p:5 rewards you with a more open view of the green, which is protected by sand and overhanging trees on the right.*

14: *(RC5, below) An uphill longish p:4 with a raised green (seen here from behind) – the fact that it is bunkerless, without compensating factors other than the greenside run-offs, makes it rather too lacking in definition.*

15: *(RC6, above) The first of a trio of well-designed closing holes, if you are to take this p:4 by storm, you will need an accurate, long downhill second over water to the contours of the green.*

16: *(RC7, below) A panoramic view of another well-conceived, if theatrical, hole – the water in front of the green can change the course of a match.*

17: *(RC8, left) The final p:3 (seen from behind) is attractively close to the Liffey.*

18: *(RC18, right) A longish p:5 (seen from behind) with strategic options to close.*

SMURFIT ★★

Palmer, Seay & Minchew   2003
€€€ **H:** M 28, L 36

Caddies
on request

	y	p		y	p
1	449	4	10	551	5
2	179	3	11	365	4
3	603	5	12	214	3
4	394	4	13	468	4
5	403	4	14	394	4
6	436	4	15	376	4
7	600	5	16	457	4
8	144	3	17	202	3
9	464	4	18	578	5
	3672	36		3605	36
				7277	72

Linksy feel to challenging layout well routed over subtly undulating land. Occasional lack of definition off the tee, but the well-shaped fairways are consistently characterful throughout. Superb green-sites, testing angles and bunkering. Remarkably three-dimensional for site without big hills. Water. The best Palmer design we've seen (including the Theme Park 7th!).

The Smurfit starts gently enough, but one glimpse of glorious p:3 2 (most effectively bunkered at the front and mounded behind) suggests that this might turn into rather more than an ordinary round of golf. Everything works here: from the well-bunkered large undulating greens with multitudinous pin positions, sand-up-face flowing yet traditional-feel bunkering style and sympathetically designed lakes, through to the

A wintry view of downhill long p:4 13: as the water crosses the hole diagonally running down to the green, several choices are left if you find yourself uncertain as to whether to go for the green in two.

dramatic folds in the fairways. Smurfit's only real weakness is the way a few fairways seem from the tee to disappear over brows. This is most noticeable at the 3rd, where the angles don't really work.

Medium p:3 2 earns gold for the combination of excellent bunkering, greenside slopes and undulating putting surface.

The winning features of downhill long p:3 12 are the large, flowing green, the attractive bunkering and the surrounding banks.

An exacting water-in-front-of-green shorter p:4, another testing p:4 with an excellently bunkered raised greensite, and a switchback p:4 over the top of the course lead us to the controversial long p:5 7. This hole must have had its own budget (if not screenplay), but while its lack of full stylistic integrity with the other 17 holes loses the course marks, we confess to liking it. The grey cliffs of the water-filled canyon on the right side of the hole is reminiscent of 'The Lost World' ride at Universal Studios, but (regardless of its appearance) it is a good hazard in the right place, and the sympathetically designed bunkers on the left balance out the view. (Don't attempt to play out of the water: the local T-Rex has his own definition of a full Irish!) If you look carefully at the slabs of rock around the bunkers on the left, you will notice a difference between 'concrete rock' and 'rock rock'. Theme park it may be, but it is an excellent and attractive golf hole. We also like the way the canyon allows you to see a short trailer for the next hole. As it doesn't allow you to see much, the mystery adds to the sense of expectation, fully justified by the excellent raised-tee-to-raised-green p:3 that reveals itself to you a few minutes later. Back to the clubhouse with a better than it first appears right-to-left p:4.

If you're a group of course-design junkies like us, when you play the front 9, which is generally on the higher part of the site, you can see the lower, potentially less interesting ground of the back 9, and so have reason to fear that you have seen the best of the course. Wrong! The quality is sustained to the end: the greensite at p:5 10, one of the lowest points of the course, is superbly crafted, and so it goes on, through gold-rated p:3 12, and the generally watery holes that follow . . . Having first seen right-to-left sweeping p:5 18 from behind, we feared that, for ★★s, Smurfit might fall at the last fence, but (despite the visual intrusion of the houses on the right, and the bunkering on the outside of the dogleg) there is just enough strategic balance between the water all down the left and the movement of land to redeem it. The Smurfit has already hosted the European Open – to mixed reaction from the players maybe, but we like it.

Egg yourself on to taste both K courses: even if they both eat you at golf, the overall experience is worth the money.

KILKEA CASTLE

Gilbert & Cassidy   1994   €

✉ Kilkea Castle Golf Club, Castledermot, Co. Kildare, RoI

☎ +353 599 145 555

✎ kilkeacastlegolfclub@eircom.net   www.kilkeacastlehotelgolf.com

🚗 ✈ Dublin: M1/M50 south; exit N7/M7/M9/N9 until Castledermot,
thence R and follow signs to Kilkea; club just before Kilkea on R.

Selected hole		
	m	p
14	168	3
Total	6097	70

Generally rather flat, low-budget parkland course, with some water, in grounds of (but under separate ownership from) the oldest inhabited castle in Ireland (1180). There is just enough movement in the land for a few holes to hint at the potential for upgrading, including: p:4 3 (right-to-left dogleg over stream); p:3 14 (an attractive stone bridge behind); 17 – cries out to be shortened into a go-for-it-in-one short p:4 over water (and is close to red, as it is); attractive 18th – with water on the left and a green set immediately below the castle.

Morning light bathes its own hue on Kikea Castle's p:4 18th, which sweeps right to left around the pond. The slopes of the green lie immediately below the castle.

KILKEE

DIY/Hackett   1896/1990   €

✉ Kilkee Golf Club, East End, Kilkee, Co. Clare, RoI
☎ +353 65 905 6048
✎ kilkeegolfclub@eircom.net www.kilkeegolfclub.ie
🚗 ✈ Shannon: N19/N18 to Ennis; N68 to Kilrush;
N67 for Kilkee; at seafront, R after Waterworld and
Dive Centre, club on R.

Selected holes		
	m	p
3	292	4
4	165	3
Total	5555	70

Rather simple and bland links course over mainly gradually sloping
ground running down to cliffs, but the view from the clifftop at the far
end (p:3 4) is *awesome*. Wind!

KILKEEL

Lord Babington/Hackett   1949/1993   £

✉ Kilkeel Golf Club, Mourne Park, Newry Rd, Kilkeel,
Co. Down BT34 4LB, NI
☎ +44 284 176 2296
✎ info@kilkeelgolfclub.org www.kilkeelgolfclub.org
🚗 ✈ Belfast Int: A26 south to M1 J9; M1 for
Belfast, exit J7; A49 to Ballynahinch; A24/A2 to
Newcastle; A2 to 2 miles beyond Kilkeel; club on R.

Selected holes		
	y	p
5	288	4
9	388	4
10	395	4
13	378	4
14	411	4
Total	6579	72

Red – short p:4 5: too much uphill with too little definition to compensate.

Set in the grounds of a grand estate under the mountains of Mourne with
stunning scenery, a sometimes hilly parkland/woodland course with some
rather eccentric, if occasionally extreme, holes (most notably p:4 5). You may
choose to ignore the coolness of our review, as the course was selected in
1999 by the Royal and Ancient Golf Club of St Andrews to be a qualifying
course for the Amateur Championship with the final 36 holes at nearby Royal
County Down, Newcastle, and likewise twice for the British Seniors Open.

*The view to the dark cliffs (and headland to the left, out of shot) from Kilkee's p:3 4 is
amazing – the cliffs are much higher than any photo from the golf course could convey.*

Killarney: Castlerosse's reply to Sir Guy's 18th (now on Mahony's Point, but originally the two holes were on the same course), Killeen's p:3 3 (seen on the direct line of play in front of the tee) is, if anything, a stronger golfing challenge. Measuring the same length, and also over the edge of water, its gilding is crowned by the superbly placed bunker at the front left of the putting surface. This photo was taken before the recent enhancement.

KILLARNEY ♉♉♉♉

✉ **Killarney Golf & Fishing Club, Mahony's Point, Killarney, Co. Kerry, RoI**
☎ **+353 64 310 34**
✉ reservations@killarney-golf.com   www.killarney-golf.com
🚗 ✈ **Kerry: L on N23/N22 to Killarney centre, then west for Killorglin on R562; club 3km on L. Note: Lackabane course on R.**

KILLEEN ★

Campbell & Castlerosse/F Hawtree etc/Steel & T Mackenzie
1939/1971/2006   €€   H: M 28, L 36

	m	p		m	p
1	345	4	10	156	3
2	351	4	11	462	5
3	183	3	12	436	4
4	382	4	13	458	4
5	415	4	14	356	4
6	193	3	15	393	4
7	469	5	16	475	5
8	375	4	17	356	4
9	359	4	18	402	4
	3072	35		3494	37
				6566	72

Mature, landscaped parkland course on gently rolling ground in beautiful lakeside setting. This former Irish Open layout will test all departments of your game. Some water, some good bunkering. Greensites more obvious, but course generally more technically challenging than Mahony's Point – especially last 6 holes. Deer. The recent enhancement looks promising.

On our original inspection in late 2004, it was difficult to separate Killarney's pair of courses with their exceptionally beautiful vistas over Lough Leane to Macgillycuddy's Reeks. Yes, Killeen seems a longer and in some ways slightly more testing course, but then Mahony's Point can be just as challenging – and since when was length a prerequisite in quality golf-course design, anyway? (If anyone disputes this last point, put them on the next plane to *Birr*…)

Castlerosse's original 7th hole, albeit from a different tee-site, Killeen's long p:4 12 gives you a flavour of the almost arboretal spacious parkland through which the 'inland' part of the course flowed. The raised, bunkered greensite can prove frustratingly elusive at the start of what can be a pivotal stage in matchplay.

Research for this article soon explained the reason for our difficulty: the two courses should really be seen as one layout of 36 holes, as they both contain the same elements. Each contains 9 holes of the original course laid out by Sir Guy Campbell, and constantly improved by Lord Castlerosse in the short time between the course's opening and his untimely death in 1943. (Castlerosse was a local aristocrat who, although spending most of his life in England and Fleet Street, was as respected as a talented course designer as he was passionate about delivering a world-class tourist product.) In addition, each has 9 holes designed by a 'conglomerate' inspired by Fred Hawtree's initial

A scenic stunner from a tee on a causeway promontory back into the water from the 3rd green, Killeen's medium p:4 4 can stun you in a rather different way if you stray to the right. The recent enhancement has seen the green move further right.

136

Castlerosse through and through, Mahony's Point's medium long p:4 3 is a good example of how the greensites dictate play more than first meets the eye: the hole swings left and the greensite is more raised that it seems from the photograph. Deer are easy prey for cameras here . . .

plans in 1969, motivated by Dr Billy O'Sullivan (captain at the time, acting rather like Castlerosse) and constructed in-house by Jim O'Meara, the head greenkeeper, who had built much of the original course, apparently including some 40 greens (yes!) for Castlerosse; Eddie Hackett acted as design consultant. The additional 9 holes on Mahony's Point are towards the main road, while Killeen was extended into a boggy area towards Killeen Point, significantly extending the golf's exposure to the lake. This was a major feat of engineering, requiring scrub clearance, all-important drainage and replanting of trees. Many of the new greens, raised to assist drainage, were built using gravel found in the area of the 8th hole (notice the drop in the ground height, highlighted by the mounds that sustain some trees at their original level).

The space and grandeur of the trees on Mahony's Point's medium p:5 8 show how its 'conglomerate' holes blend with the original. Leave yourself room here: the trees either side of the fairway can influence play significantly.

The remaining holes comprised adjustments to enable Killeen to start and finish by the clubhouse – so Killeen's first is played from a new tee round a dogleg to the original 4th green, and the last two holes are new. Overall, the new holes were built so much in sympathy with the old that it is difficult to notice the difference, except perhaps that the new Killeen Point holes are routed a little less spaciously than the rest of the course.

Since our first visit, Killeen has been enhanced by Steel & T Mackenzie – mainly greensite improvements (notably at 4, 6-9 and 13-18) and re-bunkering, with the routing unchanged. Initial impressions suggest that the revised course merits at least ★ (helped by the removal

of a birch tree in the middle of the fairway at p:4 5, which has changed
its rating from red to green).

For clarity, we summarise the provenance of the routing of each hole:

Course Killeen		Mahony's Point
Hole	Provenance	
1	Castlerosse green, played from new dogleg tee (4)	Campbell (1)
2	Campbell (5)	Castlerosse (Campbell to dogleg) (2)
3	Castlerosse (6)	Castlerosse (3)
4-9	Conglomerate – 4: new Steel & T Mackenzie lakeside green	Conglomerate
10	Conglomerate	Campbell/Castlerosse green from new angle (12)
11	Conglomerate	Conglomerate
12	Castlerosse green approached from new angle (7)	Conglomerate
13	Castlerosse (8)	Castlerosse (13)
14	Castlerosse (9)	Castlerosse greensite from Campbell original (14)
15	Castlerosse (10) new Steel & T Mackenzie green	Campbell with Castlerosse contoured greensite (15)
16	Castlerosse p:4 green played from new p:5 angle (11) – new Steel & T Mackenzie green on unchanged routing	Campbell (16)
17	Conglomerate	Campbell (17)
18	Conglomerate	Campbell (18)

(Brackets approximately denote the hole numbers of the Campbell/Castlerosse original.)

Who wins? A score draw overall, perhaps. Campbell will forever be known
for what is now Mahony's Point's priceless finish; Castlerosse for his
extensions eastwards and unforgettable Killeen 3; the conglomerate for the
consistency of their extensions and the additional waterside holes (Killeen
4 and 10); Steel & T Mackenzie for Killeen's modern focus (including
improvements to those same waterside holes). Perhaps it's fitting that Sir
Guy and the noble laird should share the prize – rightly so, because
without the former's vision and the latter's zeal, Killarney's quality might
never have come into being. Playing in the wrong direction after Mahony's
Point 3, it would be possible to play a semblance of their course: matched
against the conglomerate, we would conclude that they brought some
teeth to the grace of the noble original. All in all, a good balance.

MAHONY'S POINT ★

Campbell & Castlerosse/F Hawtree etc.   1939/1970   €€

	m	p		m	p
1	341	4	10	344	4
2	404	4	11	426	4
3	431	4	12	215	3
4	141	3	13	435	5
5	448	5	14	344	4
6	360	4	15	268	4
7	169	3	16	458	5
8	532	5	17	373	4
9	296	4	18	179	3
	3122	36		3042	36
				6164	72

Big trees, wide fairways, stunning lake and mountain views: everything is on the right scale on this gently rolling mature parkland course, whose often raised greensites dictate the line of play more than is initially apparent off the tee. Classy start; testing, dramatic finish. Some nice short p:4s. Ground drier than Killeen. Deer.

Sir Guy Campbell's closing three holes are a testament to his skill: Mahony's Point's p:3 18 is surely the most photogenic inland hole in Ireland, though it is being tested by a selection from the wealth of new courses. The understatement of the greensite matches the overstatement of the setting – and it is much more difficult than it looks.

LACKABANE

Steel & T Mackenzie   1999   €€

A good modern design that well handles overflow from Killarney's main courses on land overlooked by a factory – but, with two courses of such calibre as Killeen and Mahony's Point adjoining, play them first. If it were somewhere else Lackabane might receive higher acclaim for its qualities, including the waterside sloping green at p:5 11.

Selected holes

	m	p
11	502	5
17	484	5
Total	**6410**	**72**

KIRKISTOWN CASTLE 🏆🏆🏆 ↗

Bailie/Polley/Braid 1902/1929/1935 £ **H:** M 28, L 36

✉ Kirkistown Castle Golf Club, 142 Main Road, Cloughey, Co. Down BT22 1JA, NI

☎ +44 284 277 1233

✎ kirkistown@supanet.com www.kcgc.org

🚗 ✈ Belfast Int: A57/M2 to Belfast, whence A20 east to Newtownards, then A20 south for Portaferry until Kircubbin (11 miles), after which L onto B173 through Rubane; R onto A2 for Cloughey; course on R.

	m	p		m	p
1	474	5	10	398	4
2	368	4	11	116	3
3	278	4	12	397	4
4	139	3	13	402	4
5	363	4	14	177	3
6	393	4	15	323	4
7	294	4	16	150	3
8	135	3	17	402	4
9	351	4	18	479	5
	2795	35		2844	34
				5639	69

Set on linksy ground a little back from the sea, a playable-all-year course that winds up, over and round (sometimes rather eccentrically) two large mounds mid-site. Exposed to the wind, it plays differently every day. Some new bunkering being installed (DIY: so far so good . . .). Gently sloping greens, some more interesting than others.

Purple – 2 (right): *flat from the tee, this hole rises seemingly rather abruptly (and almost ridiculously) to a tiered green with a semi-blind putting surface – but somehow it works, so it can't be red and would otherwise be green.*

Purple – 10 (below): *similar to 2, but longer, doglegged and less attainable – but still not red; nor could it be yellow. The raised ground in the middle of this course, on which both these greens are sited, is the making of it (rather surprisingly, given that whether you start at 1 or 10, you are soon made to confront it – head on!).*

Knock's demanding p:4 3, slanted towards the politics of Stormont Castle, requires centrist golf from tee to green: too capitalist a policy with your drive and you join the wets; too socialist an approach risks the greenside bunker sleazing you into joining the wrong kind of party . . .

KNOCK ♟♟♟

Alison   1920   £

✉   Knock Golf Club, Summerfield, Dundonald, Belfast BT16 2QX, NI

☎   +44 289 048 3251

✐   knockgolfclub@btconnect.com   no website

🚗 ✈ Belfast Int: A57/M2/A2 to Belfast; immediately after City Airport, R onto ring road (A55 for Newcastle, etc – street is Parkway, then Hawthornden Way); L onto A20 for Newtownards; club on L 1/2 mile past Stormont Castle entrance.

Selected holes		
	y	p
3	457	4
17	270	4
18	396	4
Total	6402	70

A compact, shortish, mature, tree-lined parkland course touched by the famous firm of Mackenzie, Colt and Alison (we understand that it was the latter who did the work) in the shadow of Stormont Castle. Some holes run over a small hill to the north of the clubhouse, others are on flatter ground with water occasionally in play. Note long p:4 3 (photo above), short p:4 17 and p:4 18 over stream. Despite its small scale, don't knock Knock: who's there will enjoy it . . .

LAHINCH

✉ Lahinch Golf Club, Lahinch, Co. Clare, RoI

☎ +353 65 708 1003

✎ info@lahinchgolf.com   www.lahinchgolf.com

🚗 ✈ Shannon: N19/N18 to Ennis, whence N85 to Ennistimon, then N67 to Lahinch; at bottom of hill down into town, R onto R478; club immediately on L.

OLD ★★★

Morris (Old)/Gibson/A Mackenzie/M Hawtree   1895/1907/1928/2003

€€€ **H:** M 24, L 32

	y	p		y	p
1	381	4	10	441	4
2	534	5	11	170	3
3	446	4	12	577	5
4	475	5	13	279	4
5	154	3	14	461	4
6	424	4	15	466	4
7	411	4	16	195	3
8	166	3	17	436	4
9	400	4	18	534	5
	3391	36		3559	36
				6950	72

Historic, beautiful, undulating links. Recently ungraded in sympathy with Mackenzie's artistry and perceived 'old-fashioned' eccentricities – blind shots, surprises and all. Superb routing: dune after dune renders gem after gem – sublime rolling links quality is retained over inland holes. Superb bunkering and excellent natural greensites reward wizardry. Wind!!

Lahinch is the home of the famous South of Ireland Championship (as old as the course) and site of one of the better recent revisions to a golf course anywhere. Although there is very little of Old Tom Morris's design left except the 5th, and the most notable part of Gibson's still extant is the 4th, in sketching out his canvas Alister Mackenzie must have been influenced by what his distinguished predecessors had done (though it should be noted that golf here began on the area now covered by the

Downhill p:5 2 takes us slightly left to right back past the clubhouse. Extended close to the old Mackenzie greensite as part of Hawtree's enhancement, it is just reachable in two by longer hitters, but the superb bunkering and excellent greensite makes this a comprehensive test of their skills – with seemingly the whole of Lahinch playing grandstand. Yet all can play it, however many shots to the green.

Longish (into the wind) p:4 6 runs back into and through a milder mid-dune trough approximately parallel to the 4th. As you walk up to your teeshot, another stunning sea view unfolds, but concentrate: it's the deep, bunkered pit in the middle of the fairway (rather than the waves) that should distract you – play over this to a raised sloping green.

'Up and over' p:4 3 is a classic Lahinch hole: as you walk over the brow of the hill that renders your drive blind, you are rewarded with extensive sea views and the challenge of a longish second to a green protected by all the traditional links challenges at their best. Hawtree made the hill less severe, but the greensite more challenging and Mackenzie-like.

Castle course). However, by the end of the 20th century, much of Mackenzie's inspiration had been lost to various ad hoc alterations mainly by golfers connected with the club. While it would be understating Martin Hawtree's skills to say that his recent work comprises a 'restoration' of Mackenzie's design, his philosophy has primarily been to give the course the feel that Mackenzie might have given it, had he lived in

Purple – short p:5 4: *'Klondyke' is the first of Lahinch's two most eccentric, yet classic, holes – drive through a trough between the dunes (below), closed out by another dune, over which hopefully your second will go. But the hole is not unfair: you could play your second to the right, risking bunkers, to obtain a view for a third to a green (right) in full view of the houses beyond.*

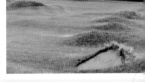

Did you find the 3rd a challenge? Now you will realise it was only training for the 7th. Up and over, with a seawards second shot, it's shorter than the 3rd – but no less difficult. Hawtree moved the green left to an exposed, raised position above the sea – a place to celebrate a par.

the world of titanium (and relatively more aerial) golf. This is not to say that the course has been stretched to over 7000yds – few links courses really need this: the wind rather than length makes the difference here. Rather, that special efforts have been made, through research and by just leaving some holes as they were, to give the course the character and, as much as possible (particularly since the titanium age has imposed more space requirements for safety), routing the holes on the general lines of Mackenzie's design.

Lahinch is often compared with its ★★★ near-ish neighbour, *Ballybunion (Old)*. We say that the latter is the benchmark against which all natural golf courses should be tested. Yet, in the same article we say there is no right answer as to which is better. You must play both, and make up your own mind, even if a tie has to be decided by whose 19th serves the better Guinness. The two are close enough to be played by enthusiasts as 36 holes in one day (but start early and expect to finish late – midsummer, perhaps). Let *Ballybunion (Old)* be the 'front 18': as a newcomer, even if

Hawtree rightly preserved the shortness of p:4 13, whose eponymous mine protects the right front of the tricky tiers of the green. As often reachable in three as it is in one, respect it: 13 wins gold on every count – a supreme strategic challenge, its terrain and hazards will reward and/or penalise you as you deserve, before you putt your way to glory (or humiliation!) – all in a beautiful duneland setting.

underwhelmed by 4 and 5 (which deserve more respect than some give), you will be awestruck by the natural feel and huge dimension of the subsequent dunes, and surprised at how such a fair course could have been routed through them (i.e. fair if you play the course tee-fairway-green – off line, you deserve what you get). Quickly test that 19th and off to Lahinch. The dunes are not as dramatic, but the quality of the course just goes on and on, and it also feels playable by all standards. The easily underestimatable 1st looks relatively uninspiring; give it respect: there seems room to drive almost anywhere (good for an opener), but for a low score position will matter. The more interesting undulations begin halfway along the 2nd, and continue, and continue, and continue . . . If you are familiar with links courses, by the time you reach the 7th green you could be

forgiven for thinking that you must have reached the end – how could there possibly be any more of this before you turn back? But no: round the corner another dune rises with the tricky bunkered p:3 8th green (pure new Hawtree) nestling on its shoulder. Yes, you will turn for home at the 9th tee (even higher). But not before you've noticed that the course later goes out even further – enjoy the preview of Hawtree's new p:3 11th, set in the lower dunes, the estuary beyond, the 12th (down towards the bridge) and 13th (coming back – photo, left), all laid out below. And it goes on . . .

Purple – shortish p:3 5: *'The Dell' is unique – although a very small section of the putting surface is visible at the right, the rest is completely blind from the tee. Unfair? – in the New World of Golf, maybe. The greenkeeper leaves a white stone on the front dune to indicate the pin position, and all the surrounding banks generally gather the ball. Remember: golf is a sport!*

The bottom line: everyone should play both courses and decide for themselves. Our own vote goes to Ballybunion . . . but only just, and then only because there is nothing (in golf design terms) quite like it.

CASTLE

Harris   1963 & 1975   €

As a starter or dessert to the main course across the road, Castle is more fun than it looks, with most interest nearest the castle ruins. Ideal for beginners and those not quite ready to eat at the big table. (The two design dates refer to the construction of the original 9 and their extension to 18, all overseen by William McCavery, the professional. Plans to upgrade the whole course are afoot . . .)

Selected holes

	y	p
6	211	3
8	275	4
10	170	3
12	442	4
Total	5556	70

LEE VALLEY 🏆🏆🏆

O'Connor Jnr   1993   €

✉ Lee Valley Golf and Country Club, Clashanure, Ovens, Co. Cork, RoI

☎ + 353 21 733 1721

✎ leevalleygolfclub@eircom.net   www.leevalleygcc.ie

🚕 ✈ Cork: N27/N22 for Killarney; signs to course on R after Ballincolig.

Selected holes

	y	p	
8	528	5	Hillside parkland course northwest of Cork that may
9	315	4	improve aesthetically with maturity. Some widespread
15	536	5	country views mid-back 9. Some reasonable holes,
17	407	4	others less so.
Total 6725		**72**	

LIMERICK 🏆🏆🏆🏆

Ballingall/A Mackenzie   1919/1927   €

✉ Limerick Golf Club, Ballyclough, Co. Limerick, RoI

☎ +353 61 415 146

✎ lgc@eircom.net   www.limerickgc.com

🚕 ✈ Shannon: N19/N18 to Limerick; R at Coonagh rbt for Cork;
cross Shannon Bridge; R for 3km then left at Cement Factory rbt for Cork;
L at next rbt but one (opposite South Court Hotel); after 100m R by
Raheen church; club on L after 3km.

Selected holes

	m	p	
1	304	4	Limerick Golf Club (aka Ballyclough) is built on a
3	406	4	compact site and features tight, tree-lined fairways and
4	371	4	small, well-bunkered, lightly undulating greensites. A
6	462	5	serpentine stream crosses the fairway twice on p:5 6,
7	392	4	but this is the only water on this old-fashioned, but
8	124	3	attractive, members' course. The scene of a famous
9	483	5	visit by Tiger Woods to play in the JP McManus Pro-
10	396	4	Am in 2000, Walter Hagen and Joe Kirkwood also
Total 5965		**72**	played the course during their World Tour in 1937.

LIMERICK COUNTY 🏆🏆🏆

Smyth/Brannigan   1994/2005   €

✉ Limerick County Golf and Country Club, Ballyneety, Co. Limerick, RoI

☎ +353 61 351 881

✎ teetimes@limerickcounty.com   www.limerickcounty.com

🚕 ✈ Shannon: N19/N18 for Limerick then N7 for Dublin; R at
Parkway rbt; over next rbt; L at Killmallock rbt; club on R after 8km.

Modern parkland course over rolling ground, which has recently been improved, including some re-routing modifications. Several challenging holes with raised greens, defended by bunkers and occasional water.

LISBURN

F Hawtree   1973   £

✉ **Lisburn Golf Club, 68 Eglantine Road, Lisburn, Co. Down BT27 5RQ, NI**

☎ **+44 289 267 7216**

✎ info@lisburngolfclub.com   www.lisburngolfclub.com

🚗 ✈ **Belfast Int: A57/M2 to Belfast; follow signs for M1 to Lisburn taking exit 7; follow A1 for Newry; immediately after rbt R over dual c'way into club. (Direct route via A26 and B101, through Lisburn.)**

Selected holes

	y	p
4	157	3
5	349	4
6	164	3
12	493	5
13	160	3
Total	6647	72

Flatish, compact, sometimes gently rolling parkland layout with good par 3s (including downhill 18 in front of the clubhouse) and some water, but also with some occasional stylistic inconsistencies. Some pretty holes, especially with shrubs in spring bloom.

Red – p:5 12 (a token red to illustrate a point): trees have been planted in a neat ring behind the green, which is, and looks, completely unnatural (particularly when seen from the next hole).

You would be right to focus on the green rather than be distracted by the blossom at Lisburn's p:3 4th – the bunkering here is a challenge in all seasons.

LUTTRELLSTOWN CASTLE   🏆🏆🏆🏆🏆

Bielenberg/Steel & T Mackenzie   1993/2006   €€€

✉   Luttrellstown Castle Golf Club, Clonsilla, Castleknock, Co. Dublin, RoI

☎   +353 1 808 9988

✎   enquiries@luttrellstown.ie   www.luttrellstown.ie

🚗 ✈ Dublin: M1/M50 south; exit Castleknock; at rbt R to Castleknock/ Auburn Avenue; over rbt at top of Auburn Av; R at T-junction lights; after 500m L at Myos Pub direction Chapelizod; R at next lights and follow road; club on L before hotel.

Set in rolling parkland, as we went to press this course was in the process of being completely rebuilt by Tom Mackenzie, Donald Steel's former associate. It was difficult to assess exactly what the results will yield, but the location is pretty.

MALAHIDE   🏆🏆🏆🏆

Hackett   1990   €

✉   Malahide Golf Club, Beechwood, The Grange, Malahide, Co. Dublin, RoI

☎   +353 1 846 1611

✎   manager@malahidegolfclub.ie   www.malahidegolfclub.ie

🚗 ✈ Dublin: M1 for Dublin; L at exit 3 onto N32 for Malahide; after 3km L onto Malahide Rd (R107); after 2/3km R onto Balgriffin Rd (R123); after 1.5km L onto Drumnigh Rd (R124); after 2km R onto Blackwood Lane; club entrance road 500m on R.

Selected holes

	m	p
6	141	3
10	300	4
16	355	4
Total	6066 71 (1–18)	
	2940 36 (19–27)	

Three 9-hole loops of parkland golf (the third 9 remodelled by Craddock in 2002) over mildly rolling ground with maturing trees and occasional water. The generally raised greensites yield several testing holes. Relatively minor modifications (especially if including skilful rebunkering) could lead to higher rating.

Do not be distracted by the beautiful setting of Malahide's short p:4 10th: there is too much trouble around the green . . .

To reach Malone's p:5 3rd in two, you will need to carry the valley that runs across the hole some 70yds before the green.

MALONE ♔♔♔♔ ★

Harris/F Hawtree   1962/1965   ££   H: M 28, L 36

✉ Malone Golf Club, 240 Upper Malone Road, Dunmurry, Belfast BT17 9LB, NI

☎ +44 28 90 612 758

✎ manager@malonegolfclub.co.uk   www.malonegolfclub.co.uk

🚗 ✈ Belfast Int: A57/M2/M1 south; exit 2 L onto A55 ring road for Newcastle, Bangor etc; follow A55 (Stockman's Lane, Balmoral Ave, R onto Malone Rd); stay in outside lane; at Upper Malone rbt, 2nd exit onto Upper Malone Rd B103; club 2 miles on L.

Drumbridge		Ballydrain		Edenderry				
	y	p		y	p		y	p
1	382	4	10	420	4	19	527	5
2	543	5	11	394	4	20	403	4
3	522	5	12	193	3	21	389	4
4	158	3	13	428	4	22	313	4
5	438	4	14	419	4	23	173	3
6	195	3	15	132	3	24	303	4
7	487	4	16	309	4	25	382	4	Totals
8	365	4	17	525	5	26	503	5	D & B	6706
9	365	4	18	431	4	27	167	3	D & E	6615
	3455	36		3251	35		3160	36	B & E	6411

Mature undulating parkland course, defended by a healthy mix of older and newer trees (several specimens) in tranquil and beautiful surroundings close to central Belfast. Something for everyone here: everything is in the right place (plentiful bunkering and water included). Third 9-hole loop is in a slightly newer style, slightly hillier and almost as good.

An old club in relatively new surroundings: formed in 1895, it is only since 1962 that Malone has enjoyed the delights of the sumptious 270

The lake at Malone comes into play most at short p:3 15, which often comes as a critical point in a match

acres of the Ballydrain estate, which includes the magnificent lake (27 acres' worth, in front of the clubhouse) that adjoins the back 9 loop of the main 18-hole course, originally laid out by John Harris. As with some other features here, understatement has been employed in the use of the lake. There are a couple of good carries from the tee, but only at the 15th (introduced by F. Hawtree) are there any noticeable adjustments to the landscape, where tees and green have been edged out into the water (not a place for that recurring hook of yours . . .).

There were several modifications, particularly in the early days. A third 9 was opened in 1964, inside the original 18, which then covered some of the lower ground – approximately comprising what are now 6–9 of the current 9-hole layout. However, these lower holes suffered from drainage problems and in late 1965 the club appointed Fred Hawtree to revise the course, although it took some time and discussion before the work was carried out.

Red – 22: *a right to left dogleg with a severe adverse camber and blind uphill 2nd shot.*

Bar moving the first short hole on the front 9 to address more drainage problems, the main 18-hole course has seen little change since and thus remains a testament to the middle member of the Hawtree golf-design dynasty: this (along with the Red and Blue courses at St-Nom-La-Bretèche, Versailles, laid out a few years earlier and which in many ways Malone resembles) represents some of Fred's finest work, though his most individual design was perhaps the narrow fairways of *Platja de Pals**, near Girona, Catalunya. Frederick G. Hawtree, Fred's father, began the firm with J. H. Taylor (one of the famous British golfing 'triumvirate', together with Braid and Vardon) and became well known for his remodelling of Royal Birkdale in 1932, and also enterprisingly building a 27-hole pay-and-play facility at Addington, London. His son Martin is gaining much respect – recently and most notably in Ireland for his work at *Lahinch (Old)* and *Dooks*.

Malone was the site of Tony Jacklin's first significant professional victory, only three years before he won the Open at Royal Lytham and St Anne's in 1969 and followed it with the US Open title in 1970.

MASSEREENE

F Hawtree   1964   £

✉ Massereene Golf Club, 51 Lough Road, Antrim BT41 4DQ, NI

☎ +44 289 442 8096

✎ info@massereene.com   www.massereene.com

🚗 ✈ Belfast Int: A26 for Antrim; L onto, and follow, A6 (avoiding Antrim centre) for 2 miles; L at leisure centre; club on L after 1/2 mile.

Selected holes

	y	p
2	401	4
4	365	4
5	378	4
7	552	5
11	198	3
15	387	4
17	426	4
Total	**6605**	**72**

Nestled on the shores of Loch Neagh, a mixture of parkland and tree-lined holes, the better ones generally being on some rolling higher ground (notably 4 and 5), the flatter holes across the road (10–12) generally less harmonious. Challenging long p:4 17 (with a few trees left rather haphazardly in fairway) is a new addition.

MILLICENT

Halpin   2001   €

✉ Millicent Golf Club, Millicent Road, Clane, Co. Kildare, RoI

☎ +353 45 893 279

✎ info@millicentgolfclub.com   www.millicentgolfclub.com

🚗 ✈ Dublin: M1/M50 south; exit 9 onto N7 to Naas, whence R on R407 to Clane; from centre of village follow signs to Naas Livestock; club is 3km on L.

Selected hole

	y	p
5	320	4
Total	**7063**	**73**

Rather long but open modern course with best hole p:4 5 skirting the river Liffey with internal lakes and bunkers for hazards. p:3 17 with a 190yd carry over water to a small green, bunkered at the rear, is considered to be one of the toughest holes.

MILLTOWN

✉ Milltown Golf Club, Lower Churchtown Road, Dublin 14, RoI

☎ +353 1 497 6090

✎ info@milltowngolfclub.ie   www.milltowngolfclub.ie

🚗 ✈ Dublin: M1/M50 south; at exit 11 (Tallaght), L on to Tallaght Rd (N81); after approx 1.5km (200m after post office), R onto Springfield Ave (R112); straight over next major junction (after 1km – becomes Dodder Park Rd); after approx 2km (becomes Braemor Rd), L onto Churchtown Rd; club 1km on L (200m before junction with Milltown Rd).

This course, which has a distinguished history, is undergoing major reconstruction by Mackenzie & Ebert Ltd. Phase 1, which comprises remodelling 7 holes, is due for completion in 2006, and Phase 2 in 2008 after the club's centenary. We hope to be able to review this course in a later edition.

MOUNT JULIET

Nicklaus   1991   €€€   **H:** M 28, L 36

✉ Mount Juliet Golf Club, Thomastown, Co. Kilkenny, RoI

☎ +353 56 77 73000

✎ info@mountjuliet.ie   www.mountjuliet.ie

🚗 ✈ Dublin: M1/M50 south; exit 9 N7/M7/M9/N9 past Carlow for Waterford; approx 2km past Thomastown, R at Ava Maria statue; club 2.5km on R.

	y	p		y	p
1	364	4	10	569	5
2	429	4	11	169	3
3	182	3	12	429	4
4	404	4	13	433	4
5	558	5	14	195	3
6	229	3	15	370	4
7	438	4	16	452	4
8	603	5	17	534	5
9	426	4	18	480	4
	3633	36		3631	36
				7264	72

A well conceived, spacious, often undulating, very playable layout in a pleasant mix of tree-lined and parkland settings with occasional distant vistas – one of Nicklaus' best courses in Europe. Characteristically strong bunkering and large, often multi-sloping greens. Good p:3s. Water. Much ado about nothing? Not!

Juliet is as impressive as the land through which she runs. Scene of several professional tournaments, she is enjoyed primarily by a host of visitors from near and afar. Her inviting p:4 prologue clearly sets the scene: trees, space and a well-bunkered raised and sloping green. Her strongest charms follow, including the dangerous seduction of signature p:3 3 over water and p:5 5, foreshortened by a dramatic nest of bunkers which seem to be right in front of the green until you realise (too late, unless you want an excuse for that proverbial cigar break) that they are there to catch a misjudged second shot. A similar deception

Juliet begins to show her teeth at longish p:4 2, seen here from outside the corner of its left-to-right dogleg. Slightly downhill, 2 marks the start of the course's best run, with a couple of beautiful holes down to the bottom, before strongly bunkered p:5 5.

Many a happy winter's tale can unfold here, as the club offers attractive discounts out of season: even with distant mountain snow you will enjoy conquering excellent (close to gold) downhill medium-long p:4 4.

comes at p:5 10, where the fairway splits round some impressive trees (though perhaps someone should burn 'em, as, combined with the bunkers, these woods give the hole a slightly cluttered feel). 6 is another strong p:3 – longer than it looks. Then, only relatively speaking, a weaker run of holes until excellent p:3 11 over water to a sloping green high above the bank beyond – almost mirrored by bunkered longer p:3 14 on the way back. The next two longish p:4s are both all about the second shot, especially at 13 which needs precision over water to the raised sloping green.

Juliet has an excellent matchplay finish: 17 and 18 have been carefully routed round large trees (including, unless/until it is removed, a disarmingly spooky dead one in front of the 18th tee – was it struck by lightning in a tempest?). If you're, say, 1 down after 16, all this *could* give you the shakes . . .

Purple – p:4 16: *Enclosed on three sides by a wall behind the green is a most unusual flat, angular bunker. In there your lament may well indeed be: 'Where, 4, art thou?' Deny thy chinks of fear: a 'sandy' avoideth tragedy!*

Peer through the trees at 17 and 18, though, and you will see at least two chances for your opponent to drown herself.

Play the course, and your labours may not be lost: to sur*mount* Juliet is genuinely feasible, and also pleasurable. She is fair game at all levels: from World Golf Championship tigers from overseas, to gentlemen over on a midsummer night's golf trip from nearby. Dream on: she is very much as you like it.

Accommodation: Athenaeum House Hotel, Dooleys Hotel, The Granville Hotel

The flat bunkers in front of Mount Temple's 18th green exemplify the simplistic style of the course. Note how the green appears to be just a more closely mown extension of the fairway.

MOUNT TEMPLE 🏆🏆

Nolan   1991   €

✉ Mount Temple Golf Club, Mount Temple Village, Moate, Co. Westmeath, RoI

☎ +353 90 648 1841

✎ mttemple@iol.ie   www.mounttemplegolfclub.com

🚗 ✈ Dublin: M1/M50 south; exit N4/M4/N6 for Galway; about 95km from M50 at Moate, R for Mount Temple; club in middle of village.

Selected hole	m	p
16	453	5
Total	5927	72

A hyper-natural (or should we say 'minimalist'?) course, i.e. one where 'natural' has been taken to its extreme. The greens seem just to be mown extensions to the fairways and the bunkers flat little sandpits. Interestingly, somehow it seems to work (well, most of the time). We like the way the owners have the courage to call it a 'championship course' – somehow it is indeed its own champion. Many may disagree, but we

say what we say with primary consideration to the *art* of golf-course design. It is also a challenge to score on. A curiosity on which it is hard to match par (and which would have received our 'particularly enjoyable' accolade, had it been eligible).

MOUNT WOLSELEY

O'Connor Jnr   1996   €€   H: M 28, L 36

✉ Mount Wolseley Hilton Spa and C. C., Tullow, Co. Carlow, RoI

☎ +353 59 915 1674

✎ sales@hilton.com   www.mountwolseley.ie

🚗 ✈ Dublin: M1/M50 south; exit 9 N7/M7/M9/N9 for Carlow; at Castledermot L onto R418 to Tullow, where L, over bridge and R – hotel and course on R at edge of town (signs).

	y	p		y	p
1	411	4	10	553	5
2	447	4	11	207	3
3	447	4	12	519	5
4	345	4	13	427	4
5	520	5	14	339	4
6	210	3	15	466	4
7	542	5	16	226	3
8	440	4	17	457	4
9	203	3	18	413	4
	3565	36		3607	36
				7172	72

One of O'Connor Jnr's better designs, especially given a relatively bland site: a lengthy hotel course over rolling parkland with consistently undulating greens, defended by some testing bunkers and some recent upgrading. A few semi-blind shots, and why the blind bunkers on p:5 7? Strong start and tough finish (e.g. p:3 16 226 yds to long thin raised green). Some water.

The best hole at Mount Wolseley, the strength of longish p:3 11 is the way the green is set against the water: the more forward your tee, the more you play towards the water; the further back, the more you play across it – lose your head here and your sin will indeed have been cardinal.

When Braid first built the raised, bunkered green of gold-rated p:3 2, he was challenged by members who had been unable to stop their balls on the green and thus thought it too difficult. In reply, Braid simply hit three consecutive shots, each stopping crisply on the green. End of debate.

MULLINGAR 🏆🏆🏆 ↗

Braid/D Jones   1937/2005   €   H: M 28, L 36

✉ Mullingar Golf Club, Belevedere, Mullingar, Co. Westmeath, RoI
☎ +353 449 348 366
✒ mullingargolfclub@hotmail.com www.mullingargolfclub.com
🚗 ✈ Dublin: M1/M50 south; exit N4/M4/N4 to Mullingar, whence L onto N52 for Kilbeggan; club on R before Belevedere.

	y	p			y	p
1	343	4		10	474	4
2	209	3		11	409	4
3	390	4		12	165	3
4	530	5		13	398	4
5	192	3		14	498	5
6	332	4		15	170	3
7	454	4		16	493	5
8	369	4		17	406	4
9	345	4		18	504	5
	3164	35			3519	37
					6683	72

James Braid's classic layout has been sympathetically upgraded by David Jones, with the main work comprising rerouting of the second 9 of this gently undulating parkland course, which has been done without significant disturbance to the majestic trees on site. Some challenging holes, good bunkering and several raised greensites (notably at p:3s). Potential for higher rating.

Red – p:5 18: *We understand that there was a mound blocking a clear view of this reachable-in-two green. This has been removed, but now we see a water hazard in front of the green, faced with sleepers. These make it look completely unnatural, out of character with anything else on the course, and ugly – all reminiscent of a similar hazard in front of the 18th green at The European; while we dislike that hazard, it is at least in style with the rest of the course, and thus doesn't attract our red card.*

MUSKERRY ♟♟♟

Hudson & McNamara/A Mackenzie/DIY
1907/1925/over the years, incl 1968 €

✉ Muskerry Golf Club, Carrigrohane, Co. Cork, RoI
☎ +353 21 438 5297
✎ muskgc@eircom.net   no website
🚗 ✈ Cork: N27/N25 for Cork/Killarney; at N25 Sarsfield rbt R onto N71 (Sarsfield Rd) for Killarney (N22); over next rbt on N71 (Wilton Rd); after 1km L onto N22 for Killarney; after 5km R onto R618 for Kanturk/Blarney; after 1km R onto R579; at junction after passing (on R) Angler's Rest pub, R for Blarney (sign); club 2nd turning on R (after hump back bridge).

Selected holes

y	p	
3	391	4
6	200	3
8	171	3
12	171	3
15	167	3
16	430	4
17	445	4
18	389	4
Total	**6388**	**71**

Set on a site part of which is very hilly, this course has been extended to 18 from Mackenzie's original 9, a few details of which are still evident (including bunkers and the old greensite halfway up steep uphill p:4 9 – the greensite has been moved, but not the bunkers!). Distant views, some spectacular p:3s (notably 6 and 15) and downhill holes compensate for the climbs. Strong finish featuring the stream that runs through the bottom of the course. (The club also has 5 extra holes, by Howes, built in 1999.)

Longish p:3 6, seen here from the left near the clubhouse, is played across a valley to a green shelved into the opposing hillside

Short-ish p:5 15 at Naas wins gold for Howes' excellent use of a flat piece of land, by placing bunkers in the line of play at strategic points along the hole.

NAAS ♛♛♛ ↗

Travers/Howes   1947/2003   €   H: M 28, L 36

✉ **Naas Golf Club, Kerdiffstown, Naas, Co. Kildare, RoI**

☎ **+353 45 897 509**

✎ **info@naasgolfclub.com   www.naasgolfclub.com**

🚗 ✈ Dublin: M1/M50 south; exit 9 N7 for Naas, exit at Johnstown; U-turn back for Dublin (N.B. sliproad off N7 being reconfigured); immediately L at lights; uphill to car park and range L, club on R.

	y	p			y	p
1	425	4		10	178	3
2	361	4		11	394	4
3	160	3		12	382	4
4	404	4		13	518	5
5	381	4		14	175	3
6	383	4		15	500	5
7	493	5		16	401	4
8	132	3		17	178	3
9	315	4		18	498	5
	3054	35			3224	36
					6278	71

Parkland course of two halves (part on lower flatter ground, the rest on slopes taking you up from or down to it), and of two styles, with Howes' enhancement (notably bunkering and greensites) of holes nearer the clubhouse so good that ** came to mind. But the other 9 holes are as weak as the Howes ones are strong. Potential for much higher rating, if he can finish the job.

Accommodation: *Naas:* Citywest, Rathsallagh; *Narin & Portnoo:* Lake House

NARIN & PORTNOO

Wallace & McNeill/DIY/Connaughton 1930/1965/2006 € **H:** M 28, L 36

✉ Narin & Portnoo Golf Club, Narin Portnoo, Co. Donegal, RoI

☎ +353 74 954 5107

✎ narinportnoo@eircom.net   www.narinportnoogolfclub.ie

🚗 ✈ Donegal: R259 past Annagary; R onto N56 south through
Dunglo to Maas; R and follow signs to club near sea in Portnoo.

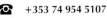

	m	p		m	p
1	289	4	10	356	4
2	479	5	11	180	3
3	176	3	12	389	4
4	417	4	13	176	3
5	367	4	14	476	5
6	198	3	15	463	5
7	255	4	16	110	3
8	130	3	17	380	4
9	294	4	18	349	4
	2605	34		2879	35
				5484	69

Undulating out-and-back links with stunning scenery and a spectacular mid-round climax as close to seaweed as you'll ever tee it. Pleasant to see the flatter, weaker land got out of the way at the start, with the return in higher dunes by the sea, including some new holes nearing completion as we go to press. Potential for higher rating when finished. Wind!

Note: the scorecard will change when the new holes are opened.

Played from one dune to another across an abyss, golden medium short p:3 8 is an excellent natural hole in exposed, scenic surroundings.

159

NENAGH

A Mackenzie/Hackett/Merrigan 1929/1973/2001 € **H:** M 28, L 36

Nenagh Golf Club, Beechwood, Neneagh, Co. Tipperary, RoI

+353 67 314 76

nenaghgolfclub@eircom.net www.nenaghgolfclub.com

Shannon: N19/N18 to Limerick, whence N7 (for Dublin) to Nenagh; from town centre, northeast on Old Birr Rd; club on R after 5km.

	m	p		m	p
1	374	4	10	326	4
2	362	4	11	129	3
3	457	5	12	460	5
4	360	4	13	314	4
5	387	4	14	339	4
6	177	3	15	178	3
7	460	5	16	399	4
8	155	3	17	463	5
9	319	4	18	370	4
	3051	36		2978	36
				6029	72

A parkland mix of older and newer holes with widespread views on a moderately undulating site. The newer holes are well conceived and complement the rest. With maturity the course should become a more homogenous whole. Some excellent greensites (especially at older holes) and a good batch of p:3s (notably 6, 8 and 15). Uncertain if any of Mackenzie design survives.

NORTH WEST

Thompson/Hackett 1889/Unknown €

North West Golf Club, Lisfannon, Buncrana, Co. Donegal, RoI

+353 74 936 1027

secretary@northwestgolfclub.com www.northwestgolfclub.com

Derry: A2 for Derry, thence A2/N13 just over border to Bridge End, whence R and immediately L for Burnfoot; thence R238; club 2km past Fahan on L between road and sea.

Selected holes

	m	p
4	314	4
15	338	4
16	85	3
17	372	4
Total	5759	70

Natural links running to and fro by sea on a relatively flat plain with scenic views, certainly worth a visit from all links devotees. The most highly rated holes tend to be the few that run across the line of the rest, i.e. not parallel with the shoreline. It is not known how much, if any, of the original by Thompson (pro at Portrush) survives. Wind!

Nenagh's medium p:3 15 is played slightly downhill to a well-bunkered green.

The direct view from tee to green at Old Head's golden p:4 2nd: played out to the right and round to the clifftop green, cut off as much as you dare . . .

OLD HEAD OF KINSALE

O'Shea, Hackett, Higgins, Carr, Merrigan & Kirby   1997   €€€€

H: M 22, L 24

✉ Old Head Golf Links, Kinsale, Co. Cork, RoI

☎ +353 21 477 8444

✎ info@oldheadgolf.ie   www.oldheadgolflinks.com

🚗 ✈ Cork: N27 becomes R600 south to Kinsale; on R600 follow signs for Bandon/Garrettstown to estuary bridge, then after 3km L onto R604, past Speckled Door pub (after 5km); straight on 1.5km to club.

	y	p		y	p
1	446	4	10	518	5
2	406	4	11	198	3
3	178	3	12	564	5
4	427	4	13	258	3
5	430	4	14	452	4
6	495	5	15	342	4
7	192	3	16	190	3
8	549	5	17	632	5
9	475	4	18	460	4
	3598	36		3614	36
				7212	72

Challenging clifftop (not links) course on often rather windswept Atlantic peninsula. With a couple of sublime exceptions, the rather muddled design, with mounding and several raised, bunkered greensites, fails to match the spectacular scenery. Savour the demanding p:3s and shorter p:4s. Must play... well, once – if the weather's good you'll probably return. If not...

The green at Old Head's long-ish p:3 16 has been sunk into a bowl immediately above the Atlantic. This hole is all about the wind.

Accommodation: White House

161

Oughterard's p:5 14th, seen near sunset through the trees which line the fairway.

OUGHTERARD

Harris/Merrigan   1973/1983 & 1997   €

✉ Oughterard Golf Club, Gortreevagh, Oughterard, Co. Galway, RoI

☎ +353 91 552 131

✎ oughterardgc@eircom.net   www.oughterardgolf.com

🚗 ✈ Galway: L onto R339 to Galway, thence N59 for Clifden; after some 25km, club on R (1km before Oughterard).

Selected holes

	m	p
1	371	4
4	376	4
6	306	4
7	294	4
8	444	5
13	185	3
16	394	4
17	155	3
18	393	4
Total	5876	70

Set on a mildly sloping site, a challenging tree-lined course, whose holes mainly run parallel to each other (in the absence of which the rating would be higher). Generally good greensites and some watery tests. Two challenging p:4s astride the tough p:3 17th greensite give it a testing finish, while the most intriguing hole is double dogleg tree-lined p:5 8.

PALMERSTOWN (PGA NATIONAL) ★

O'Connor Jnr & Nicklaus   2004   €€€   **H:** M 28, L 36

Caddies on request

✉ PGA National Ireland, Palmerstown House, Johnstown, Co. Kildare, RoI

☎ +353 45 871 404

✎ pganational@palmerstownhouse.com
www.palmerstownhouse.com

🚗 ✈ Dublin: M1/M50 south; exit 9 N7 for Naas; at Johnstown exit (just before Naas), U-turn back for Dublin (N.B. sliproad off N7 being reconfigured); club on L (after turning to Naas).

	y	p			y	p
1	422	4		10	178	3
2	408	4		11	447	4
3	198	3		12	183	3
4	428	4		13	477	4
5	465	4		14	588	5
6	565	5		15	409	4
7	427	4		16	560	5
8	205	3		17	431	4
9	580	5		18	448	4
	3698	36			3721	36
					7419	72

Set in beautiful, gently undulating grounds of a former estate, challenging modern-style 'championship course', much of which feels instantly mature, routed out-and-back. Some attractive use of water and bunkering. Large, undulating, generally well-defended greensites. Peaceful atmosphere.

This testing new course lies in a quiet mix of woods and former farmland across the Palmerstown estate, within an hour's (non-rush-hour) drive of Dublin. Its design is an interesting compilation: the original intention had been for Payne Stewart and Jack Nicklaus to have designed it together, but the former's untimely death came too soon for the course to qualify as his Irish testament. Nicklaus continued the project by himself and had completed the routing before he was joined by Christy O'Connor Jnr, who effectively took over responsibility for most of the rest of the design. The resultant layout is therefore a hybrid: Nicklaus with O'Connor on top.

The different stylistic approach of the two designers is most noticeable in the bunkering. O'Connor uses relatively shallow, generally rounded, open splashes of white sand, while Nicklaus' bunkers are more three-dimensional, less regular in appearance and backed by mounding. (Compare the bunkering at the many O'Connor courses over Ireland with Nicklaus' at *Mount Juliet*.)

Although the overall style here is generally uniform, several different features mark out the strengths and weaknesses of the course. The strengths lie in the variety within the predominantly O'Connor style – a strong but not unwelcoming opening p:4 with a large green, a similar feel to the p:4 2nd, spiced up by a more challenging greensite (defended by

The teeshot over water at the previous hole prepares you for the 2nd shot at p:4 4 over the red brick-fronted pond. The red brick picks up on part of the design of the boathouse just visible left of the rear greenside bunker.

The style of the fairway and greenside bunkers at p:5 6 feels as if it owes something to Nicklaus as well as O'Connor (if in doubt, compare with Mount Juliet's p:5 5th).

water), developed further at deceptive tee-water-green p:3 3 (the green is much deeper than it looks). The scene begins to change into more open ground in front of Palmerstown House at p:4 5, where the fairway moves attractively, leading to a potentially elusive raised green.

So far so good: the variety works admirably and it continues with an excellent p:5. Left-to-right dogleg p:4 7 is home of Christy's 'fun' green, one of Palmerstown's best, raised with banks from the fairway and edged into the rising ground round which the hole has turned (but the use of land on the rest of this hole is weak). The bank in the middle of the hourglass-shaped lakeside green at downhill p:3 8 gives us almost two different greensites, according to the pin position.

Although the back 9 is on generally less interesting land, the exacting level of challenge is maintained, not least at 13 and 14, excellently sculpted round a lake. Two other holes have unusual features: medium p:3 10 with its raised green surrounded almost entirely by sand and framed with pampas grasses; p:3 12 bounded on two sides by a wall as if in a garden (continuing the genre of McEvoy's remarkable walled garden p:3 12 at *Coollattin*). Note also the design of the putting green and the quality of the course furniture.

Note: *Citywest* (page 71) is part of the same group.

Palmerstown's long p:5 14 wins gold primarily for its strategic qualities – under pressure here and a thumping second shot could send you towards victory or disaster.

Played downhill to a green raised above the shore, Parknasilla's longish p:4 11th is one of the most visually appealing holes in Munster.

PARKNASILLA

Unknown/Hackett   Unknown/1995   €

✉ **Parknasilla Golf Club, Sneem, Co. Kerry, RoI**

☎ **+353 64 451 22**

✎ **parknasilla@golfnet.ie www.greatsouthernhotels/parknasilla**

🚗 ✈ **Kerry: L onto N23/N22 to Killarney, whence N71 Ring of Kerry route south to Kenmare; then R onto N70 for Sneem for about 25km; club on L before Great Southern Hotel.**

Selected holes

	m	p
1	303	4
2	120	3
5	286	4
10	346	4
11	386	4
12	324	4
Total	5284	69 (for 1-12 + 1-6)

On the way to Waterville from Killarney, Parknasilla and its hotel make a good base for exploring the Ring of Kerry. A slightly eccentric, if not occasionally old-fashioned, undulating, mostly tree- and shrub-lined 12-hole course, with some stunning sea views, to boot.

PORTMARNOCK ★★★

Pickeman, Ross & Cairnes/F Hawtree/M Hawtree
1894/1971/2003   €€€   **H:** M 28, L 36

✉   Portmarnock Golf Club, Portmarnock, Co. Dublin, RoI

☎   +353 1 846 2968

✈   Reservations via website   www.portmarnockgolfclub.ie

🚗 ✈ Dublin: M1 for Dublin; L at exit 3 onto N32 for
Malahide; after 3km L onto Malahide Rd (R107); after 0.75km R
onto Balgriffin Rd (R123); after 1.5km L onto Drumnigh Rd (R124);
after 0.5km R onto Station Rd; after 0.75km R into Strand Rd
(R106); after 0.5km R at Golf Links pub; club 1km on R.

	Championship							
	Red			**Blue**			**Yellow**	
	y	p		y	p		y	p
1	405	4	10	370	4	19	427	4
2	411	4	11	428	4	20	398	4
3	398	4	12	160	3	21	155	3
4	474	4	13	565	5	22	300	4
5	442	4	14	411	4	23	503	5
6	603	5	15	190	3	24	448	4
7	184	3	16	577	5	25	540	5
8	427	4	17	472	4	26	190	3
9	437	4	18	411	4	27	500	5
	3781	36		3584	36		3461	37
				7365	72			

Note: ★★★ rating
is for 1–18;

19–27 merit ★.

Ireland's superlative grand-scale world-class links: fascinating
movement of land; superb, vast, often raised greensites (who
said short grass isn't a hazard?); classic bunkering; superbly
natural; sea views; understatement, overstatement …
everything. Premium on short game. Wind! Best course in
northern hemisphere ineligible to host the Open
Championship (if only…).

*The closing hole on
the Championship
course requires you
to avoid the
approach bunkers in
finding a raised
green, now further
away from the
clubhouse than it
once was.*

This shot from behind the green at longish golden p:4 8, shows how the greens here must be approached with skill: with short grass as a hazard, misjudged or mishit shots will roll off to bogeyland . . .

Although we ascribe the names of the three pioneering members who led the creation of this remarkable links and show the date they began, the 18 hole course at Portmarnock has, effectively, evolved over the a longer period. Before Messrs Goss and Pickeman famously rowed from Sutton to the island spit opposite, some of the land had already been used for golf by the Jameson family, and John, the local landlord, was the first president of the club. Countless professional tournaments have been held here (ever since Vardon won the first one in 1899), and the course has been upgraded to retain its pedigree. (Vardon won over 5810yds, compared with the present layout of more than 7000.) Suffice it to say that many of the current members will recall the addition of the often no less challenging third 9

The superbly positioned bunkers on the inside of the dogleg at p:4 14 interact with those greenside to yield gold.

(completed in 1971, by F Hawtree), the construction and loss (partly to the sea) of a 4th 9 (late 1970s, primarily DIY), the shortening of the 18th (the green used to be hard by the clubhouse), a new 6th hole (replacing what is now the 2nd on the 9-hole course), and the recent lengthening and modifications (such as of the 1st into its current form) by Martin Hawtree.

Why is it so good? It is not one of those links courses with spectacular shots among high dunes, such as both at *Ballybunion*. Portmarnock, by contrast, oozes understatement. There are no Himalayan features – indeed, the maximum overall height difference cannot be much more than 20ft. What we do have here is something grand-scale, spacious, extremely fair

A view of the excellently bunkered p:5 7th hole on Portmarnock's Yellow Course, which only just misses a gold rating.

and transparent (i.e. you are shown very clearly what is asked of you), which pits you against every links-golf challenge you can imagine, and more. Don't underestimate the psychological effect of the furze (gorse) which bedecks a good proportion of the site, either. The greensites are superb, fast and generally vast (think of three putts being par and see how many putting 'birdies' you get), edged by many often steep, short grass swales and run-offs (the greensite of gilt-edged p:4 8 being just one example). The routing also quietly ensures you get the best of golfing tests. Building to a climax late in the round at the shoreside tee of Cairnes'

The raised, sloping dramatically bunkered p:3 12th green on Portmarnock's Championship Course. We prefer this to the famous p:3 15th. More gold.

famous p:3 15, it quietly shows off every facet of the links, changing direction (sometimes subtly) at every hole – but it won't feel so subtle in the wind. Exuding quality at every corner, this is a sublime links that fits into its landscape completely naturally, yet serves its purpose with stylish efficacy.

All of which prompts a romantic issue. There has long been debate as to whether golf's annual links world championship should continue to be known as 'The Open Championship' or whether the word 'British' should be inserted before 'Open'. (It seems to be common media, if not US, practice to call it by the wrong name, i.e. inserting the word 'British', but can you correctly call something which is capable of being held *outside* Britain 'British' – The Open was played over *Royal Portrush (Dunluce)* in 1951?) Keeping it as plain 'The Open', and building also on the precedent of the 1949 Amateur Championship (held here), why not play it at Portmarnock? The course is good enough.

Moreover, why not at Royal Melbourne or even Paraparaumu? (They're good enough too.) If someone had told you 50 years ago that the European Tour would now be playing in China, you wouldn't have believed it. Of course, 50 years hence, maybe Majors will be history and the Open will have been bribed inland, having been outstaged by the $trillion 'World Links Championship', which by then may have been played several times over Portmarnock …

Caddies
on request

PORTMARNOCK LINKS ★★

Langer   1995   €€€   H: M 28, L 36

✉   Portmarnock Links Hotel and Golf Course,
     Strand Road, Portmarnock, Co. Dublin, RoI

See also: The Dublin Coast – Golf and Craic, pages 22–23.

☎   +353 1 846 1800

✎   Reserve via website   www.portmarnock.com

🚗 ✈ Dublin: M1 for Dublin; L at exit 3 onto N32 for Malahide; after 3km L onto Malahide Rd (R107); after 0.75km R onto Balgriffin Rd (R123); after 1.5km L onto Drumnigh Rd (R124); after 0.5km R onto Station Rd; after 0.75km R into Strand Rd (R106); club/hotel on R after 1km.

	m	p		c	m	p
1	320	4	10		484	5
2	329	4	11		419	4
3	178	3	12		329	4
4	527	5	13		137	3
5	431	4	14		317	4
6	486	5	15		392	4
7	412	4	16		371	4
8	374	4	17		185	3
9	156	3	18		408	4
	3213	36			3042	35
					6255	71

Superbly bunkered modern links that hits the spot, growing from a (relatively) weak start in a crescendo to its sparkling finish in the highest dunes near the sea. It is fortunate that it's not too long, as it plays best from the new raised back tees, whence the golfing challenges of each hole are most visible. Often testing raised greens, swales and run-offs. Wind!

The raised green of challenging right to left dogleg p:4 8 at Portmarnock Links; not a long hole, but you can get into a lot of trouble with it . . .

The menacing sand below the raised green of long-ish p:3 17 well exemplifies
Langer's excellent bunkering, which is the single most memorable feature of
Portmarnock Links.

We first played Portmarnock Links in June 1995: only just open, its
reputation was climbing fast. Along with *The European,* this was one of
the first true links new courses of the modern era of Irish golf design. In
those days impenetrably tall dune-grass rough lined the fast-running
fairways, and balls were all too easily lost.

Ten years on, the course has matured and is rather less frightening, so
one wants to play it all the more. Portmarnock Links provides further
support for our thesis that there is a big difference between a course that
runs naturally and sympathetically through duneland, and one imposed
on top of it by computer and bulldozer. Langer is to be congratulated for
his routing (which sensibly uses the flatter, more inland section first,
allowing the charm of the course to build as the round develops), for
the character of his greens and for the well-defined incision of his bunkering.
It is the combination of all this, harmoniously, intimately and naturally
fitted into the dunes, that is the key to success here. Compare this with
the fairways of *Ballyliffin (Glashedy),* for example, which are driven
almost like motorways through equally, if not rather more, impressive
duneland, and maybe you'll understand what we are getting at.

*The undulating fairway of golden longish p:4 16 turns left to right around the well-
positioned fairway bunkers; more sand defends the green.*

The direct view from tee to green at Portsalon's gold-rated p:4 2, a classic 'Cape' hole (i.e. where one is invited to decide how much of a corner to cut, with more or less risk) – and there's water before the green as well.

PORTSALON ★

Thompson/Ruddy   1891/2003   €   **H:** M 28, L 36

✉   **Portsalon Golf Club, Portsalon, Fanad, Co. Donegal, RoI**
☎   +353 74 594 59
✎   portsalongolfclub@eircom.net   No website
🚗 ✈ Derry: A2/N13 to Letterkenny, R245 to Rathmelton and Milford, whence R246 to Portsalon; club on R.

	m	p			m	p
1	349	4		10	141	3
2	396	4		11	497	5
3	327	4		12	166	3
4	470	5		13	322	4
5	180	3		14	387	4
6	408	4		15	140	3
7	343	4		16	355	4
8	467	5		17	477	5
9	409	4		18	364	4
	3349	37			2849	35
					6198	72

Fun to play on, but rather more than a holiday course, this out-and-back links overlooks, and once plays across, a stunningly beautiful beach. Generally lower front 9 are set more in duneland, while the back 9 (probably the better part of the course) are more inland. Greensites (including two double greens) vary in size and degree of undulation. Beware hidden bunkers. Wind!

In 1891, when the Barton family appointed Mr Thompson, the Portrush professional, to build a course at Portsalon, they could have had little idea how popular it would become. Laid out alongside one of the most beautiful beaches in, they say, the world, but Ireland for sure, the views over Lough Swilly from this course are spectacular.

The double green at which Portsalon's 3rd meets its 9th, seen with the 3rd pin to the right of the shot.

Portsalon has recently been lengthened to modern standards, with effectively 8 new holes (including challenging long p:4 6), at the hand of Pat Ruddy. This has generally been achieved within the superb natural duneland in which the course is fortunate to reside. Many courses around the world have the occasional double green, in homage to the 8 at the Old Course, St Andrews, which are played consecutively out and back, with only single greens at 9 and 18. Rare is it that double greens on other courses are played consecutively, but here there are two double greens in the heart of the course, joining together the 3rd & 9th and 4th & 8th holes, which means that twice in a round you will play consecutively on these large putting surfaces. Other old features remain: a club brochure includes a photo from the 1890s showing play over the famously testing Strand p:4 2nd, requiring a Cape-style teeshot over the beach and another water carry to the green; also retained is the longish p:4 14th (appropriately named Matterhorn) which tumbles down from an exhilarating tee at the top of the course over an uneven fairway to a green far below in the middle of the links. In addition to the blind shot to the 1st green, one tip: watch out for several hidden bunkers in and around the fairways.

Since 1986 the club has been owned by its members, who built a new clubhouse in 1991.

With its green raised above the fairway, Portsalon's long p:4 6 can play even longer, especially in the wind.

PORTSTEWART ♟♟♟

✉ Portstewart Golf Club, 117 Strand Road, Portstewart BT55 7PG, NI
☎ +44 287 083 2549 (Old); +44 287 083 2015 (Strand/Riverside)
✎ reservations via website   www.portstewartgc.co.uk
🚗 ✈ Belfast Int: go to Royal Portrush; follow road past clubhouse and take signs for Portstewart, with Old Links on R entering town; follow road into centre of town; at next mini rbt after passing seafront on R, R into Strand Rd at end of which R; club on L.

OLD

McLaughlin   1894   £

Some simple but truly spectacular holes over uneven natural shoreline links ground near clubhouse (including long p:3 4 over the ocean), plus a rather less entertaining mid-round section on land across road away from the sea. The seaside holes give a good flavour of what golf would have been like 100 years ago. This is the site of the original Portstewart course, 9 holes inspired by Dave McLaughlin, a local solicitor, who sought to attract visitors to come over from Portrush. Although the course was enlarged in 1904, it was too small and the club moved to its main site at the other end of the town in 1908.

Selected holes

	y	p
1	186	3
2	366	4
4	190	3
17	339	4
18	124	3
Total	4822	64

Note: facility rating assumes main Portstewart clubhouse is used by visitors to the Old Course.

RIVERSIDE

Gow/DIY   1908/2004   £

Compared with *Portstewart (Strand)* a relatively mild and tranquil layout, with some well-positioned bunkers and an assortment of testing water challenges on land that gently slopes towards the river Bann. Suitable for players of all levels.

Selected hole

	y	p
9	277	4
Total	5725	68

Short p:4 9 at Portstewart's Riverside Course is a left to right dogleg, turning around the pond. A stream (hidden) runs in front of the green.

STRAND ★

Gow/Harris/Giffin   1908/1960s/1992   £££   **H:** M 28, L 36

Caddies on request

	y	p		y	p
1	427	4	10	407	4
2	366	4	11	390	4
3	218	3	12	167	3
4	538	5	13	498	5
5	461	4	14	493	5
6	143	3	15	168	3
7	516	5	16	418	4
8	427	4	17	436	4
9	361	4	18	461	4
	3457	36		3438	36
				6895	72

Testing links with awesome front 9 magically routed down, up and between some massive dunes, with minimal but effective bunkering and wonderfully natural, entertaining greensites. To say that the back 9 (with two excellent p:3s) are relatively ordinary would be unfair: it just seems that way, as the land is not nearly so dramatic (especially near the end). Wind!

The background to the addition of what are now the front 9 of the Strand Course at Portstewart (which, by themselves, would cruise to ★★★), should be an education to anyone interested in building new golf holes, however many or few.

In a paramount illustration of the maxim 'less is more', it is sobering and reassuring to learn that the remodelling of the entire Strand course, including the spectacular front 9 in the dunes, irrigation, everything, cost less than £100,000 (and this price is less than 15 years old). How? We do not have access to the details, but the story is told that it was done by an (effectively) in-house team, led by a local schoolteacher who was also a golf-course architect, the club's manager, its pro and its

From a tee high above the shore, Portstewart (Strand)'s 2nd drops into a fairway below massive sandhills, and runs up to a sloping green sheltering in the dunes.

Portstewart Strand's 12th is a drop p:3 with a slightly raised bunkered green, set against the Bann estuary.

bank manager. Of course, they did have the most wonderful natural site, which they used to its best. In a sense they had no choice, as they couldn't afford to do anything but make the best of what nature had given them. And that is precisely the point: by definition, the less you do, the more natural your course will be. If you can combine the technical challenge of having to produce something good for golf, with an artistic flair in placing it within the landscape, then the result may be noticeably better than if you bring out a fleet of bulldozers (e.g. compare these 9 holes with some of the newer courses to the west).

The raised green of medium p:3 6 is more difficult to find than it looks, especially in the wind.

In some ways our point is illustrated by Portstewart's second course, the Riverside. While it is both bland and milder and, to be a little blunt, set on relatively boring land, the natural features have been well used (especially the streams and the border with the river Bann). The result: a course that is better than it might have been, and indeed better than it looks from a distance (e.g. when playing the back 9 of the Strand).

We would have liked to give the Strand an honorary ★★, but the weaker back 9 doesn't permit it, mainly because of the last three holes, despite their length and the challenging shot to the green at 17.

Accommodation: Brown Trout, Bushmills Inn

PORTUMNA 🏆🏆

O'Keefe/O'Connor Jnr/Connaughton   1934/1992/1998   €

✉ Portumna Golf Club, Ennis Road, Portumna, Co. Galway, RoI

☎ +353 90 974 1059

✎ portumnagc@eircom.net   www.portumnagolfclub.ie

🚗 ✈ Galway: R onto R339 away from Galway; R onto N18; L onto N6; 3km past Loughrea, R onto N65 to Portumna, whence R onto R353 for Abbey/Gort; club 2km on L.

Selected holes		
	m	p
3	405	4
17	500	5
18	181	3
Total	6341	72

Running through the rolling land of Portumna Forest Park, a very attractive woodland course with plenty of mature trees and water. p:5 17 is probably the best hole, with the green tucked round a pond on the right of the second shot, and p:3 18 plays tough to an elevated green. Watch out for the deer.

POWERSCOURT 🏆🏆🏆🏆🏆

✉ Powerscourt Golf Club, Powerscourt Estate, Enniskerry, Co. Wicklow, RoI

☎ +353 1 204 6033

✎ golfclub@powerscourt.net   www.powerscourt.ie

🚗 ✈ Dublin: M1/M50 south (becomes M11 for Wexford); exit R117 for Enniskerry; club within Powerscourt Estate (signs), just south of Enniskerry on R760.

EAST

McEvoy   1996   €€€

See also: *The Garden of Ireland*, pages 24–25.

Caddies on request

Selected holes		
	m	p
1	401	4
3	154	3
4	332	4
16	145	3
18	390	4
Total	6421	72

A long undulating course set in some wonderfully natural valleys of the Powerscourt Estate (with a moorland feel to the back 9), full of beauty (notably with the trees to start and vistas to finish), but also some tough playing challenges. Use your yardage chart carefully as you often don't see the bottom of the flag on the fairly large undulating greens. Some good p:3s.

Red – 18: You can't see the flag properly, if at all, from anywhere when you need to – all unnecessary on a piece of ground where it could have been avoided.

The meadows of the rough on Powerscourt (East)'s p:4 10th add a rustic feel to this beautiful course.

Accommodation:
Powerscourt: Druids Glen; Porterhouse Inn, Powerscourt

The direct line from tee to green on Powerscourt (West)'s downhill p:5 18th, but the sensible play (in three shots) is around the tree to the right.

WEST ↗

Kidd 2003 €€€ H: M 28, L 36

	m	p		m	p
1	544	5	10	356	4
2	196	3	11	153	3
3	329	4	12	358	4
4	412	4	13	392	4
5	309	4	14	368	4
6	155	3	15	336	4
7	490	5	16	525	5
8	379	4	17	187	3
9	370	4	18	493	5
	3184	36		3168	36
				6352	72

Large-scale, challenging, well-bunkered modern course set on fairly hilly open ground between occasional copses with views of the dramatic Sugar Loaf mountain and, to finish, the Powerscourt mansion. Pleasantly and sympathetically folded into the landscape, the course feels as if it belongs. Large, gently but distinctly undulating, often raised greens. Water.

The classic view of the mansion at Powerscourt looks down over the attractively bunkered fairway and approach to Powerscourt (West)'s p:5 16.

Rathcore's gold-rated p:3 11: this surprisingly mature modern course merges well with the rustic charms of its setting.

RATHCORE ♙♙♙ ★

Flannigan   2004   €   **H:** M 28, L 36

✉ Rathcore Golf and Country Club, Enfield, Co. Meath, RoI

☎ +353 46 954 1855

✐ info@rathcoregolfandcountryclub.com
www.rathcoregolfandcountryclub.com

🚗 ✈ Dublin: M1/M50 south; exit N4/M4/N4 for Galway; some 33km from M50, R to Enfield, where R onto R159; club entrance on R after 5km.

	y	p		y	p
1	543	5	10	515	5
2	390	4	11	165	3
3	311	4	12	442	4
4	188	3	13	557	5
5	425	4	14	367	4
6	317	4	15	406	4
7	311	4	16	197	3
8	443	4	17	337	4
9	138	3	18	481	5
	3066	35		3467	37
				6533	72

More mature than its youth suggests, a well-routed and generally well-bunkered course with a slight heathland feel, although much is over moderately undulating former farmland, with plenty of natural water hazards and the occasional specimen tree. Good greensites with gently but distinctly sloping putting surfaces. Two golden p:3 gems.

It was nice to find a really good new course that didn't have 8,000yds in its sights. Those living close to the Dublin–Galway road (and indeed those prepared to drive about an hour west of the capital) have long been blessed with several choices for quality golf. Here is another one.

In creating the course, a sensitive touch was required, to respect archaeological and environmental issues on-site. Before construction the site comprised grassland, hillocks that turn yellow in the spring with the furze (gorse) in flower, natural springs and ponds. In addition, there are three recorded archaeological sites (two hillforts and a motte). The course

Accommodation: *Rathcore:* Castleknock;
Rathsallagh: Clanard Court, Rathsallagh

has been woven through all of this with a delicate panache, but don't be lulled: extra long it may not be, but it will test your game, especially around the greens. Sensitivity also in the design of the stylish rotunda clubhouse, which has been cleverly sunk below the level of the adjoining 18th fairway, leaving only the roof, upper floor and veranda visible from the course, yet you can approach it on the level from the car park.

RATHSALLAGH ♟♟♟♟♟ ↗

Caddies on request

McEvoy & O'Connor Jnr   1995   €€   **H:** M 28, L 36

✉ Rathsallagh House Golf and Country Club, Dunlavin, Co. Wicklow, RoI

☎ +353 45 40 3316

✎ info@rathsallagh.com   www.rathsallagh.com

🚗 ✈ Dublin: M1/M50 south; exit 9 N7/M7/M9/N9 for Carlow; 1.5km after Ballymount church, L for Dunlavin and Rathsallagh (signs); L after 1km, L after 2km, R fork back after 500m, L into club after 500m. Hotel: straight on instead of R fork back; entrance soon on R.

Note: children under 12 years of age are not permitted in hotel.

	y	p		y	p
1	571	5	10	465	4
2	454	4	11	519	5
3	400	4	12	390	4
4	173	3	13	153	3
5	396	4	14	351	4
6	502	5	15	382	4
7	176	3	16	536	5
8	382	4	17	169	3
9	416	4	18	450	4
	3470	36		3415	36
				6885	72

Beautiful, fairly open parkland course set among some splendid mature trees in tranquil rolling grounds of Rathsallagh House, an excellent country house hotel. Play here for aesthetics (dominant feature in our rating), relaxing setting and some testing p:4s, rather than for the subtleties of golf-course design. Some semi-blind shots and blind hazards. Water.

Red – 6: *at this beautiful downhill p:5, the yuccas on the right conceal ponds and there's a hidden wall and ditch 50yds short of a green fronted by two blind bunkers. The design could have been fairer to the player.* **N.B.** *Photo of p:4 10 on pages 18–19.*

RING OF KERRY 🏆🏆🏆

Hackett   1998   €€

📧 Ring of Kerry Golf and Country Club, Templenoe, Kenmare, Co. Kerry, RoI

☎ +353 64 420 00

✎ reservations@ringofkerrygolf.com   www.ringofkerrygolf.com

🚗 ✈ Kerry: L onto N23/N22 to Killarney, whence N71 Ring of Kerry route south to Kenmare, then R onto N70 for Sneem; club signs in Templenoe after some 10km.

Selected holes

	y	p
3	162	3
10	450	4
17	435	4
Total	6820	72

A feat of golf-course construction on a hillside site, with extensive sea and mountain views. Although the bunkers are generally well positioned, the design is not Hackett's best. Hilly.

Ring of Kerry's p:4 11th cascades from this point down onto the lower fairway visible in this shot, before rising to a green slightly round to the right.

An early spring panoramic view of Roganstown's medium p:3 2nd green (played from the right). The trees give it maturity beyond its years.

ROGANSTOWN 🏆🏆🏆🏆🏆🏆🏆 ↗

See also: *O'Connor's Welcome*, pages 20–21.

O'Connor Jnr   2004   €€   **H:** M 28, L 36

✉ Roganstown Golf and Country Club, Swords, Co. Dublin, RoI

☎ +353 1 843 3118

✎ info@roganstown.com   www.roganstown.com

🚗 ✈ Dublin: R132 north for Swords; past Coachman's Inn on R; L at 1st (Cloghran) rbt onto Naul Rd; after 2km R at next rbt onto R108; follow road for 5km past housing estate; L at T junction; R after 50m for Ballyboughal and Naul (sign); club/hotel 500m on L.

	y	p			y	p
1	434	4		10	532	5
2	195	3		11	419	4
3	441	4		12	206	3
4	544	5		13	446	4
5	519	5		14	409	4
6	196	3		15	417	4
7	445	4		16	446	4
8	388	4		17	199	3
9	172	3		18	592	5
	3334	35			3666	36
					7000	71

Roganstown's attractive tee-pond-green p:3 9th, from the water's edge.

Challenging water, good bunkering and routing (sometimes rather parallel, but also sensitive, e.g. siting the 2nd green beneath a standing semi-circle of trees, producing an instant feel of maturity) bring a touch of style to a long course (many 3-wood/iron second shots here) over gently sloping former farmland. Generally good greensites with gently but noticeably contoured putting surfaces.

Accommodation: Roganstown   **181**

ROSAPENNA 🏆🏆🏆🏆

✉ Rosapenna Hotel and Golf Links, Downings, Co. Donegal, RoI
☎ +353 74 915 5301
✎ rosapenna@eircom.net   www.rosapennagolflinks.com
🚗 ✈ Derry: A2 for Derry, whence A2/N13 to Letterkenny, then R245 to Rathmelton, Milford, Cranford and Carrigart; then R248 for Rosapenna; club on L before hotel.

OLD TOM MORRIS 9 + 9/RUDDY 9 ↗

Morris (Old)/Vardon & Braid/Colt/Hackett/Ruddy
1893/1906/1916/1993/2006 €   **H:** M 28, L 36

Caddies on request

New Morris-Ruddy layout (may be known as 'Old Links')						Old Tom Morris (alternative 9)		
	y	p		y	p		y	p
1	391	4	10	415	4	1	423	4
2	132	3	11	455	4	2	340	4
3	413	4	12	392	4	3	481	5
4	385	4	13	323	4	4	126	3
5	522	5	14	198	3	5	412	4
6	403	4	15	419	4	6	167	3
7	201	3	16	515	5	7	362	4
8	512	5	17	191	3	8	383	4
9	427	4	18	552	5	9	380*	4
	3386	36		3460	36		3074	35
				6846	72			

* provisional length of new hole

Important note: at the time of going to press the 'Old Tom Morris' course was in the process of being adjusted with the addition of 9 holes built by Ruddy to open in 2006. We have made assumptions based on the latest information supplied to us by the club.

Bunkers abound in front of the medium p:3 17th green – this hole comes near the end of the loop of older holes formerly known as Old Tom Morris.

The best hole on the Morris-Ruddy layout is golden p:3 14 – with almost 200 yards worth of carry from the tee above the shore to a raised green, a proper golf shot is required here.

In and out of dunes, a part traditional/part modern links bearing relatively little resemblance to the original Morris layout, but mostly the better for it, enhanced by the new Ruddy holes (better than the alternative 9 downland holes, now playable separately). The fun-to-play old links holes in the valley (10-18) excel, with slightly haphazard bunkering and irregularly shaped greens.

Rosapenna has a rich history as a golf facility, dating back to 1892 when the 4th Earl of Leitrim commissioned Old Tom Morris to build a course there (the earl sadly died of food poisoning before it was completed). Little could either have dreamed that some 110 years later, Rosapenna would host 45 holes, 27 of which lie in an ocean of dunes that then would have been considered impractical for the construction of a golf course. For this reason, Morris routed his course into part of the valley between dunes and sea, and over a hilltop (with a more downland feel), before running back to the site of the original hotel (which was burnt down in 1962), in the proximity of the today's brand new clubhouse. (These hilltop holes now comprise the 9 hole course and it is there that some of Morris' routing survives, particularly on the way out to the hilltop, i.e. the area of 1-4 on the alternative 9 hole course, and some of the flatter greens amongst the valley holes nearest the clubhouse are also probably his.) Later designers extended the routing further down the valley (with the holes being renumbered when today's hotel was built). The land in this valley is the best natural land for golf at Rosapenna (hence the early designers' use of it) and it undoubtedly contains the most entertaining of all 45 holes.

This means that, despite the lower rating, we encourage you to play at least the valley loop (i.e. back 9 of the Morris-Ruddy course). Appreciate the uneven surfaces and see how the designers have fitted their work into the land nature gave them: you cannot avoid having a course of character this way (sloping greens and all).

Sandy Hills' left to right golden dogleg longish p:4 4 requires your best golf for a par. Unlike most of this course, it also offers a beautiful vista of the Morris links below and the sea beyond.

SANDY HILLS ★

Caddies on request

Ruddy 2004 €€ H: M 24, L 36

	y	p			y	p
1	495	4		10	405	4
2	463	4		11	186	3
3	188	3		12	409	4
4	438	4		13	522	5
5	493	4		14	354	4
6	420	4		15	468	4
7	196	3		16	167	3
8	536	5		17	487	5
9	441	4		18	487	4
	3670	35			3485	36
					7155	71

Fun to play but rather challenging modern course set over a vast wasteland of dunes, with occasional sea views coming from best holes. Essential to play off correct tee to match your ability or the long carries will prove too penal. Generally tough, mostly raised greensites with undulating putting surfaces. Some excellent p:3s. Beware hidden bunkers. Wind!

In the age of the bulldozer the modern designer has a greater choice over the type of land that can successfully be used for golf. The duneland over which Ruddy laid out the 18 holes of Sandy Hills was a feast for a modern golf designer, and it has been fashioned into a fabulous arena. We prefer to call this 'dunes' golf rather than 'links' golf, because of the way the course feels more as if it has been laid out on top of the topography, rather than fitted into it. This may be an academic issue, but have no doubt: your game will be challenged at Rosapenna in every way by a cross-section of ancient and modern golf design. Make the most of it!

Sandy Hill's p:4 10th – after a drive from high in the dunes (from the right in this shot), your second will play every yard of its length up to the raised green.

184

ROSCREA ♟♟♟

Unknown/Spring 1911/1992 €

✉ Roscrea Golf Club, Derryvale, Roscrea, Co. Tipperary, RoI

☎ +353 505 211 30

✎ roscreagolfclub@eircom.net no website

🚗 ✈ Dublin: M1/M50 south; exit N7/M7 for Limerick; club on L 2km before Roscrea (some 110km from M50).

Selected holes

	m	p
4	150	3
6	311	4
17	189	3
Total	5862	71

Parkland course over some reasonably interesting land with some undulation. The present course is Spring's extension and remodelling of the original 9 holes, all done for the club's centenary in 1992. Roscrea is a good place to stop over, halfway across Ireland, if you are travelling from Dublin to the west coast courses of Munster. The clubhouse was renovated in early 2006.

ROSSLARE ♟♟♟

✉ Rosslare Golf Club, Rosslare Strand, Co. Wicklow, RoI

☎ +353 533 2203

✎ office@rosslaregolf.com www.rosslaregolf.com

🚗 ✈ Dublin: M1/M50 south (becomes M11; then N11) to Wexford, whence N25 towards Rosslare Harbour; 1km after Killinick, L onto R740 through Rosslare; club on R on road to Burrow.

BURROW

O'Connor Jnr
1992 & 2000

Selected holes

	y	p
8	360	4
9	140	3
Total	3956	46

O'Connor Jnr built 9 holes in 1992, and extended them to 12 in 2000. Set on more inland and generally less interesting ground than the Old links, this is an ideal facility for those preferring a gentler round. But p:4 8 and p:3 9 break the mould, extending north beyond the end of the Old links into dunes full of character and good views across the bay to Wexford.

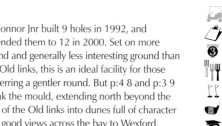

The links at Rosslare are full of history, beginning with the enterprise of its original promoter, JJ Farrell, who effectively bankrupted himself to save the club and in doing so probably self-inflicted his sudden and untimely death. It is a testament to him and George Baillie, the original designer of the course, that 15–18 of today's Old links would still be recognisable to them.

But what has changed, and is not untypical of the problems encountered by many seaside courses, is the appearance of the land that lay seawards of these holes. The Old has been on the move, ever since the first 9 holes were laid out, due to the perennial battle with the sea. (The erosion problems in this area were referred to as long ago 1654 in Dr Simington's 'The Civil Survey, Co. Wexford'.) Although this golf course is particularly vulnerable to

OLD ★★

Baillie/Pickeman/
FG Hawtree & Taylor/DIY
1905/1912/1928/1992
€   **H:** M 28, L 36

	y	p			y	p
1	382	4		10	167	3
2	198	3		11	481	5
3	542	5		12	494	5
4	398	4		13	282	4
5	455	4		14	172	3
6	365	4		15	403	4
7	554	5		16	400	4
8	177	3		17	429	4
9	414	4		18	482	5
	3485	36			3310	36
					6795	72

Outstanding natural golf, primarily over linksland inshore from seaside dunes, which are occasionally used to give height to tees. The ground contains some delightfully eccentric folds, used to their best in creating an historic links of character and a good length. The few bunkers that are needed are well placed. Greensites full of character. Wind!

storms from the northeast and southeast, man has had a hand in it. The construction of Rosslare Harbour in 1873 unsettled the natural equilibrium, and the worst period of erosion on record coincided with the reclamation of the harbour. Today, the dunes are estimated to erode at approximately 0.6m a year. The relevance of this: those closing holes may still be recognisable, but Baillie would be asking where his holes seawards of them were. Lost! As was the clubhouse, which used to stand south of the 17th green – washed away in 1950. Worse was to come in the winter 1989/1990 storms. Something had to be done.

It is not difficult to see how Rosslare (Old)'s long p:4 5 earns gold: the rest of the hole easily matches the quality of the approach to the green.

The approach to the impressive greensite at Rosslare Old's longish p:5 7, seen from right of the fairway.

Rock revetments and other obstacles have been placed along the shoreside of the dunes, and as the club history, appropriately named *Fairways of the Sea* (ISBN 095253763X, Tom Williams, 2004), says, '*it is hoped* [this] will arrest the loss of foreshore and stabilise the erosion'. This problem also undoubtedly influenced the club in its decision to build the Burrow course, which is more inland and gives further assurance for the longer-term future of a golf club on this site.

We write at length on this subject here, but the majority of Irish seaside courses suffer from the same problem, to a greater or lesser extent. Look out for sea walls and/or other defences next time you play one.

We conclude here with another extract from *Fairways of the Sea*, which any fan of links golf should take to heart: 'But the sea created it and the sea endeavours to reclaim it. In this never-ending battle between man and sea, man must continually be alert to ensure that the treasure that is [any links] is protected for future generations.'

THE ROYAL BELFAST ♟♟♟♟ ★

Colt & Murray   **1925**   **££**   **H:** M 24, L 36

✉ Royal Belfast Golf Club, Station Road, Craigavad, Holywood,
Co. Down BT18 0BP, NI

☎ +44 289 042 8165

✎ royalbelfastgc@btconnect.com   www.royalbelfast.com

🚗 ✈ Belfast Int: A57/M2 to Belfast; A2 for Bangor, past
Culloden Hotel and Transport Museum then L into Station Rd,
under bridge; club immediately on R.

	y	p			y	p
1	415	4		10	308	4
2	408	4		11	174	3
3	370	4		12	431	4
4	142	3		13	369	4
5	553	5		14	186	3
6	351	4		15	411	4
7	183	3		16	483	5
8	409	4		17	195	3
9	408	4		18	510	5
	3239	35			3067	35
					6306	70

Classic mature, compact, almost arboretal parkland layout over partially wooded slopes down to Belfast Lough – more mildly bunkered than Colt's original conception, but with more trees. Although frequently inviting from the tee, place your drives carefully for rewards at impressive, often raised greensites that test your approach shots. Sea views.

The name Harry Shapland Colt is synonymous with the advent of golf course design as a profession – in its own right. Most of the more illustrious of his predecessors were professional golfers, who obliged when asked to peg out new courses. In those awful days of 'gentlemen and players', with Colt and his various partners over the years all being Oxbridge men, one wonders if Braid and his pro-shop-based designer peers must have felt some resentment at the prospect of amateur golfers (professionally qualified in other fields – Colt was a lawyer,

Gold from the first: everything is in the right place at this longish p:4, and the slopes of the land have been expertly used to accommodate fairway and sloping green, alike.

The classic bunkering, superbly crafted greensite, setting beneath the trees and lough vista from the top of the course combine to gild Royal Belfast's shortish p:3 4th.

Alister Mackenzie a doctor, Hugh Alison a journalist and John Morrison a WW1 RAF pilot) creating the new profession of 'golf architect'. Between them (admittedly with growing competition across the world) they changed the status of golf-course design – for ever. (We should note, in passing, that much credit goes to CB Macdonald, the father of American golf course design. He too was not a golf pro, and indeed may have been the first designer to have called himself 'golf architect'; however, he was an amateur designer – in the sense only that he never charged a fee for his services.)

Shortish p:4 10 is played up from near the shore to a small green tucked around to the left hidden from the tee by trees.

This change also saw the development of collaboration in course design. Although he first mapped out a plan for Rye, East Sussex by himself as early as 1894, Colt was in partnership (with one or more of his colleagues) for most of his career. Maybe we shouldn't be surprised – as a lawyer he would have been very familiar with the concept of partnership and in a position to create such entities without difficulty. As a result, when the name 'Colt' is associated with a course, it could mean that one of his partners did the work. (Alison, for example, bunkered *County Sligo*, and did most of the firm's work in America.)

What is less well known is that Colt also worked with the Walker Cup player WA Murray, and that The Royal Belfast is one of the greatest examples of their collaboration. This is the oldest golf *club* in Ireland (whereas The Curragh is the oldest *course*): founded in 1881, the first Belfast course was designed by George Baillie, then recently appointed an English master at Royal Academy, but the club moved in 1925 and his course was lost.

A postscript: the oldest continuously active *firm* of golf course designers is Hawtree (FG began his practice in 1912).

Uphill p:3s are one of the most difficult types of hole to design successfully. This one (11th, a visual tease) really works!

Accommodation: Malone Lodge, Shelleven House

THE ROYAL COUNTY DOWN

✉ The Royal County Down Golf Club, 36 Golf Links Road, Newcastle, Co. Down BT33 0AN, NI

☎ +44 28 4372 3314

✎ golf@royalcountydown.org   www.royalcountydown.org

🚗 ✈ Belfast Int: A26 south to M1 J9; M1 for Belfast, exit J7; A49 to Ballynahinch, whence A24/A2 to Newcastle, entering which, L onto one way system, straight on (Railway Street) when one-way system turns R; L into Golf Links Road keeping Slieve Donard Hotel to R; club at end of road.

CHAMPIONSHIP ★★★

Morris (Old)/Dunn/Vardon/Steel & Ebert 1891/1905/1908 & 1919/2004 £££ **H:** M 28, L 36

	y	p			y	p
1	539	5		10	197	3
2	444	4		11	440	4
3	477	4		12	527	5
4	213	3		13	444	4
5	440	4		14	212	3
6	398	4		15	467	4
7	145	3		16	337	4
8	430	4		17	435	4
9	486	4		18	550	5
	3572	35			3609	36
					7181	71

A classic view of a classic hole: long p:4 9 is played over a huge dune down into the valley and up to the green, with the Slieve Donard hotel beyond

One of the world's most challenging links, with its own character (the home of 'wispy-grassed' bunkering) up, over and round dominating heather- and gorse-clad dunes. Closer to the sea, the front 9 is more instantly spectacular but the back 9 just as testing. Classic ingredients abound: deep bunkers, blind shots, undulating fairways. Greensites harsher than they appear. Wind!

Medium p:5 1 can be a gentle opener – in kind conditions on our first visit in 1995 we were an amazing 7 under par between four of us. But when the wind blows . . .

The last decade of the 19th century saw golf sweep across Ireland, as if it were the latest fashion – and that, to a large extent, is what it was. (Lord Annesley is said to have talked to his friend Lord Leitrim, owner of the links at *Rosapenna*, in terms of giving people 'an alternative recreation' at his new course at Newcastle.) The Royal County Down is the second oldest club in Ireland and has long been on the cherished rota of 'must-play' courses of the world. Other than those credited, many have had a hand in minor adjustments to its design (including, early on, CS Butchart, who was pro there from 1899–1904). The latest change has been Steel and Ebert's marked improvement to what many considered to be the weakest area of the course, the closing three holes, carried out in advance of the 2007 Walker Cup matches. Many other major events have been held here, including the Amateur Championships of

The green of long p:4 3 is bathed in sunlight, seen here from a little left of the tee and over the 2nd green.

One of the most photographed holes in Ireland, the classic view of longish p:3 4 is from behind the tee with the gorse in bloom.

Accommodation:
Four Seasons, Slieve Donard, Burrendale

Why gold for a hole with a blind teeshot? Long p:4 11 on Royal County Down's Championship course is one of the best of its type: plenty of room to drive into and excellent design through the green.

1970 (scene of Michael Bonallack's record-breaking third successive victory and fifth such title overall) and 1999 (won by Graeme Storm).

Although some might say the character of the whole place is a little old-fashioned, with the Steel and Ebert changes and a new wing to the clubhouse this is now an outdated sentiment – though not quite as out of date, perhaps, as the 4 guineas Old Tom Morris was paid for his design.

Much has been written about the course itself, which comprises two loops of 9 (both emanating from the clubhouse, framed by the Slieve Donard hotel and the mountains of Mourne beyond), including the general observation that the back 9 comes as a disappointment after the dramatic proportions of the front (frighteningly wild in the wind). We disagree: the second 9 represents no less a quality in golf design – it may be less spectacular, but here, more than just about anywhere, your golf (and emotions) will be tested until the final putt.

ANNESLEY

Butchart/Steel & Ebert   c1900/1995   £

Selected holes

	y	p
4	399	4
8	338	4
12	144	3
15	364	4
Total	**4708**	**66**

No match for its big brother, in the way that Royal Portrush (Valley) is for Dunluce, and playable by all, a links course generally running more inland. An exception is the 10th, a short downhill p:4, which gives the most direct straight-down-the-hole view of the sea at Royal County Down. The 8th is a brilliant medium short p:4, curving round a hill to the right, with a semi-blind tee shot leaving a short iron to a wonderful greensite, set in a hill with gorse all around and a small, sloping putting surface. Medium p:4 15 can require two drivers into the wind! The course has six p:3s, of which the best is the 12th.

The attractive 12th is the best p:3 on the Annesley course.

THE ROYAL DUBLIN ♟♟♟♟ ↗

Campbell/Colt/M Hawtree   1919/1920/2006   €€€

H: M 28, L 36

✉ The Royal Dublin Golf Club, Bull Island, Dublin 3, RoI

☎ +353 1 833 6346

✎ info@theroyaldublingolfclub.com
www.theroyaldublingolfclub.com

🚗 ✈ Dublin: M1 for Dublin; L just after end of M1 onto Collins Ave (R103, becomes Collins Ave East); after 2.5km, L onto Howth Rd (R105); after about 0.5km R into Sybil Hill Rd (becomes Vernon Ave); after about 1km L onto Seafield Rd East; after 0.5km R onto Clontarf (i.e. coast) Rd; immediately L across wooden bridge to club, on L.

	m	p		m	p
1	367	4	10	422	4
2	445	5	11	500	5
3	373	4	12	184	3
4	163	3	13	423	4
5	446	4	14	513	5
6	543	5	15	415	4
7	196	3	16	278	4
8	375	4	17	402	4
9	159	3	18	449	4
	3067	35		3586	37
				6653	72

An out-and-back relatively flat links, with most holes running parallel to the shore, with some notable exceptions, especially right-angle dogleg 18 (quaintly named 'the Garden'). Hawtree's remodelling is just complete – a significant improvement.

The twin towers seen here behind Royal Dublin's medium p:3 4th are a surprisingly endearing feature of the course: they always keep their distance, reminding you that you are at play, not work.

ROYAL PORTRUSH 🏆🏆🏆🏆

✉ Royal Portrush Golf Club, Dunluce Road,
  Portrush, Co. Antrim BT56 8JQ, NI

☎ +44 28 708 223 11   Only required at Dunluce Course

✎ info@royalportrushgolfclub.com www.royalportrushgolfclub.com

🚗 ✈ Belfast Int: A57 to M2 (J5); west on M2 for Londonderry;
exit J1, whence R onto A26 to Ballymoney bypass, then R onto B62
through Ballybogy to coast (9 miles), where L onto A2 to Portrush;
main clubhouse on R before town; Valley course starts 400yds
beyond on R near ladies' clubhouse.

DUNLUCE ★★★

Colt 1933 & 1947   £££
H: M 24, L 36

	y	p			y	p
1	392	4	10		478	5
2	505	5	11		170	3
3	155	3	12		392	4
4	457	4	13		372	4
5	411	4	14		210	3
6	189	3	15		365	4
7	431	4	16		442	4
8	384	4	17		548	5
9	475	5	18		469	4
	3399	36			3446	36
					6845	72

Large-scale links up, over and through duneland, with views to the Skerries rocks as dramatic as some of the folds in the land, which render a very natural feel. Out-and-back routing, with mid-round holes turning on themselves through waves of sandhills. Well-bunkered, moderately sized testing greens. A premium on driving for position (few holes are straight). Wind!

The Dunluce is the only golf course in Ireland to have hosted the Open Championship (1951, won by Max Faulkner) – a great distinction, if tinged by the disappointment that it has never returned. The troubled days of the

The view direct from tee to green at downhill golden p:4 5, a wonderfully natural hole, which feels as if it has been there for centuries. Don't try to cut off too much of the corner.

20th century seem now to be a thing of the past, but significant improvements in the local infrastructure would also be required. Let us hope that one day it does return to Ireland, if not Portrush.

Both courses here meet every golfing challenge on a site that would be most golf-course designers' dream, with a massive playground of dunes on different levels: on the upper Dunluce links with dramatic views to the surf breaking over the Skerries (a rocky offshore reef) and along the Antrim coast towards the nearby Giant's Causeway; in the lower Valley course yielding shelter from the stiff breezes. Although there have been minimal changes to Colt's design,

Calamity Corner is the name of Dunluce's famously demanding p:3 14th, but hopefully not for you . . .

Looking up the fairway of golden longish p:4 7.

A fabulous vista of the Skerries rocks unfolds as you come over the brow and look down at the testingly raised green of golden medium p:4 13.

Gold at Valley's short p:5 10 for the wonderful use of natural features: a double roller coaster, there are so many ways through huge waves of land to the shelter of the green – you choose the degree of risk and reward.

neither course is how Colt had originally intended. The 1st and 18th holes of Colt's original Dunluce were lost as a result of the sale of land across the road beyond what is now the 17th green. In 1946 the club bought a hotel on the site of today's modern clubhouse, changed the start and renumbered the holes. Dunluce's current 18th was the original 2nd and today's 1st the original 3rd hole. Colt returned and inserted two new holes, now played as the 8th and 9th. While the overall result is one of the highest quality, an understanding of these changes does explain why the course ends with two holes on lower, flatter ground that seem

The view from the tee at simply, but most effectively, bunkered medium short p:4 5.

VALLEY ★★

Colt   1933 & 1946   ££

	y	p			y	p
1	349	4		10	496	5
2	385	4		11	140	3
3	141	3		12	465	4
4	534	5		13	486	5
5	336	4		14	421	4
6	237	3		15	165	3
7	453	4		16	391	4
8	409	4		17	384	4
9	320	4		18	192	3
	3164	35			3140	35
					6304	70

Understated and underestimated links set on ground below the Dunluce in the lee of massive dunes (consequently often requiring careful wind judgement). Both loops of 9 cross an open area of seemingly flat links ground, whose greens and subtle eccentricities are as testing as the larger undulations elsewhere. Risk-and-reward character runs right to the card-wrecker 18th.

slightly out of character with the rest. This would have been much less the case with the original layout, but none of this affects our overall rating: the two new 1946 holes are as superb as the rest.

If, as you should, you come to Portrush, it is essential to play both courses. Rare is it for any club to have two of such quality. It would not take much adjustment for the Valley course also to receive our ★★★ rating. This course runs over lower ground, including the large open plain known as the War Hollow, where the folklore is that the Chief of Dunluce fought the King of Norway. This hollow contains no less than 7 holes and is best visible overall from Dunluce's 14th tee, whence it looks flat. Get down there, and in detail it is very much not. It is the clever way that this often wonderfully minimalist course uses the ground here (only about 20 bunkers were needed for the whole layout) that renders much of its ★★ charm, and (on your off-day) occasionally chilling brilliance. The other 11 holes run over more obviously undulating ground, but all are protected from the sea winds by massive dunes – rendering it the locals' choice, particularly on the wilder days of the winter.

Both courses have been the scene of many other events – from Amateur and Ladies Championships to Seniors Opens, via countless more or less domestic tournaments.

The first of the holes across the War Hollow, medium p:5 4 wins gold for its completely natural features, all so well used and often very subtly so.

Closing with a lengthy p:3 cross a chasm at least as effective as any water hazard, Valley goes out with a bang – a big bang, hopefully not a big score!

ST ANNE'S 🏆🏆🏆

DIY/Hackett/Connaughton 1921/unknown/2003 €€

✉ St Anne's Golf Club, Bull Island Nature Reserve, North Bull Island, Dollymount, Dublin 5, RoI

☎ +353 1 833 6471

✎ info@stanneslinksgolf.com www.stanneslinksgolf.com

🚗 ✈ Dublin: M1 for Dublin; L just after end of M1 onto Collins Ave (R103, becomes Collins Ave East); after 2.5km, L onto Howth Rd (R105); after about 1km, R into All Saints Rd; R at end into Watermill Rd; after 400m cross James Larkin Rd onto Causeway Rd; club on L after 0.5km.

Selected holes

	y	p
2	368	4
3	187	3
7	472	4
10	173	3
13	489	5
14	396	4
15	390	4
17	186	3
18	402	4
Total	6626	71

Compact links next to *The Royal Dublin* with holes running parallel to each other between fairly low dunes, which has benefitted from recent upgrading. The best holes are the two running across the general line play: right-to-left dogleg medium p:4 2 and bunkered p:3 3 over water.

ST HELEN'S BAY 🏆🏆🏆

Walton 1993 · €

✉ St Helen's Bay Golf and Country Club, Kilrane, Rosslare Harbour, Co. Wexford, RoI

☎ +353 53 332 34

✎ info@sthelensbay.com www.sthelensbay.com

🚗 ✈ Dublin: M1/M50 south, becomes M11/N11, to Wexford; thence N25 for Rosslare Harbour, 1km before which, in Kilrane, 2nd R (at new school) for St Helen's Bay; follow signs to club, on sea at end of road.

Selected holes

	y	p
3	209	3
16	405	4
17	210	3
18	266	4
Total	6641	72

Clubhouse above beach with widespread sea views serves 27 holes running inland on relatively flat and bland former farmland, with occasional water, but the course springs to life on a spectacular clifftop at 16–18 of the main 18.

The 16th tee only hints at the drama to come at St Helen's Bay's closing two holes: 17 (below) is a downhill p:3 to a green partially hidden by mounding; 18 also runs above the waves.

Late winter tree shadows stripe the green at Seafield's p:4 3rd, seen from behind.

ST MARGARET'S

Ruddy & Craddock   1992   €€

✉ St Margaret's Golf and Country Club,
  St Margaret's, Co. Dublin, RoI

☎ +353 1 864 0400

✎ info@stmargaretsgolf.com   www.stmargaretsgolf.com

🚗 ✈ Dublin: R132 north for Swords; past Coachman's Inn on R; L at 1st
(Cloghran) rbt onto Naul Rd; after 2km straight over rbt, round to right at the
next junction and follow road for 4km to club, just north of St Margaret's village.

Selected holes

	y	p
8	525	5
18	458	4
Total	6917	73

Compact mounded layout sculpted out of what appears to have been
former farmland, conveniently close to (but not in the flightpath of)
Dublin airport. Many speak highly of p:5 8, with water all down the
right waiting to bathe your second shot (if you dare) to the green – on
grounds of difficulty, we agree! p:4 18 is also challenging: your round
could finish in the water rather than the hole... This course is highly
regarded by some notable professionals, having staged the Irish PGA,
Irish Senior Open and Ladies Irish Open championships.

SEAFIELD

McEvoy   2002   €€

✉ Seafield Golf and Country Club, Ballymoney,
  Gorey, Co. Wexford, RoI

☎ +353 55 247 77

✎ info@seafieldgolf.com   www.seafieldgolf.com

Selected holes

	y	p
1	343	4
2	486	5
11	176	3
16	209	3
Total	6533	71

🚗 ✈ Dublin: M1/M50 south (becomes M11/N11) past Arklow for
Gorey; 10km after Arklow, L for Ballymoney; after 5km signs to club on L.

A promising start and a couple of holes near the clifftop are overshadowed
by the poor definition at many other holes on a site with some good sea
views and potential for much more. Excellent clubhouse. If you wish to
evaluate McEvoy's design talents, also go to *Coollattin*, nearby.

Accommodation: *St Helen's Bay:* St Helen's Bay;
Seafield: Marlfield House Hotel

Starting inland, Seapoint finally reaches the shoreline at medium p:3 17, whose green is longer than it looks

SEAPOINT ♔♔♔♔ ↗

Smyth & Brannigan   1993 & 2005   €€   **H:** M 28, L 36

✉ Seapoint Golf Club, Termonfeckin, Drogheda, Co. Louth, RoI
☎ +353 41 982 2333
✎ golflinks@seapoint.ie   www.seapointgolfclub.com
🚗 ✈ Dublin: N1/M1 north for Belfast; exit for Drogheda North after toll bridge, take Monasterboice exit on 2nd rbt following signs to Termonfeckin; then L turn, across humpbacked bridge and R; club on R after 1.5km.

	m	p		m	p
1	354	4	10	490	5
2	141	3	11	368	4
3	347	4	12	419	4
4	402	4	13	412	4
5	385	4	14	401	4
6	484	5	15	154	3
7	404	4	16	342	4
8	505	5	17	171	3
9	186	3	18	508	5
	3208	36		3625	36
				6473	72

Relatively flat modern course that becomes increasingly linksy as the round progresses, culminating in a strong finish within shoreline dunes. Gentle on the player, excellent for newcomers to links golf, its fairly flat greens and approaches encourage bump-and-run shots. Play it from the back in the wind, and it's something else . . .

SHANDON PARK ♔♔♔

Unknown/Swan   1926/2005   £

✉ Shandon Park Golf Club, 73 Shandon Park, Belfast BT5 6NY, NI
☎ +44 289 080 5030
✎ shandonpark@btconnect.com   www.shandonpark.com
🚗 ✈ Belfast Int: A57/M2/A2 to Belfast; immediately after City Airport, R onto ring road (A55 for Newcastle, etc – street is Parkway, then Hawthornden Way and, after A20, Knock Rd); approx 1/2 mile after A20 (Newtownards) junction, L into Shandon Park at lights before hill; club 1/2 mile on R.

Accommodation: *Seapoint:* Ballymascanlon, Boyne Valley; *Shandon Park:* Malone Lodge

Selected holes		
	y	p
3	542	5
6	455	4
8	188	3
10	149	3
13	173	3
15	186	3
17	404	4
18	370	4
Total 6282		70

Parkland course on lower ground with a higher section in middle of each 9-hole loop. Some good holes, especially those recently rebunkered (e.g. p:3 13 and p:4 18, with raised green); others are weaker. The course was being lengthened by approximately 640 yards in 2006. Striking new clubhouse. This is a club of considerable distinction: winners of the European Amateur Championships in 2000 and 2001, and of the Irish Senior Cup (Club Team Championship) on 10 occasions since 1960; also home to many Irish amateur internationals and to Michael Hoey, winner of the 2001 Amateur Championship.

Red – 3: Downhill sweeping right-to-left dogleg p:5, with massive adverse camber and woefully artificial greenside water feature. Maybe the 2006 revisions will make amends.

SHANNON

Selected hole		
	y	p
17	219	3
Total 6763		72

Harris 1966 €€

✉ Shannon Golf Club, Airport Road, Shannon, Co. Clare, RoI

☎ +353 61 471 849

✒ info@shannongolfclub.ie   www.shannongolfclub.ie

🚗 ✈ Shannon: L of airport; take 3rd exit at mini rbt; club at 3rd turning on L.

Landing at Shannon airport from afar, anyone wishing to try golf's antidote to jet lag could almost tee it up outside the arrivals hall, because this course immediately adjoins it. (Mercifully, flights are not so frequent as to make more than the occasional audible disruption to play.) Set on flat ground with adequate bunkering and some water, Shannon is an (occasionally tightly) tree-lined course with some testing holes, most notably long p:3 17th, where the course reaches the water's edge, over which the demanding teeshot must be played.

The camera angle exaggerates the water at Shannon's long medium p:4 16, but it awaits a bad shot in any event . . .

Downhill medium p:3 15 provides only one of several magnificent vistas at Skellig Bay, this one directly over Waterville.

SKELLIG BAY

Kirby   2005   €   H: M 28, L 36

✉   Skellig Bay Golf Club, Waterville, Co. Kerry, RoI
☎   + 353 66 947 4133
✎   info@skelligbay.com   www.skelligbay.com
🚗 ✈ Kerry: N23 into Farranfore (adjoining airport, south), whence R on R561 to Castlemaine; here L onto N70 through Killorglin for Ring of Kerry; through Waterville (some 55km from Killorglin); club on R just after village; temporary clubhouse in Waterville Hotel beyond on L.

	m	p		m	p
1	467	5	10	358	4
2	354	4	11	405	4
3	190	3	12	207	3
4	346	4	13	457	5
5	342	4	14	506	5
6	421	4	15	192	3
7	480	5	16	405	4
8	440	4	17	182	3
9	164	3	18	543	5
	3204	36		3255	36
				6459	72

Added reason for the long journey to Waterville, an open clifftop/moorland course at the southern end of the bay, over moderately sloping ground with occasional water. The impressive and extensive views and resultant high score for aesthetics (dry stone walls included) just render this rating, which may be more fully established with maturity. Wind!

SLIEVE RUSSELL ★

Merrigan   1992   €€   **H:** M 28, L 36

✉ Slieve Russell Golf Club, Ballyconnell, Co. Cavan, RoI

☎ +353 49 952 6458

✎ slieve-golf-club@quinn-hotels.com   www.quinnhotels.com

🚗 ✈ Dublin: M1/M50 south; exit 6 for N3 past Cavan; L onto
N87 at rbt after Belturbet (some 120km from M50) for Ballyconnell;
club/hotel (signs) on L after 8km.

Caddies on request

	y	p			y	p
1	428	4		10	411	4
2	434	4		11	193	3
3	398	4		12	442	4
4	167	3		13	529	5
5	436	4		14	374	4
6	512	5		15	453	4
7	220	3		16	176	3
8	389	4		17	399	4
9	552	5		18	540	5
	3536	36			3517	36
					7053	72

Large-scale, attractive parkland hotel course set over significantly undulating ground with expansive fairways and several well-placed water hazards. First impressions may suggest this is a resort course, but it is more than that, with many testing uphill shots to raised, large, sloping, occasionally challengingly bunkered greens. Extensive mountain and lough scenery.

In the depths of West Cavan, with some wonderful hill, field and lough vistas, lies one of Paddy Merrigan's best designs. The rurality of the site he was given probably also accounts for the generosity of space, yielding a tranquillity that well balances the leisure opportunities of a hotel away from it all in the middle of Ireland.

The view from tee to green at Slieve Russell's long downhill p:3 7. The vista to the distant mountains over the lake is even more spectacular: go and see it for yourself . . .

The peaceful rustic feel extends all over the course at Slieve Russell, including here at longish p:4 5

But if you are playing serious, rather than holiday, golf, you will need to put your brain into gear: while you can't avoid the pleasure of the countryside, it is all too easy here to incur displeasure at your play. The bunkering around the green at the downhill p:4 opener hints at what is to come. On the 2nd tee you begin to realise that this course is rather more than ordinary: with bunkers well placed inside the corner of the right-to-left dogleg and water not far left of them, this is an excellent heroic hole, where you will be rewarded for making the 232yd carry over the furthest sand, setting up a significantly shorter second over water to a raised two-tiered green. If you take this route and fail, you will be in trouble for a bogey . . . . And so it goes on, made all the more pleasurable by the well-conceived routing that eases you up the hill to the 6th tee, the highest point of the front 9, with a significantly milder climb than via the direct route. Thence, as you make your way from 6th tee to the 7th green, far below, unfold perhaps the best views from the course. The back 9, partly set around a large lake, doesn't disappoint, either.

Slieve Russell's tough p:3 11 – the 8th (see page 203), just visible through the trees beyond the 11th green, is only the warm up: here, you find a similarly bunkered green – add water!

SOUTH COUNTY 🏆🏆🏆

Bielenberg   2001   €€

✉ South County Golf Club, Lisheen Road, Brittas, Co. Dublin, RoI

☎ +353 1 458 2965

✎ info@southcountygolf.ie   www.southcountygolf.com

🚗 ✈ Dublin: M1/M50 south; exit 9 onto N7 for Naas; after 5km L onto N82; after 2km R onto N81 for Brittas; club on L about 12km beyond Brittas.

Selected holes		
	y	p
13	555	5
14	435	4
17	434	4
Total	7000	72

With an 'away from it all' feel in rural surrounds towards the Wicklow Hills, despite being not that far from Dublin, and good value for money, South County is an open upland course partly set on a small hill, partly on the plain below with several good golfing challenges, especially over the testing closing holes, where water, sloping greens and bunkers can easily wreck your card.

SPANISH POINT 🏆🏆

DIY/?A Mackenzie/DIY 1890s/?1928/intermittently €

✉ Spanish Point Golf Club, Spanish Point, Co. Clare, RoI

☎ +353 65 708 4198

✎ info@spanish-point.com   www.spanishpointgolf.com

Selected holes		
	m	p
7	287	4
8	82	3
9	150	3
Total	2308	32

🚗 ✈ Shannon: N19/N18 to Ennis; whence R474 to Milltown, where L on N67 and R into Spanish Point after 2km; club on R.

A 9-hole reminder of what links courses must have felt like 100+ years ago, set over rough dunes and more open sloping ground inland. The recent extension to the 1st hole is not completely consistent with the character of what went before. The club's records suggest that a sum of 50 guineas was paid to a designer in the 1920s and, given Mackenzie's involvement at nearby Lahinch and the sum of money involved, it is plausible (but by no means certain) that he redesigned an old links, which is presumed to have been created by its founding members and has since been revamped in house every so often (to the extent that probably only a couple of holes date back to the 1920s). A curiosity worth a brief visit by links fans.

STRANDHILL 🏆🏆🏆

Malone   1973   €€

✉ Strandhill Golf Club, Strandhill, Co. Sligo, RoI

☎ +353 71 916 8188

✎ strandhillgc@eircom.net   www.strandhillgc.com

🚗 ✈ Knock: N17/N4 north, 6km before Sligo L onto N59 and R at Belladrihid onto R292 to Strandhill (10km); club on L in town.

Strandhill

Occasionally eccentric natural links in two sections, one closer to, the other further from, the town – with extensive views over land and sea. Inconsistent in quality, but there are many good holes, notably wonderfully hummocked uphill p:5 5, close to gold. Worth playing if you have spare time on a trip to nearby *County Sligo*.

Purple – 13: The smallest green we've ever seen (on a full size course)!

Selected holes

	m	p
2	154	3
5	480	5
6	372	4
7	344	4
9	131	3
12	345	4
13	338	4
16	394	4
17	182	3
Total	5630	69

SUTTON

Army officers/Harris/Merrigan   1890/1971/1993   €€

✉ Sutton Golf Club, Cush Point, Sutton, Dublin 13, RoI
☎ +353 1 832 2965
✎ info@suttongolfclub.org   www.suttongolfclub.org

Selected hole

	y	p
9	383	4
Total	2889	35

🚗 ✈ Dublin: M1 for Dublin; L at exit 3 onto N32 for Malahide; straight across all jncts/rbts until (after about 6km) T-junction with coast road at Baldoyle; here R and immediately fork L onto Strand Rd (R106); 1st L after level crossing; cross railway again; then immediately L and R into club.

Nine-hole course on edge of bay with mainly linksland and rather compact holes near the clubhouse followed by an inland venture. Routing forces consecutive p:3s – we approve. Classic shoreliner links hole to finish. Sutton is most famous as the golfing home of Ireland's legendary player, JB Carr (11 Walker Cups, 3 Amateur Championships and no space here for the rest!). Carr was also responsible for Ireland's first driving range: on the site of p:3 6, which he floodlit to meet his insatiable hunger for practice.

We normally look for natural features in a golf course, and, in nature, trees generally don't grow in straight lines. The amazing use of lines at Templepatrick's p:4 10th exception more than proves the rule.

TEMPLEPATRICK

Caddies on request

D Jones & Feherty   1999   ££   **H:** M 28, L 36

✉ Hilton Templepatrick Golf Club, Castle Upton Estate, Templepatrick, Ballyclare, Co. Antrim BT39 0DD, NI

☎ +44 289 443 5542

✒ reservations.templepatrick@hilton.com

www.hilton.co.uk/templepatrick

🚗 ✈ Belfast Int: A57 for Templepatrick (signs to M2); beyond Templepatrick but before M2, L at rbt to Parkgate; club 200myds on L.

	y	p		y	p
1	395	4	10	426	4
2	435	4	11	183	3
3	564	5	12	461	4
4	170	3	13	428	4
5	568	5	14	374	4
6	450	4	15	182	3
7	200	3	16	526	5
8	434	4	17	445	4
9	392	4	18	444	4
	3608	36		3469	35
				7077	71

Competently designed, fairly flat hotel course in riverside setting, used to great effect early in the back 9, which reward patience with the front 9. The length of the p:4s can make it a challenging round, even before you are tested on the often large sloping greens. The straight rows of poplars near the clubhouse render a memorably architectural dimension. Water.

TRALEE 🏆🏆🏆🏆 ★

Palmer & Seay/Steel & T Mackenzie 1985/2005 €€€ H: M 24, L 36

✉ Tralee Golf Club, West Barrow, Ardfert, Co. Kerry, RoI

☎ +353 66 713 6379

✎ info@traleegolfclub.com   www.traleegolfclub.com

🚗 ✈ Kerry: N23/N22/N21 for Tralee, thence R551 to Ardfert, whence L and follow signs to Barrow; R fork uphill to club.

	y	p			y	p
1	404	4		10	474	4
2	596	5		11	595	5
3	194	3		12	461	4
4	426	4		13	159	3
5	430	4		14	403	4
6	427	4		15	300	4
7	157	3		16	199	3
8	399	4		17	361	4
9	504	5		18	486	4
	3537	36			3438	36
					6975	72

Must-play-at-least-once course in one of the most stunning golf settings on earth, with aesthetically clever routing. More-clifftop-than-links American feel emphasised by 'smoothed out' fairways and fairly regular bunkering. Some interesting greensites. If out is sublime, back can play tough. You can't but enjoy golf at a place like this, whatever your score. Wind!

Some will feel that this course deserves a higher rating: we would agree if our evaluation were purely on aesthetics. Tralee must be played by any golfer who is already in Ireland, as our ★ rating implies, but its aesthetics warrant a longer journey – as do those at, say, Pebble Beach, California. Indeed the 3rd at Tralee is often compared with Pebble's 7th: fair enough for aesthetics, but the latter is a better design. However, our rating system requires more than just aesthetics to earn one ★, let alone more: there's not quite enough salt and pepper at Tralee, and it is all rather too smoothed out to fit the definition of a proper links course.

At the current rate of progress (or the opposite), by 2020 golf equipment will enable us to stand on the tee of Tralee's long p:5 2nd and aim across the bay at the green. For now, you will have to go round . . .

If you go into them, the dramatic and deep bunkers at Tralee will darken your scorecard more than they darken this view from above left of the fairway of longish p:4 14.

Arnold Palmer and Ed Seay were clearly aware from the start of the site's problems, which are not unusual for courses in spectacular settings: the topography is such that it is not possible for every hole to be spectacular. Here, the available land included a mix of stunning dunes by the shore and relatively uninteresting ground towards the clubhouse. The gap had somehow to be bridged. The designers' solution on the front 9 was to give the player an initial taste of the aesthetics (*amuse-gueule* down 1, clifftop *hors d'oeuvres* on 2–3) and then to get much the weaker land out of the way (4–6), before two of the best holes for golf as well as views (7–8) are balanced by the weaker return to the clubhouse (9).

If you think you've seen it all, there's plenty for the main and dessert courses, because the back 9 routing provides the *entrée* in one of the most dramatic duneland vistas you'll ever see: indeed, its unfolding is your reward after perhaps the dullest moment on the course – the climb to the 11th green. Maybe this is what was intended?! The design teases you further by immediately turning away from the view for 12 and 13 in and among the inner sandhills, before sternly bunkered 14 brings you back to the vista. Do you like *crème* with your *dessert*? There's plenty of that: rich aesthetic

Gold-rated medium p:4 8 runs around the bay (from the left of this view) to an excellent waterside greensite in a stunning setting.

moment succeeds rich from the 15th to the 18th tees – dunes, beach, rocks, surf, all now sugared with recent enhancements to the course by Donald Steel and Tom Mackenzie of Steel and Co (rebuilding 15 greens, 10 fairways and the bunkers, and enhancing 16–18). Then enjoy looking back at it all over *café* at the 19th. (No, we didn't mention *Ryan's Daughter* on the beach below: a DVD with the *petit fours*, perhaps…?)

Medium p:4 4 turns sharply from left to right around the trees just visible on the right. The land over the stream (4th green and 5th tee) is the additional parcel Tippett insisted the club should buy.

TRAMORE ♟♟♟ ★

Tippett/Harris   1939/1968   €€   H: M 28, L 36

✉ Tramore Golf Club, Newtown Hill, Tramore, Co. Waterford, RoI

☎ +353 51 386 170

✎ tragolf@iol.ie   www.tramoregolfclub.com

🚗 ✈ Dublin: M1/M50 south exit 9, N7/M7 for Naas; M9/N9 past Carlow to Waterford, where cross bridge and L; follow N25 along quayside and R; follow signs for R675 through Tramore, just beyond which (following R675 for Fennor) club entrance is on rbt.

	m	p		m	p
1	365	4	10	174	3
2	455	5	11	366	4
3	155	3	12	315	4
4	344	4	13	366	4
5	294	4	14	406	4
6	159	3	15	122	3
7	367	4	16	500	5
8	371	4	17	346	4
9	506	5	18	449	5
	3016	36		3044	36
				6060	72

Well-balanced layout set on gently rolling round and partially on former marshland, transformed by prudent tree planting, and occasional cross-fairway ditches (attractively indicated by gorse). The simple but efficient design provides one of the closest resemblances to 'Surrey'-style heathland golf in Ireland. Excellent greensites, often subtly raised above fairways.

Tramore Golf Club was founded as long ago as 1894, making it one of the oldest clubs in Ireland, in those days with a wild 9-hole Willie Park Jnr links course at the Back Strand alongside the old racecourse. Too wild – in

210 Accommodation: Dooley's Hotel, Granville Hotel, White House

The bunkering and greensite are the key to Tramore's golden medium short p:4 5th.

December 1911, after several previous disasters in which two clubhouses had been swept away, the embankments were breached in a severe storm, leaving golf and race courses under water. How many seaside layouts have been exposed to such risks (and, in some cases remain so, such as *Rosslare*)?

After an interim move alongside the new racecourse, it was only in the mid-1930s that the club purchased the land that has become its home. Even then, in the judgement of Captain HC Tippett (of Wimbledon Golf Club), employed to design the new course over land the locals regarded as 'only fit for snipe shooting', the club was one field short. Although the extra acre cost as much as the rest of the land put together, Tippett held his ground. A good thing, as its use has yielded two gold holes.

Commander John Harris, more known for his courses abroad than in his native isles, was called in to review the design some 30 years later, but his report effectively said that there was little in Tippett's work that could be improved on. The only change was the insertion of fairway bunkers at 7 and 8. We would not normally name a designer at the top of an entry for such minor amendments, but Harris deserves credit as much for what he didn't do as for what he did do: so often with course design, less is more.

The ditches crossing golden p:4 13 are marked out for the player by the bushes, which exaggerate their appearance. An excellent greensite ensues.

TULFARRIS ♛♛♛ ↗

Merrigan   1987   €€   **H:** M 28, L 36

✉ Tulfarris Hotel and Country Club, Blessington Lakes,
Blessington, Co. Wicklow, RoI

☎ +353 45 867 600

✎ golf@tulfarris.com   www.tulfarris.com

🚗 ✈ Dublin: M1/M50 south; exit 9 N7 for Naas; after 5km L
onto N82; after 2km R onto N81 past Blessington, 7km after which
L for Valleymount; L again after 500m; L after 1km; club on L.

	y	p		y	p
1	540	5	10	447	4
2	183	3	11	174	3
3	456	4	12	405	4
4	456	4	13	511	5
5	375	4	14	409	4
6	184	3	15	520	5
7	413	4	16	200	3
8	434	4	17	369	4
9	608	5	18	481	4
	3649	36		3516	36
				7165	72

Competently designed rolling
parkland/tree-lined hotel course,
with stunning lakeside views in
Wicklow Hills setting, imbued
with tranquillity. Stronger on the
back 9, the course includes
some excellent mounded
greensites and several water
hazards. Some spectacular trees.
Aesthetics just clinch the rating
here – greater stylistic subtlety
to the hazards and it could be
earned more easily.

*A stunningly clear March sunset was
in the making when we visited
Tulfarris, seen here at longish p:4 10,
which runs down towards the water.*

The well-bunkered slightly raised green at Tullamore's left to right sweeping p:5 7th.

TULLAMORE ★

Hewson/Braid/Merrigan   1926/1938/1995   €   **H:** M 28, L 36

✉ Tullamore Golf Club, Brookfield, Tullamore, Co. Offaly, RoI

☎ +353 57 932 1439

✐ tullamoregolfclub@eircom.net   www.tullamoregolfclub.ie

🚗 ✈ Dublin: M1/M50 south; exit N4/M4/N6 for Galway; at
Kilbeggan L onto N52 for Tullamore, whence N52 for Birr; forking L
onto R421 for Kinnitty after 1km; club soon on R.

Caddies
on request

	y	p			y	p
1	359	4		10	382	4
2	177	3		11	325	4
3	429	4		12	197	3
4	492	5		13	387	4
5	439	4		14	474	4
6	189	3		15	548	5
7	489	5		16	419	4
8	338	4		17	184	3
9	148	3		18	452	4
	3060	35			3368	35
					6428	70

A parkland midlands gem, over
gently sloping ground, whose
remodelling by Merrigan is
reaching maturity, though
Braid's mark is still apparent.
Thus some holes exude history
(e.g. p:3 2), while others feel
more modern (e.g. the watery
touch to the newer holes at 5–8,
perhaps with one too many left-
to-right doglegs). Good
greensites. Strong finish.

Golf was played by a Colonel
Craig and his friends at Tullamore
as long ago as 1886, only five years after the formation of Ireland's first golf
club (*The Royal Belfast*), but it took five moves (and a certain amount of grief)
before what became Tullamore Golf Club settled on part of the Charleville
Estate, employing Captain Hewson to lay out a course. The grief arose during
the civil war, when the club was targeted and its clubhouse destroyed by fire.

Little of Hewson's course remains: it was comprehensively redesigned by James Braid in the late 1930s, to bring it in line with the requirements of contemporary championship play, while also respecting the splendid tree specimens found on the site. Braid was so

successful that it was still up to the challenge some 30 years later, when the club hosted the Native Irish Championship (1967) and the Dunlop Tournament (1970). Both were won by the same man: Hugh Boyle, one of Ireland's respected list of Ryder Cup players.

However, by the 1990s the course did need further upgrading to retain the challenge. The club had an excellent excuse in that it was looking for a good way to celebrate the centenary in 1996 of its affiliation to the GUI. Patrick Merrigan, the designer appointed, has respected Braid's original: several holes remain basically unchanged, although the order of play has been changed – the area near the clubhouse now contains the closing rather than opening holes. Braid would still recognise his 5th hole, an excellent left-to-right sweeping longish p:4 around the splendid clump of trees in front of the clubhouse, but it is now played as the 18th.

The longish p:4 16th, with water running across the front of the green, is apparently one of the members' favourites at Tullamore.

Our reservations over Merrigan's routing, which includes (in 5, 7 and 8) three left-to-right doglegs all with water within the angle, may be misplaced. As it is, these are all holes of different lengths, including the tempting short p:4 8. Often golf-course designers are confronted with the question of whether to accept a weakness in routing (and therefore design) just to serve up one spectacular hole, or whether it is more satisfactory to present a series of consistently better holes at the sacrifice of the one spectacular one. Merrigan may have rightly concluded that this routing was the best solution for the site. Whatever the case, the overall result is a course one wants to play again, so our reservations may be no more than academic.

A side on view of Tullamore's long p:4 18th (and 19th) from the woods lying to the left of the 1st fairway.

We hope your golf here is as pretty as the shrubs at Warrenpoint's downhill medium p:3 6th.

WARRENPOINT

Unknown/Hewson/Ruddy & Craddock
1904/1925/1997   £

✉ Warrenpoint Golf Club, Lower Dromore Road,
Warrenpoint, Co. Down, BT34 3LN, NI

☎ +44 284 175 2371

✎ office@warrenpointgolf.com   www.warrenpointgolf.com

🚗 ✈ Belfast Int: A57/M2/M1 south from Belfast; exit J7 onto A1 for
Newry, whence A2 for Warrenpoint; club on outskirts on L.

Selected holes

	y	p
9	315	4
13	364	4
17	426	4
Total	6173	71

This course shows how golf can be played over a very cramped site (only 90 acres) – well, just. The length balls can now be hit is likely to be testing the boundaries of this intriguing parkland layout over moderately undulating ground. There are also several crossovers, which add to the pressure on busy days. Short p:4 9 requires careful thought at the tee: a burn crosses the fairway 200yds from the back and tests the mind further around the sloping green. The raised green at p:4 13 requires an accurate second from the fairway above. Some pretty shrubs, especially when in bloom in the spring.

Accommodation: *Warrenpoint:* Burrendale Hotel, Slieve Donard Hotel

Your second shot at Waterford Castle's longish downhill p:4 12 needs to avoid the bunkers down the right hand side.

WATERFORD CASTLE

Caddies on request

Smyth & Brannigan   1992   €€   H: M 28, L 36

✉ Waterford Castle Hotel and Golf Club, The Island, Ballinakill, Co. Waterford, RoI

☎ +353 51 871 633

✎ golf@waterfordcastle.com   www.waterfordcastle.com

🚗 ✈ Dublin: M1/M50 south; exit 9 N7/M7 for Naas; M9/N9 past Carlow to Waterford; where cross bridge and L; follow N25 along quayside and R; then L onto R683 for Clohernagh/Dunmore; L for ferry to Waterford Castle (sign); L after ferry crossing; club R of hotel.

	m	p		m	p
1	385	4	10	160	3
2	176	3	11	346	4
3	372	4	12	415	4
4	356	4	13	463	5
5	476	5	14	343	4
6	337	4	15	468	5
7	193	3	16	187	3
8	452	5	17	368	4
9	381	4	18	353	4
	3128	36		3103	36
				6231	72

On an island only reachable by a free chain ferry, adjoining Waterford Castle (hotel), a spacious parkland course with extensive views over Waterford harbour. The well-routed design is as solid as the castle, with only small blemishes (notably 18), and many good holes, including two challenging watery p:3s (2 and 16). Generally good bunkering and greensites. Excellent 19th.

Accommodation: *Waterford Castle:* Athenaeum House. Dooley's Hotel, Granville Hotel; *Waterville:* Butler Arms Hotel

WATERVILLE ★

Caddies
on request

Hackett, Harmon & Mulcahy/T Fazio   1973/2004   €€€
H: M 28, L 36

✉ Waterville Golf Club, Waterville, Co. Kerry, RoI
☎ +353 66 947 4102
✎ wvgolf@iol.ie   www.watervillegolflinks.ie
🚗 ✈ Kerry: N23 into Farranfore (adjoining airport, south),
whence R on R561 to Castlemaine; here L onto N70 through
Killorglin for Ring of Kerry; approaching Waterville (some 55km
from Killorglin), follow signs R to club.

	y	p		y	p
1	430	4	10	475	4
2	464	4	11	506	5
3	417	4	12	200	3
4	179	3	13	488	5
5	595	5	14	456	4
6	194	3	15	428	4
7	424	4	16	386	4
8	463	4	17	194	3
9	445	4	18	594	5
	3584	35		3727	37
				7311	72

As scenic as the long journey
there, a modern links laid over
a duneswept promontory,
whose initial relatively mild
undulations make way for more
dramatic movement nearer the
sea. Strewn with grass-whisped
bunkering, with some
entertaining greens, the course
is a very popular destination.
Check distances to greens
carefully. Some water. Wind!

The history of golf at Ireland's
remotest golfing mecca goes back to 1880, even before the heyday of
the transatlantic wireless station whose employees' leisure allowed golf
to flourish here in the early 20th century. Advances in technology
eventually killed off the station, but the golf was revived by the
construction of one the first of Ireland's 'modern' links, the vision of
Irish American John Mulcahy, implemented by Eddie Hackett and

The snaking 11th fairway unfolds as you walk up the gentle incline from the tee.
Without even a view of the sea, this hole is as beautiful as it is perilous, should you
stray off the fairway. Three good shots do make an eagle, but more often it is
played in two over par.

A view of long p:4 2 with its impressive fairway bunkering: best to keep left, but you must also respect the subtle undulations of the land and be prepared for the depth of the raised green – almost 40yds.

Claude Harmon (1948 US Masters Champion) and more than face-lifted since 2002 by Tom Fazio (including major changes to 1, 2, 6, 7, 12, 16 and 17) with subsequent modifications (including, sadly, weakening the previously excellent bunkering at 8).

As for the playing of it, this favourite of US visitors starts as tough as it finishes: it (and the elements) will test anyone. At over 7300yds, its back tees have pre-Open-softened up the Woodses, Elses and O'Mearas of this world, and the Stewarts of the next (club captain elect at the time of his death, a statue of Payne overlooks the putting green). Even at a more modest length the members' tees are challenging. The key is to use the conditions, not to fight them.

Waterville is undoubtedly a course on linksland, but it doesn't feature the subtleties of traditional links: it is more American (e.g. 18: tough p:5, but only the greensite has design finesse). It also contains a 1970s hint towards the 'dunes' courses of the future. An illustration of what we mean: the most famous point at Waterville is its highest point, Mulcahy's Peak at the 17th tee, named after the American golf pioneer John Mulcahy (who also inspired *Ashford Castle*). We are aware that Fazio has made adjustments to 17, but its concept (and the recent further heightening of the tee) is demonstrative. At some 200yds from the back this is a downhill p:3 to a green immediately above the beach, with relatively flat surrounds all fully exposed to the wind, especially as the protective yuccas between green and beach have recently been removed. Would an old master of links golf have built such a hole? We doubt it: i) he wouldn't have 'built' it, but fashioned it from what nature had given him, and ii) his tee and green would almost certainly been lower. Lower partly because shortcomings in contemporary equipment prevented much alternative, but also because leaving the folds of the dunes close to their natural state would almost certainly have presented more subtle golfing challenges than laying a new green on top of them.

(The old masters also preferred to use land within the dunes for greens as it generally was less exposed to the wind, easing maintenance and minimising erosion.) None of this would have detracted from the sense of spectacle. Even at a lower level, an old master would have ensured a visual sense of drama from the juxtaposition of golf, dunes, beach and sea. (We do not deny that Waterville's 17th is a supreme and spectacular challenge, but it does illustrate different approaches to course design.)

Ultimately the reasons why Waterville does not achieve a higher rating relate to some weaknesses in bunkering and to the routing of Hackett's original layout. A site often presents designers with a choice: whether to sacrifice quality on the rest of a course to achieve a few spectacular holes, or to sacrifice such holes for a more consistent whole. Too high a high price may have been paid for the spectacle of the closing 3 holes above the beach. We do not deny that they bring a climax to the round, but this has inevitably resulted in weaknesses elsewhere, e.g. two p:5s (5 and 13) running parallel to each other and routed rather against the natural flow of the land.

Fazio's revised medium p:4 16. Debits are always supposed to equal credits – the revision exposes the hole and its raised green to the full blast of the elements, while giving us the benefit of a stunning sea view. No need for bunkers: there are already hazards enough. Gold for golf and view.

There are undoubtedly several memorable holes here (notably 2, 11 and 16 – note that the shortest p:4 is also the best). We also highly endorse the concept of Mulcahy's Peak – not as a site for a tee, but as a viewpoint perfectly timed within the routing as a memorial to a man who, in many ways, began the transformation of golf in late-20th-century Ireland, and from which to review the challenges of what undoubtedly will have been a memorable round.

WESTPORT

F Hawtree 1973 € **H:** M 28, L 36

✉ Westport Golf Club, Carrowholly, Westport, Co. Mayo, RoI

☎ +353 98 282 62

✎ wpgolf@eircom.net www.golfwestport.com

🚗 ✈ Knock: N17 north; L onto N5 at Charlestown through Castlebar to Westport, whence N59 for Newport; L after 2km onto Golf Course Rd; club 4km from Westport on L.

	y	p		y	p
1	348	4	10	500	5
2	342	4	11	434	4
3	164	3	12	231	3
4	496	5	13	449	4
5	356	4	14	191	3
6	455	4	15	560	5
7	520	5	16	363	4
8	472	4	17	355	4
9	204	3	18	560	5
	3357	36		3643	37
				7000	73

Well-designed parkland course over fairly mildly sloping land with gentle start building to tougher challenge from 6 onwards, especially from back tees. Generally well-placed bunkers and some water (notably at p:4 15). Extensive views of the famous Croagh Patrick mountain and surrounding hills. Fairly flat greens. Can play very long when wet.

Golden p:5 15 offers a multitude of alternative strategies to the player: cutting the corners and going for it in two is not necessarily the wisest. Croagh Patrick (exeunt serpentes: see page 28, top) watches you choose.

Medium p:4 8 at Wicklow makes good use of natural features, including the division of the fairway by the swale (visible mid-shot) and an excellent, slightly raised greensite.

WICKLOW ♔♔♔ ↗

DIY/Ruddy   1904/2003   €   **H:** M 28, L 36

✉ Wicklow Golf Club, Dunbur Road, Wicklow, Co. Wicklow, RoI

☎ +353 40 467 379

✎ info@wicklowgolfclub.com   www.wicklowgolfclub.com

🚗 ✈ Dublin: M1/M50 south, becomes M11/N11, to Wicklow; from town centre, south along R750 coast road; club in Wicklow town, facing sea.

	y	p		y	p
1	522	5	10	363	4
2	397	4	11	170	3
3	258	4	12	397	4
4	296	4	13	348	4
5	301	4	14	545	5
6	406	4	15	305	4
7	137	3	16	456	5
8	393	4	17	161	3
9	143	3	18	348	4
	2853	35		3093	36
				5946	71

With outstanding sea views, a clifftop links, on a site where the inevitable cramping of some holes in some parts has nonetheless inspired excellent holes in other parts; on balance it works. Despite some hillier sections, its character makes it fun to play, particularly off the back tees. Some interesting putting surfaces. Wind!

Accommodation: Druids Glen, Porterhouse Inn, Powerscourt, Rathsallagh   **221**

Your golfing cruise at Woodbrook reaches its midpoint above the cliffs at medium p:3 9, the furthest point from the clubhouse: the wind here can make havoc of what appears to be a simple task.

WOODBROOK 🏆🏆🏆 ↗

?DIY/F & M Hawtree & Jiggens/McEvoy   1926/Unknown/1995

€€   **H:** M 28, L 36

✉   Woodbrook Golf Club, Bray, Co. Wicklow, RoI

☎   +353 1 282 4799

✎   golf@woodbrook.ie   www.woodbrook.ie

🚗 ✈ Dublin: M1/M50 south, becomes N11/M11; exit for Bray; at exit rbt, L (north) onto R119 for Shankhill; club entrance road on r after 250m.

	y	p			y	p
1	506	5		10	443	4
2	194	3		11	196	3
3	383	4		12	542	5
4	449	4		13	230	3
5	576	5		14	551	5
6	401	4		15	447	4
7	482	4		16	507	5
8	385	4		17	136	3
9	157	3		18	371	4
	3533	36			3423	36
					6956	72

Flat course with subtle undulations (including some raised, well-bunkered greens) mainly running along cliffs above the shore with extensive sea views. Several parkland holes, especially 1–4 and 18 inland of railway. Some challenging holes, notably mid-round. Rich in history (many tournaments, incl. Irish Open). Wind!

WOODENBRIDGE 🏆🏆🏆 ↗

Merrigan   1994 & 2005   €€   **H:** M 28, L 36

✉ Woodenbridge Golf Club, Vale of Avoca, Arklow, Co. Wicklow, RoI

☎ +353 40 235 202

✉ wgc@eircom.net   www.woodenbridgegolfclub.com

🚗 ✈ Dublin: M1/M50 south, becomes M11/N11, to Arklow; cross river into town and follow signs to Woodenbridge (R747); in Woodenbridge club on R (walk across railway and river from car park).

	y	p		y	p
1	360	4	10	455	4
2	411	4	11	194	3
3	374	4	12	353	4
4	190	3	13	386	4
5	407	4	14	295	4
6	448	4	15	500	5
7	322	4	16	357	4
8	121	3	17	167	3
9	502	5	18	551	5
	3135	35		3258	36
				6393	71

A flat parkland relatively tranquil alternative to the many links nearby, and recently upgraded with good, unobtrusively bunkered greensites and undulating putting surfaces. You will also remember this course for its setting: stately trees, four crossings of a wide river flowing through its midst, and several holes that are rather more difficult than they appear.

Modern equipment has made Woodenbridge's 14th into a driveable p:4. The tree is superbly positioned and the land falls away around a green set on a promontory above the river. Is it worth the risk?

Useful Information

Designers of Rated Courses

We list those involved in design of ★★★ and ★★ courses and a few other leading designers involved with Irish courses. We have not been able to obtain all the information, especially in respect of dates of birth and death of some of the earlier designers. We would be grateful for help from readers who could help us fill in the gaps for future editions. Emails to look@pocket-golf.com, please.

Hugh Alison (GB 1882–1952) *Designer* Oxford-educated journalist and talented cricketer/golfer. As secretary to newly formed Stoke Poges (England), Hugh Alison met H.S. Colt, who invited him to help with its design and that of several other London area courses. After WW1 20 year partnership with Colt: responsible for most of their work in North America and Far East. J.S.F. Morrison and A. Mackenzie also worked for the firm. Alison's Irish work included *County Sligo,* notably its bunkering.

George Baillie (GB 18??–19??) *Designer* A Scot from Musselburgh, who learnt golf as a boy and played to scratch in 1885, Baillie moved to Belfast and was a schoolteacher by profession (taught English at Royal Academy). The most prolific late Victorian designer of Irish golf courses, he was also involved in their promotion (e.g. at *Rosslare*). Founder Secretary (1881–1888) and designer of *Royal Belfast's* original course (now defunct). Small elements of his work survive at *Greenore and Rosslare (Old)*. Other involvement in courses now lost/superseded includes *Bundoran, Castlerock,* Leapordstown, *Lisburn* and Omagh.

Mr Bancroft (IR 18??–19??) *Designer* Reputed (rightly, it would seem) to be the 'expert of experts', Bancroft designed the original 9 holes at *Birr* (1893) and was invited back to extend it to a full 18 (1911). We know nothing further – unless our source has confused an 'n' with an 'r' in which case might 'Mr Bancroft' be Cecil Barcroft?

Cecil Barcroft (IR 1871–1924) *Designer* A barrister, member of *Royal Portrush* in 1892, captain of Dublin University and Dungannon golf clubs in 1897 and Secretary of *The Royal Dublin* (1905–1924), he was a pioneer of golf, designing several courses, including *Carlow (Deerpark), Castle* and input into *County Louth*. His obituary credits him also with work (now extinct) at *Tullamore* and *Naas*, and with 20–30 other courses. Also a golf journalist (incl. for The Daily Express).

Cuthbert Butchart (GB 1876–1955) *Player* A Scot from Carnoustie, who was appointed pro at *The Royal County Down* at the young age of 23, marked out a few Irish courses (e.g. *Bundoran* and *The Royal County Down (Annesley)*) and contributed to others (most notably *The Royal County Down (Championship)*), before leaving Ireland in 1904. Golf teacher to the German royal family, he won the 1913 German PGA championship, only to be interned in 1914. Emigrated to America, enhancing the name of his club-making family, while pro at the Westchester Biltmore, New York.

James Braid (GB 1870–1950) *Player* 5 times Open Champion who dominated competitive golf along with H Vardon and JH Taylor (1900–1920). Pro at Walton Heath GC (England) from 1904, he was responsible for laying out many courses (mainly in GB as he feared the sea). Wrote knowledgeably re course design. Irish credits include *Ballybunion (Old), Bangor, Howth, Kirkistown Castle, Mullingar* and *Tullamore*.

Sir Guy Campbell (GB 1885–1960) *Designer* Eton educated grandson of Robert Chambers (co-designer of original 9 holes at Hoylake, England). Sports editor of The Times under legendary Bernard Darwin, he wrote countless magazine articles and several books, notably "A History of Golf in Britain". Began designing courses in late 1920s with C.K. Hutchinson and S.V. Hotchkin, continuing until his death. Courses include *Killarney (Killeen & Mahony's Point)* and *The Royal Dublin*.

Valentine Browne, **Lord Castlerosse** (6th Earl of Kenmare) (IR 1891–1943) *Designer* Landowner and press baron with a passion for golf (good enough to get through the 1st round of the 1913 French Amateur Championship). Employed Sir Guy Campbell to design the original course at Killarney and forever continued revising it. A friend of Edward VIII and Wallis Simpson, and clearly a character: once, at Baden–Baden, he visited a florist to buy orchids for his dinner date that evening; luxuries were scarce then, and the shop only had one spray – 'Get me more,' he demanded, 'more, more, more. Wire for them. Send planes for them.' It was done!

Harry Colt (GB 1869–1951) *Designer* Cambridge-educated solicitor and distinguished amateur golfer, first assisted Douglas Rolland in design of Rye Golf Club, 1894. Secretary at Sunningdale, 1901–1913. Soon abandoned law practice and became one of the world's leading course designers before WW1. Colt brought on many first-rate golf architects, including C.H. Alison and A. Mackenzie. The first truly professional course architect – first to use a drawing board in preparing layout plans, and first to prepare tree planting plans. Many famous courses worldwide; in Ireland, most notably: *Castle, County Sligo* and both courses at *Royal Portrush*.

Tom Craddock (IR 1932–1998) *Player* First rate Irish amateur golfer (Walker Cup 1967 & 1969) who began designing in 1982 when he joined Pat Ruddy. Many collaborations with Ruddy, e.g. *Ballyliffin* and *Druids Glen* and some solo work (including the 3rd 9 at *Connemara* taken up after Hackett died; sadly, he also died before its completion).

Seymour Dunn (GB 1882–1959) *Player* Best known for his teaching of (and writing about) the fundamentals of golf (pupils included Hagen and Sarazen) and a member of a famous golfing dynasty (father, Tom, was the most prolific designer of GB courses in the late Victorian era; grandfather laid out Royal Wimbledon, England). With a transatlantic career, he was one of the early pro's at *The Royal County Down* and had input into its design. Most of his courses were in the USA and on the Continent (notably Ugolino, near Florence, Italy).

Stan Eby (US 1948–) *Designer* Qualified in Landscape Architecture, Project Management and Construction Administration from Wisconsin University, with experience of many courses in US, working under Dick Nugent. Joined European Golf Design (EGD), specialist in working with tour players on design, in 1992. Irish work: *Portmarnock Links* (with Langer), and *Carton House – Montgomerie* (with Montgomerie).

Martin Ebert (GB 1966–) *Designer* Cambridge University golfer, graduating with degree in Engineering and joining Donald Steel in 1990. Travelled extensively with firm until formation of Mackenzie & Ebert, who are now remodelling *Milltown* and *Luttrellstown Castle*. Worked with Steel on *Enniscrone* and *The Royal County Down*.

Charles Gibson (GB 1864–1932) *Designer* Famous clubmaker/pro at Westward Ho!, England. From 1888 he trained J.H. Taylor (amongst others) and is also known to have designed several holes at *Lahinch* in 1904.

Mary 'Molly' Gourlay (GB 1898–1990) *Player* Represented Great Britain in the 1932 and 1934 Curtis Cup, and won many major amateur tournaments. At the height of her playing career assisted Tom Simpson in designing several courses including *Carlow*, *County Louth* and *Ballybunion*.

Eddie Hackett (IR 1910–1996) *Designer* Club pro at many Irish clubs, but also worked in England and Belgium with Henry Cotton, and subsequently assisted F.W. Hawtree who was designing courses at *Westport* and *Killarney*. Hackett's own first design was in 1964 and his last was the extra nine holes at Connemara which he never saw finished. Prolific in Ireland, designing/remodelling over 100 courses, notably *Ashford Castle, Ballyliffin (Old), Bellmullet, Connemara, Donegal, Dooks* and *Waterville*.

John Harris (GB 1912–1977) *Designer* Low handicapper, who took his education in civil engineering into the specialized golf course construction firm (run by father and uncle). On father's death became director and worked closely with all the top British designers before WW2, during which he became naval Commander. Having returned to business, formed partnership with C.K. Cotton in early 1950s and set up own firm in 1960. By 1970s his associates include Bryan Griffiths, Michael Wolveridge, Peter Thomson and Ronald Fream. Most of his some 450 courses are outside British Isles but include *Lahinch (Castle), Shannon* and minor work at *Tramore*.

Frederick George Hawtree (GB 1883–1955) *Designer* First began designing courses in 1912, and after service in WW1 practised alone until formed partnership with J.H. Taylor (1922). Hawtree and Taylor continued in business until WW2, after which formed Hawtree & Son with F.W. Hawtree. Created first pay and play course in 1931. Irish work includes *Arklow* and *Carlow*.

Frederick William Hawtree (GB 1916–2000) *Designer* Educated Oxford. Joined father's firm Hawtree & Taylor, 1938. Captured by Japanese, WW2. Upon release started practice as Hawtree & Son, and continued after father's death (1955), designing courses worldwide. Joined in firm by A.H.F. Jiggens (1969) and by son Martin (1974). Irish work includes *Killarney, Portmarnock, Westport* and *Woodbrook*.

Martin Hawtree (GB 1947–) *Designer* Educated Liverpool University. Joined father's firm in 1973 becoming third generation in the longest standing golf course design firm (effectively in business in peacetime since 1912). Became director on father's death in 2000. Irish work has primarily been links restoration/remodeling, notably at *Dooks* and *Lahinch (Old)*.

Jeff Howes (CAN 1945–) *Designer* Former scratch golfer from Calgary, with degree in Physical Geography (Alberta) and Diploma in Turf Management (Massachusetts), now based in Ireland, where work includes *Gowran Park, The Heritage* and remodelling at *Castle* and *Naas*. Assisted Nicklaus at *Mount Juliet*.

Robert Trent Jones Snr (US 1906 –2000) *Designer* British born, but moved to US aged 5. Scratch player, educated Cornell. 1930 – joined Stanley Thompson at Thompson, Jones & Co, a firm influential in promoting strategic design, with the principle "hard par easy bogey". By 1960s had become the most known and influential designer in history: by 1980 over 400 courses in play worldwide. Two sons, Robert Jnr. and Rees, are both successful designers. In Ireland: *Adare* and *Ballybunion (Cashen)*.

Bernhard Langer (GER 1957–) *Player* Undoubtedly Germany's greatest golfer, twice Masters Champion and victorious Ryder Cup Captain in 2002. Responsible for many courses including Ireland's *Portmarnock Links* (with Stan Eby).

Alister Mackenzie (GB 1870–1934) *Designer* Arguably the greatest and most artistic course designer of the 20th century, 'The Doctor' graduated from Cambridge with degrees in Medicine, Natural Science, and Chemistry. Surgeon in Boer War also studying Boer soldiers' use of camouflage to avoid detection in treeless veldts. Returned to medicine in Leeds. In 1907 at nearby Alwoodley met Harry Colt, who was so impressed with his models for greens and bunkers that he invited him to collaborate on its revision. Mackenzie gradually became full time designer. In 1914 earned worldwide publicity with winning design for best "two shot hole" for Lido GC, New York. Further developed camouflage techniques in WW1, after which designed extensively (most famously at Royal Melbourne, Australia, and Augusta National and Cypress Point, USA) including 1920s visits to Ireland, where courses include *Cork and Lahinch (Old)*. See *Design Principles* (page 17).

Tom Mackenzie (GB 1966–) *Designer* Low handicap golf at Dornoch kindled interest in course design. After university golf and a spell as a Tour caddy, upon graduation (Landscape Architecture) joined firm of Donald Steel with whom enhanceed *Tralee, County Louth* and *Killarney*. Since recent formation of Mackenzie & Ebert involved in remodelling of *Luttrellstown Castle* and *Milltown*.

Patrick Merrigan (IR 1942–) *Designer* Graduating from University College, Dublin in Agricultural Science, worked in course design since 1971 when he assisted Eddie Hackett at Waterville. Based in Dublin, portfolio includes *Faithlegg, Slieve Russell* and *Tulfarris*.

Harrison G Minchew (US 1956–) *Designer* Began golf at Forest Hills, Augusta where student work on course maintenance crew, curried his interest in design. Graduated in Landscape Architecture (University of Georgia, 1979, whose course included work for Kirby & Griffiths), joined Ron Fream and in 1982 became associate of Ed Seay in Palmer Course Design Company, where projects included remodeling Forest Hills. Irish courses include both at *K Club* and assisting at *Tralee*.

Tom Morris (Old) (GB 1821–1908) *Player* Assistant to Allan Robertson at St Andrews Old Course from 1839 to 1851, when moved to Prestwick as Pro/Greenkeeper after a dispute over use of "gutta percha ball" (Robertson disapproved). Returned to St Andrews in similar post (1865) until retirement in 1904. 4 times Open Champion in 1860s and top links designer in second half of 19th century, when design necessitated expertise at utilizing every natural feature of terrain, passing skill on to his assistant Donald Ross. Irish courses include *Lahinch (Old), Rosapenna* and *Royal County Down.*

Jack Nicklaus (US 1940–) *Player* The golfer of the 20th century. Formed design company in 1974, renowned for big budget projects worldwide. *Mount Juliet* his only Irish course to date though he routed *Palmerstown* (finished off by Christy O'Connor Jnr.).

Greg Norman (AUS 1955–) *Player* Starting golf at 16, turned pro in 1976. Successful career through 1980s and 1990s – the only player ever to win order of merit either side of the Atlantic. >80 wins worldwide, including The Open. Heads Great White Shark Enterprises, which includes a course design company. *Doonbeg* is his first design in Ireland.

Christy O'Connor Jnr (IR 1948–) *Player* Nephew of famous namesake, a successful playing career was capped in 1989 with famous 2 iron shot to beat Fred Couples in Ryder Cup. Prolific Irish course design career, resulting in over 30 courses including *Headfort (New)* and *Palmerstown* .

Arnold Palmer (US 1929–) *Player* Charismatic attitude made him the people's champion through 1960s and 1970s. Bought Bay Hill in late 1960s, remodelling many holes. First worked as design consultant with Francis Duane, 1969–74; then joined Edwin Seay, forming Palmer Course Design, delegating much of work to professionals in his firm. Many courses in the US and a few elsewhere, notably the first course in Communist China and in Ireland *The K Club* (both courses) and *Tralee.*

William Pickeman (GB 18??–19??) *Designer* On Christmas Eve 1893 Pickeman, a Scottish insurance broker, and his friend George Ross famously rowed over from Sutton to the peninsula of *Portmarnock* to scout out land for golf links. The rest is history . . . Became Honorary Secretary and Honorary Treasurer of the club. He went on to work on some 30 courses (though little of his input is left), including *Castle* and *Rosslare (Old).*

Pat Ruddy (IR 1945–) *Designer* Characterful golf writer since 1963, who first became involved in course design in 1972 (*Castlecomer*). He has completed 36 others since then including many collaborations with Tom Craddock. They include *Ballyliffin* and *Druids Glen* and many more like *Druids Heath* and *Rosapenna (Sandy Hills)* in his own right. His "*pièce de resistance*" is undoubtedly *The European,* which he runs with his family.

Edwin Seay (US 1938–) *Designer* Graduated from Florida University with degree in Landscape Architecture and entered US Marine Corps. In 1964 joined Ellis Maples designing and constructing 27 courses. Began private practice in 1972, later forming design company with Arnold Palmer, where, as Director of Design, work has included *The K Club* (both courses) and *Tralee.*

Tom Simpson (GB 1877–1964) *Designer* Wealthy Cambridge-educated lawyer and scratch golfer. Became interested in design when home club of Woking, England, was remodelled by its members. By 1910 closed legal practice and joined Herbert Fowler. After WW1 joined by Abercromby &

Croome. Hired P.M. Ross as assistant in 1920s and soon split from Fowler, forming partnership with Ross. In 1930s often worked with Molly Gourlay, becoming first designer to solicit a woman's opinion on the art. Always oversaw construction, which restricted his design output. Colourful character: made site visits in Silver Rolls Royce, wearing embroidered cape and beret. Retired at outbreak of WW2, but continued to write into 1950s. In Ireland, most notably: *Ballybunion (Old)* and *County Louth*.

Donald Steel (GB 1937–) *Designer* Scratch amateur golfer. Educated Cambridge, became golf writer in 1961. Then joined firm of Cotton (C.K.), Pennink, Lawrie, 1965. Full partner from 1971, responsible for many courses in UK and Europe (notably Iberia). Subsequently founded own firm. Close connection with The Open, in that having played in it in 1970, he has subsequently has advised re every course over which it has been played. Courses revised in Ireland include: *Carlow, Enniscrone, The Royal County Down* and *Tralee*.

John (J.H.) Taylor (GB 1871–1963) *Player* Originally trained as a gardener and served as greenkeeper at Westward Ho!, then pro/greenkeeper at Burnham, Winchester, and Royal Mid Surrey, England. Won The Open 5 times. Designed several courses before WW1 and in 1924 formed Hawtree & Taylor, designing actively until WW2. Irish work included *Arklow, Carlow and Rosslare (Old)*.

Harry Vardon (GB 1870–1937) *Player* Six times Open champion, much in demand as course designer but his work was limited by ill health. Irish input included *Bundoran and The Royal County Down*.

Tom Watson (US 1949–) *Player* Glittering playing career: 5 Open wins highlight his affinity with links courses. Formed design company 1990. A long time fan of *Ballybunion (Old)*, it was natural he was asked to assist with its remodelling.

RECOMMENDED READING

There is a whole library of books on golf design. We include only a brief listing, to get you further into the subject.

The Anatomy of a Golf Course, Tom Doak, 1992
The Architects of Golf, Geoffrey Cornish & Ronald Whitten,
  (formerly published as *The Golf Course*, 1988)
    We are indebted to the authors of this book, which we have used as a
    principal source for many of the designer biographies
Golf Architecture, Dr Alister MacKenzie, 1920
The Links, Robert Hunter, (reprinted) 1999
Some Essays on Golf Course Architecture, Colt & Alison, 1920
The World Atlas of Golf, Hamlyn (ed Ward–Thomas and Rowlinson, 2001

Many of these books are out of print, but a good source for second hand books on golf design is Rhod McEwan Golf Books – www.rhodmcewan.com

GLOSSARY OF GOLF DESIGN TERMS

Aesthetics The quality of the visual, sensual (and occasionally aural) impression provided during the experience of playing individual holes and the golf course as a whole.

Blind (or blind shot) Situation in which the player cannot see the target from any point on a hole where the player should be if playing the hole reasonably as intended by the designer.

Cape An heroic feature: players are invited to shorten a hole by driving across the corner of a hazard – the more they attempt to cut off, the more the risk.

Dogleg Golf hole which turns a distinct corner from the original line of play from the tee.

Double dogleg Golf hole which turns two distinct corners from the initial line of play – the second turn normally being in the opposite direction to the first.

Dunes Course A course laid out generally over sand dunes (often rather smoothed over), using modern equipment.

Enhancement Embellishment of an existing design, generally without re-routing, nor to the extent that the course is so changed as for the work to constitute remodelling (e.g. addition of bunkers and tees, or tree amendment).

Esker A geological rather than golf term. See article on *Birr*, page 55.

Fair A course or a hole is fair when its features are openly presented to the player, so that playing errors are due to the player himself making such errors, rather than due to an aspect of the course of which the player is not given reasonable notice.

Greensite The whole complex of a green and its immediate surroundings, including humps, swales, bunkers and other immediately adjoining features.

Hazard Design feature (whose definition has widened with developments in design), which makes the playing of a hole more challenging, e.g. bunkers, water, trees, swales (especially when combined with short grass), humps, and long grass (i.e. longer than normal rough – undesirable because of ball searches).

Heroic design A type of design which gives the player an opportunity to take on risks (e.g. cutting corner of dogleg by driving over bunkers, water or even rough) resulting in higher chances of lower score; success should render heroic satisfaction. There should always be room for an alternative stratgey. (A classic example of such a hole is do-I-have-a-go-for-the-green-in-1-but-then-I-must-carry-the-water? p4:10 at The Brabazon Course, The Belfry, England.)

Holiday Course Related to, and in some ways the forerunner of, the Resort Course, often shorter and less demanding than a traditional design, also intended to be fun and more relaxing; generally to be found in holiday locations.

Links The original terrain of golf: ground which 'links' the land to the sea, also often used for common grazing. Its sandy soil, giving a base for springy turf, was generally formed by the sea, wind, and animals that lived there. The often uneven surfaces mean that links golf can seem a little unfair to the uninitiated but such courses really test the player's resolve to keep going, despite bad luck – on such courses, the best player inevitably wins. There is little such ground outside Great Britain, Ireland and land adjoining the North Sea and English Channel. The term is often misused (generally for marketing purposes) to denote land adjoining the sea, on which golf is played (e.g. *Alcaidesa* Links, near Gibraltar), or artificially manufactured, inaccurate replicas (e.g. *Carton House (Montgomerie)*).

Penal design A type of design where the perfect shot is rewarded but almost anything else is severely punished; in such design, the designer gives the player no option but to take on risks (the do-or-die island green p3:17 at TPC Sawgrass, Florida is a classic example).

Remodel A golf course is remodelled when the work carried out significantly changes the design of holes, although not necessarily involving re-routing (e.g. changing the bunkering, moving tees and/or significantly changing greens)

Renovation Making good defects to the design and condition of a golf course – a process more of repair than change.

Re-routing Adjustment to a course layout involving significant changes in the sites of tees and greens, so that the course (or parts of it) takes a different route around the land on which it is sited.

Resort Course A golf course designed to be more user friendly than a traditional course, often without significant rough, generally found in lavish holiday locations and designed to be appealing, fun and bold in appearance.

Restore A golf course is restored if the work carried out generally returns it to how its designer originally designed it (though increasingly with sensitive and sympathetic adjustments to allow for the extra distance achievable with modern equipment).

Reverse camber On a dogleg hole, land which slopes in the opposite direction to the turn in the hole and therefore does not help the ball go round the corner – generally an undesirable feature.

Routing The way the holes are laid out over the land used for the golf course, and how the holes relate to the terrain and its opportunities or restrictions. The quality of the routing is crucial and generally closely related to the overall quality of the course because of the strong influence it can have on both the golfing test and aesthetic merits (or demerits).

Run offs Short grass slopes on, and immediately adjoining, greens which cause misplaced shots to run off the green into nearby fairway, rough or hazards. The concept of short grass as a hazard should not be undervalued in golf design.

Semi-blind (or semi-blind shot) As for blind shot, except the player can see part but not all of the target (or relevant ground between himself and the target).

Strategic design The type of design which offers the player a choice of different ways to play a golf hole, ideally where risk and reward are balanced (i.e. riskier option may result in fewer strokes if successfully executed). St Andrews (Old) is the classic example of a strategic golf course.

Swales Gentle depressions (often near greens) designed to catch or deflect the slightly errant shot and sometimes also test a player's distance judgment.

WHERE TO STAY

We offer a list of hotels, guesthouses and B&Bs, noting some of the nearby courses in the guide. We are not accommodation inspectors so we refer readers to specialist accommodation guides and the internet for more critical comment. As we have generally only listed establishments in which we have stayed (between September 2004 and April 2006) and which we found fit for purpose, this list is not comprehensive for the whole of Ireland. (We accept no responsibility in connection with this listing.)

Adare Manor Hotel & Golf Resort Spacious and sumptuous 5 star hotel accommodation in majestic manor and nearby clubhouse, or self-catering townhouses and villas - all in an amazing inland setting. Adare, Co. Limerick. Tel: +353 61 396 566 reservations@adaremanor.com www.adaremanor.com *Adare* and *Limerick*, en route for *Ballybunion, Doonbeg* and *Lahinch*.

Aghadoe Heights Hotel & Spa

Quietly located just outside Killarney with breathtaking views of the lakes and mountains, a top notch hotel in every respect, including Ireland's only Aveda Resort Spa, with bespoke treatments including Ayurvedic, reki, reflexology choices, etc. Irish Golf Hotel of the Year, 2004. 73 rooms and suites with excellent lake or garden views and private balconies. Aghadoe Heights Hotel & Spa, Lakes of Killarney, Co. Kerry. Tel: +353 64 31 766 info@aghadoeheights.com www.aghadoeheights.com *Beaufort, Dooks* and *Killarney*.

The Athenaeum House Hotel Boutique Hotel with 10 acres fronting River Suir. All mod cons, great food. Christendom, Ferrybank, Waterford, Co. Waterford. Tel: +353 51 833 999 info@athenaeumhousehotel.com www.athenaeumhousehotel.com *Faithlegg, Mount Juliet, Tramore* and *Waterford Castle*.

Ballyliffin Self Catering 6 quaint cottages in village close to golf. Ballyliffin, Inishowen, Co. Donegal. Tel: +353 74 937 6498 info@ballyliffinselfcatering.com www.ballyliffinselfcatering.com *Ballyliffin*.

Ballymascanlon House Hotel Comfortable and well appointed, with leisure club and scenic 18 hole course and dolmen. Dundalk, Co. Louth. Tel: +353 42 395 8200 info@ballymascanlon.com www.ballymascanlon.com *County Louth, The Royal Co. Down* and *Seapoint*.

Boyne Valley Hotel & County Club Hotel and leisure club with pleasant garden. Drogheda, Co. Louth. Tel: +353 41 983 7737 admin@boyne-valley-hotel.ie www.boyne-valley-hotel.ie *Ardee, Dundalk, County Louth, Headfort New* and *Seapoint*.

Bridge House Hotel & Leisure Club Town centre. Good craic (award winning bar) and breakfasts. Tullamore, Co. Offaly. Tel: +353 50 622 000 info@bridgehousehotel.com www.bridgehousehotel.com *Mullingar, Tullamore* and en route for *Birr*.

The Brown Trout Pleasantly quaint and spacious cottages adjoining pub with 9 hole course. 209 Agivey Road, Aghadowey, Coleraine, Co. Londonderry BT51 4AD. Tel: +44 287 086 8209 bill@browntroutinn.com www.browntroutinn.com *Castlerock, Portstewart* and *Royal Portrush.*

Burke's Armada Hotel Atlantic seaside hotel - taste the sea and nearby quirky 9 hole course. Spanish Point, Miltown Malbay, Co. Clare. Tel: +353 65 708 4110 info@burkesarmadahotel.com www.burkesarmadahotel.com *Doonbeg, Kilkee, Lahinch* and *Spanish Point.*

Burrendale Hotel & Country Club Comfortable edge of town hotel with large rooms. 51 Castlewellan Road, Newcastle, Co. Down BT33 0JY. Tel: +44 284 372 2599 reservations@burrendale.com www.burrendale.com *Ardglass, Kilkeel, The Royal County Down* and *Warrenpoint.*

Bushmills Inn Hotel Whiskey, fires, food, comfort and golf. Bliss! 9 Dunluce Road, Bushmills, Co. Antrim BT57 8QG. Tel: +44 282 073 3000 mail@bushmillsinn.com www.bushmillsinn.com *Portstewart* and *Royal Portrush.* (See *The North – Golf, spirits and more for giants,* pages 30–31.)

The Butler Arms Hotel Family run with good food (fish!) and wine. Waterville, Co. Kerry. Tel: +353 66 947 4144 reservations@butlerarms.com www.butlerarms.com *Skellig Bay* and *Waterville.*

Castleknock Hotel & Country Club Large new 4 star hotel on western outskirts of Dublin. Porterstown Road, Castleknock, Dublin 15. Tel: +353 1 640 6300 info@chcc.ie www.castleknockhotel.com *Carton House, Castleknock, Luttrellstown Castle* and en route for *Rathcore.*

Castlerosse Hotel & Leisure Centre Budget hotel with 9 hole course adjoining Killarney Golf Club. Killarney, Co. Kerry. Tel: +353 643 1144 res@castlerosse.ie www.castlerosse.com *Beaufort, Dooks* and *Killarney.*

Citywest Hotel & Golf Resort Conveniently close to the road to Munster, a busy hotel with 36 holes on site, plus Palmerstown. Saggart, Co. Dublin. Tel: +353 1 401 0500 res@citywesthotel.com www.citywesthotel.com *Castle, Citywest, The K Club, Naas* and *Palmerstown.*

Clanard Court Set in 8 acres of landscaped gardens in the verdant, rolling countryside of the Midlands, 1 mile from heritage town Athy - an ideal base for equestrian sports in Country Kildare and Ryder Cup golf. Elegant and luxurious, the hotel exudes warmth in its welcome and friendliness. 38 de luxe bedrooms, bistro, bar and function suites; complimentary parking. Clanard Court Hotel, Dublin Road, Athy, Co. Kildare. Tel: +353 59 864 0666 sales@clanardcourt.ie www.clanardcourt.ie *Athy, Carlow, The Heritage, Kilkea Castle* and *Rathsallagh.*

Connemara Gateway Hotel Mature gardens and peat fires close to golf at, Oughterard, Co. Galway. Tel: +353 91 552 328 info@connemaragateway.com www.connemaragateway.com *Connemara Isles, Galway, Oughterard.* En route for *Ashford Castle* and *Connemara.*

Dooleys Hotel Family run - central waterfront location. The Quay, Waterford, Co. Waterford. Tel: +353 51 873 531 hotel@dooleys-hotel.ie www.dooleys-hotel.ie *Faithlegg, Mount Juliet, Tramore* and *Waterford Castle.*

The Lodge at Doonbeg Golf Club Luxury suites, fine dining, spa, and golf shop adjoining golf and beach. Tel: +353 65 905 5246 reservations@doonbeggolfclub.com www.doonbeggolfclub.com *Doonbeg, Kilkee* and *Lahinch.* (See *The Wild West – Ballybunion, Doonbeg, Lahinch, Spanish Point and much more,* pages 28–29.)

Links Lodge Doonbeg Family run B&B, conveniently close to golf and beach. Warm welcome. Tel: +353 65 905 5108 linkslg@eircom.net *Doonbeg, Kilkee, Lahinch* and *Spanish Point.*

Dromoland Castle Luxury castle hotel in beautiful grounds with golf course. Newmarket-on-Fergus, Co. Clare. Tel: +353 61 368 144 sales@dromoland.ie www.dromoland.ie *Adare, Doonbeg, Dromoland Castle* and *Lahinch.*

Marriott Hotel Druids Glen & Country Club All facilities and 36 holes on site. Newtownmountkennedy, Co. Wicklow. Tel: +353 1 287 0800 mhrs.dubgs.reservations@marriotthotels.com www.marriott.ie/dubgs *Druids Glen, Druids Heath, The European, Glen of the Downs* and *Powerscourt.*

Dunraven Arms Hotel Classy olde worlde hotel in pretty village. Adare, Co. Limerick. Tel: +353 61 396 633 reservations@dunravenhotel.com www.dunravenhotel.com *Adare, Limerick* and *Limerick County,* en route for *Ballybunion, Doonbeg* and *Lahinch.*

Fitzgerald's Woodlands House Hotel Budget accommodation, pretty village and quality golf. Knockanes, Adare, Co. Limerick. Tel: +353 61 605 100 reception@woodlands-hotel.ie www.woodlands-hotel.ie *Adare and Limerick,* en route for *Ballybunion, Doonbeg* and *Lahinch.*

Four Seasons Hotel & Leisure Club Fabulous food. Convenient for visits to north. Carlingford, Co. Louth. Tel: +353 42 937 3530 info@4seasonshotel.ie www.4 seasonshotel.ie *County Louth* and *Greenore,* en route for *The Royal County Down.*

Marriott Courtyard Galway All facilities on outskirts of Galway. Headfort Point, Galway, Co. Galway. Tel: +353 91 513 200 galway.reservations@courtyard.com www.marriott.com/gwycy *Galway* and en route for *Connemara* and *Connemara Isles.*

Glenroyal Hotel & Leisure Club All facilities in busy village on Straffan Road. Glenroyal Centre, Maynooth, Co. Kildare. Tel: +353 1 629 0909 info@glenroyal.ie www.glenroyal.ie *Carton House, The K Club* and *Rathcore.*

The Granville Hotel 100 thoughtfully designed bedrooms. Meaghers Quay, Waterford City, Co. Waterford. Tel: +353 51 305 555 info@granville-hotel.ie www.granville-hotel.ie *Faithlegg, Mount Juliet, Tramore* and *Waterford Castle.*

The Heritage at Killenard Luxury hotel with sumptuous cuisine, conference facilities, spa and bowls arena. The Heritage at Killenard, Killenard, Co. Laois. Tel: +353 157 864 5500 reservations@theheritage.com www.theheritage.com *The Curragh, The Heritage, Tullamore*

Killeen House Hotel Small and family run, with great food and golf pub atmosphere. Aghadoe, Lakes of Killarney, Co. Kerry. Tel: +353 643 1711 charming@indigo.ie www.killeenhousehotel.com *Beaufort, Dooks* and *Killarney.*

Marriott Johnstown House Hotel & Spa All facilities on main Dublin-Galway route. Enfield, Co. Meath. Tel: +353 46 954 0000 info@johnstownhouse.com www.marriott.ie/dubjh *Rathcore* and not far from *The K Club.*

Lake House Hotel Blue flag beach and golf nearby. Friendly atmosphere. Narin, Portnoo, Co. Donegal. Tel: +353 74 954 5123 lakehouse@iol.ie www.lakehousehotel.ie *Donegal* and *Narin & Portnoo.*

Malone Lodge Hotel & Apartments Victorian terrace hotel in quiet area. 60 Eglantine Avenue, Malone Road, Belfast BT9 6DY. Tel: +44 289 038 8000 info@malonelodgehotel.com www.malonelodgehotel.com *Belvoir Park, Malone, Royal Belfast* and *Shandon Park.*

Marlfield House Hotel Luxurious, family run regency period house, with antiques and excellent food. Gorey, Co. Wexford. Tel: +353 552 1124 info@marlfieldhouse.ie www.marlfieldhouse.com *Coollattin, The European Rosslare* and *Seafield.*

Mount Wolseley Hilton 18 holes on site, plus all facilities and spa. Tullow, Co. Carlow. Tel: +353 59 915 1674 reservations.mountwolseley@hilton.com www.hilton.co.uk/mountwolseley *Carlow, Coollattin* and *Mount Wolseley.*

The Porterhouse Inn On seafront with stylish rooms and plenty of craic downstairs. Strand Road, Bray, Co. Wicklow Tel: +353 1 286 0688 bray@portehousebrewco.com *Druids Glen, Druids Heath, Powerscourt* and *Woodbrook.*

Portmarnock Hotel & Golf Links Next to fabulous beach and course. Full conference, banqueting and golf facilities in centre of golfing hotspot. Portmarnock, Co. Dublin. Tel: +353 1 846 0611 res@portmarnockhotel.com www.portmarnockhotel.com *Howth, Portmarnock, Portmarnock Links, The Royal Dublin, St Anne's* and *Sutton.* (See *The Dublin Coast: Golf and Craic*, page 22–23.)

Ritz Carlton Powerscourt From autumn 2007, 203 suite luxury hotel in stunning setting with state-of-the-art spa. Enniskerry, Co. Wicklow. www.ritzcarlton.com/resorts/powerscourt Limited accommodation is available on the Powerscourt Estate by arrangement through the golf club. Tel: +353 1 204 6033 www.powerscourt.ie *Castle, Druids Glen, Druids Heath, The European, Powerscourt* and *Woodbrook.* (See *The Garden of Ireland*, page 24–25.)

Rathsallagh House, Golf & Country Club Converted from Queen Anne stables in 1798, a must visit luxury country house in 530 acres, sporting 18 holes in a beautiful parkland setting. Friendly staff make you feel at home. Excellent cuisine, including wonderful breakfasts. Individually styled and spacious rooms add to the calm and relaxing atmosphere

inside and out (turn off that mobile phone and enjoy…). A favourite haunt of Ireland's horse-breeders. Dunlavin, Co. Wicklow. Tel: +353 45 403 112 info@rathsallagh.com www.rathsallagh.com *The Curragh, The K Club, Mount Wolseley, Naas, Palmerstown, Rathsallagh, South County* and *Tulfarris*. See also photo pages 18–19.

Roganstown Golf & Country Club Close to Dublin airport, modern accommodation, good food, pool, gym, spa and a challenging O'Connor Jnr golf course. Swords. Co. Dublin. Tel: +353 1 843 3118 info@roganstown.com www.roganstown.com *Malahide, The Island, Portmarnock, Portmarnock Links, Roganstown* and *St Margaret's*. (See *O'Connor's Welcome*, page 20–21.)

Rosapenna Hotel & Golf Links A traditional hotel with sea views, extensive golf facilities and a warm welcome. Downings, Co. Donegal. Tel: +353 74 915 5301 rosapenna@eircom.net www.rosapenna.ie *Portsalon* and *Rosapenna*.

Shelleven House Comfortable family run Victorian guesthouse in Bangor. 61 Princetown Road, Bangor, Co. Down. Tel: +44 289 127 1777 shellevenhouse@aol.com www.shellevenhouse.com *Bangor, Clandeboye, Kirkistown Castle* and *Royal Belfast*.

Slieve Donard Hotel Splendid Victorian architecture combines with all modern facilities, including spa, immediately adjoining one of the world's best courses. Downs Road, Newcastle, Co. Down BT33 0AH. Tel: +44 284 372 1066 res@sdh.hastingshotels.com www.hastingshotels.com *Ardglass, Kilkeel, The Royal County Down* and *Warrenpoint*.

St Helen's Bay Clifftop clubhouse serves holiday cottages overlooking 27 hole course with spectacular finish. Kilrane, Rosslare Harbour, Co. Wexford. Tel: 353 53 33 234 golfing@sthelensbay.com www.sthelensbay.com *Rosslare* and *St Helen's Bay*.

Tower Guesthouse Bar & Restaurant Wysiwyg - convenient inn halfway between Dublin and the west coast, not far from local golf. Church Street, Roscrea, Co. Tipperary. Tel: +353 50 521 774 thetower@eircom.net *Birr, Nenagh* and *Roscrea*.

Vaughan Lodge Comfortable modern golf lodge in town Lahinch, Co. Clare. Tel: +353 65 708 1111 info@vaughanlodge.ie www.vaughanlodge.ie *Doonbeg* and *Lahinch*.

Watersedge Hotel Waterfront, award-winning boutique hotel with wonderful food. Cobh, Co. Cork. Tel: +353 21 481 5566 info@watersedgehotel.ie www.watersedgehotel.ie *Cork* and *Fota Island*.

White House Good food and craic in centre of Kinsale. Pearse St. & The Glen, Kinsale, Co. Cork. Tel: +353 21 477 2125 whitehse@indigo.ie www.whitehouse-kinsale.ie *Old Head of Kinsale* and *Tramore*.

Whitesands Hotel On beach, Irish pub with all mod cons. Coast Road Portmarnock, Co. Dublin. Tel: +353 1 846 0003 info@whitesandshotel.ie www.whitesandshotel.ie *Malahide, Portmarnock* and *Portmarnock Links*.

The GOLF HOUSE

Golf Breaks with a Difference

Bespoke golf based at our beautiful houses

Marbella (Spain)
Tuscany (Italy)
Cornwall (UK)

We are well connected with local golf markets – arrange a special break with us to suit you and your team

Free Tuition!

4somes to 20somes – fully staffed or self-catering

Packages: play & study the art of course design with Greg Turner

Golf and Sun

The Golf House, Marbella, Spain (sleeps 4 to 12 ensuite)

Marbella, on the Costa del Sol, is one of Europe's top golfing destinations – see our *Spain & Portugal* volume or www.pocket-golf.com.

With immediate access to two courses, beaches, swimming pool and stunning views, Greg Turner's luxurious Spanish base is within easy driving distance of the mountain city of Ronda, The Alhambra at Granada and the glories of Seville. Marble, a/c and under-floor heating throughout. Golf design library. Home cinema. Also available for non-golf holidays.

Málaga airport 45 minutes.

Original art by Sarah Sanderson ▶ (sarah@sportingred.com) adorns the walls of the 80m² main room, also boasting a grand piano

▲ p:5 2 at Marbella GC, which adjoins the house

Mediterranean views of ▶ mountains, Gibraltar and Morocco – available throughout the year